J. Arthur Heck
1502 North Twelfth St.,
Reading, Penna.

WHAT IS
CHRISTIAN EDUCATION?

WHAT IS
CHRISTIAN EDUCATION.?

BY
GEORGE A. COE

CHARLES SCRIBNER'S SONS
NEW YORK · LONDON
1930

PREFACE

The theme of this book is not religious education taken generically, but Christian education taken specifically.

What I have attempted is a critical examination of present Christian practice and of the better practice that would ensue if Christian principles were more fully to control the teaching work of the churches.

By "critical examination" I do not mean the scholastic and largely sterile procedure that first constructs a formal definition, and then tests concrete situations by means of it. The method here pursued is the reverse of this. It starts with actual situations, particularly those in which there is awareness of confusion, difficulty, or defeat, and from them it endeavors to ascertain what are the forces at work, and what are the issues that need to be met.

Much that calls itself Christian is a survival, and it is becoming anachronistic. The education that expresses it is consciously or unconsciously feeble. Meantime, the world's need of religious enlightenment, quickening, and spiritual discipline mounts higher and higher.

The whole situation, ecclesiastical and extra-ecclesiastical, is here confronted with a principle, already within historical Christianity, that could re-create Christian education, and by doing so make an indispensable contribution to the healing of our sick society.

This principle is neither dogmatic nor ecclesiastical, but dynamic. It is most intimately personal, and therefore most intensely social. If the reader, as a consequence, finds here little apparent concern for the systems of doctrine that "Christian teaching" usually connotes, and little attention to the machinery of the church, let him not infer that they are regarded as unimportant. I do regard them, however, as products of the spiritual life, not the source of it. They are not the starting-point for Christian education, nor a control for it. That which gives to Christian education its true and proper life is an experience that is obviously worth repeating and developing. The worth thus found and developed in present experience is that which first makes vital the problems of doctrine, and it is the same experienced worth that furnishes the true test of all our ecclesiastical machinery.

In short, the radicalism that has been implicit in Christianity from its beginning is here applied to Christian education. Our churches are ailing, and our religious nurture is feeble, because they are not Christian enough; and their influence upon world-events and the movements of society is disappointingly small, not because of any unwillingness to put on modern dress, but because old, obvious, and acknowledged principles of our religion have not been erected into a steady discipline of our spirits.

In the Fondren Lectures, delivered at the Southern Methodist University, Dallas, Texas, in March, 1928, I discussed the present theme in somewhat the same way, but more briefly. The thoughtful and friendly hearing that was then accorded to my unconventional and rather troublesome views furnished a material part of the stimulus for going on with the work that is here and now brought to completion. The spoken material of the lectures is not reproduced except in a few paragraphs and scattered sentences.

GEORGE A. COE.

GLENDORA, CALIFORNIA,
February 28, 1929.

CONTENTS

vii

INTRODUCTION

1. Meanings of "Christian" and of "Christianity" as They Are Used in This Work

An eminent historian said in my presence that a satisfactory definition of Christianity could not be constructed—he could prove from history the inadequacy of any formula whatever. What am I, then, that I dare essay an answer to the question, "What is Christian education?"

Happily for my purpose, it does not require me to untangle historical threads, nor to prove anything about origins, nor to assume that there is an "essence" of Christianity that includes just so much and excludes all else. On the other hand, I am unwilling either openly or covertly to select from a complex tradition the part that most appeals to me and for this reason insist that it is the heart of the Christian religion.

What I have in mind when I use the term "Christian" is so simple and straightforward that ambiguity can scarcely arise, certainly no controversy over definitions. Organizations that in common parlance are called Christian churches maintain schools of various sorts. Here is Christian education in one unmistakable meaning of the term.

These churches, though they disagree upon many points, trace their lineage to a common historical source, and they hold in common, as parts of their religion, various standards and ideals. Any item of this sort that is commonly professed is a part of Christianity in a sense that is entirely free from ambiguity.

When we use the terms "Christian" and "Christianity" in these homespun ways, no question concerning the boundary between our religion and something else need arise, nor need we assume anything as to the correspondence between our present religion and the sources whence it sprang; it is here as a going concern, whatever its origin or its past may have been.

It is in this sense that I inquire what Christian education is and might be. I ask what the churches commonly called Christian are doing in this field, and when I call attention to defects and to possible improvements, I do so from standpoints already accepted as Christian within the system itself. I propose no importation into Christianity, no accommodation to anything outside itself.

Through much of the discussion similarities and contrasts between Catholic and Protestant education either appear or are near the surface. Yet my speech is mostly of Protestant conditions and policies. The reason is not that I identify Protestantism with Christianity, nor that I lack information concerning the principles and the methods of Catholic education, but rather that Protestantism, having gone farther upon certain routes of exploration, exhibits more in detail the difficulties of these routes, as also the kind of landscapes through which they lead. At appropriate points the policies of the Roman Church will receive specific attention, and here, as everywhere, judgments favorable or unfavorable will be based upon principles that Catholics and Protestants hold in common.

WHAT IS
CHRISTIAN EDUCATION?

CHAPTER I

THE UNSOLVED PROBLEM

2. *The Jerusalem Meeting of the International Missionary Council Hunts for the Meaning of Christian Education*

What constitutes really Christian education is an unsolved problem. Through many centuries, to be sure, the churches have taught the people, but is teaching the same as educating? Moreover, though any teaching by the churches called Christian is in a proper sense Christian teaching, the question remains, To what extent is the total effect thereof upon the personality of pupils a genuinely Christian effect? In respect to both these question marks—education (?) and Christian (?)—the churches are at sea.

Lest the "gentle reader" should say to himself, "This is the ill-considered judgment of an educational enthusiast," let evidence be brought from an entirely different quarter, namely, the world conference on missions that was held at Jerusalem in the spring of 1928.[1] Here the mission lands and the home lands were represented by a select company of men who were alive and quivering with religious interest, and with first-hand knowledge of religious actualities. This was not a meeting of educational theorizers, but of experienced religious leaders who were in contact with the stern realities of the field.

One of the leading purposes of the conference was that of reconsidering the whole policy and practice

[1] The lectures referred to in the last paragraph of the Preface were delivered while the Jerusalem conference was in session.

of foreign missions in the field of education. Elaborate preparation was made for fresh thinking on the subject. In various cities and countries preliminary conferences were held, and preliminary studies were made; then, expressing the results of these studies, a preliminary statement of more than 70 pages was printed for the purpose of defining issues and securing fundamental thinking at Jerusalem.

With what, then, was this statement chiefly occupied? With two questions: What is education? and, How is the Christian Gospel to express itself in and through educational processes? Both these questions were discussed in the light of a frank confession that neither in mission lands nor in the home churches has a solution for the problem of religious education been found.

It may well startle Christians to hear these experienced and trusted leaders affirm that we do not really know what it is that makes, or would make, any education Christian. One would suppose that the much-talked-of topic of the teaching function of the church must by this time be squeezed dry. But the Jerusalem conference warns us that the old answers are embodied in certain types of schools and schooling with which informed and thinking Christians can no longer be satisfied.

The outlook for the future, as it took shape at Jerusalem, will in due time claim our attention. But first it is needful that we who were not of the conference should realize that Protestantism as a whole has upon its hands an unsolved problem of the greatest magnitude—a problem not merely of means and methods for doing something that we understand, but also of understanding what it is that we have to do.

That this truly is our condition will become clear if, with matter-of-fact eyes, we look at some of the troublesome phases of the schools and schooling called Christian in both mission lands and the home land.

3. *The Plight of Protestant Mission Schools in the Orient*

That an acute crisis has been reached in mission schools in the Orient is known to every observer. Not every observer, however, realizes the entire nature of the crisis. It is customary to say that external causes, such as the rise of national systems of schools, or the politico-economic entanglements between East and West, are causing embarrassment. This is true enough, but it does not go to the bottom of the trouble. The crisis is due, even more, to inherent religious deficiencies in these schools themselves, deficiencies that have been there all along, but now are clearly exposed by the social changes and emergencies of the day. I do not refer, of course, to any lack of sincere devotion upon the part of missionaries, but to the misdirection of their energies. Here is a summary of some of the pertinent facts:

(1) These mission schools have, as a rule, no inclusive plan for the development of Christian character in their pupils, no real curriculum in religion. Hence there never has been any rationally justified expectation of religious results.

Instead of an inclusive plan expressive of the Christian purpose, we behold a few religious fragments, such as Bible study and a chapel service, set within a school framework that is imitatively borrowed from western secular schools.

Moreover, to a great extent it has been assumed that to teach religion is to do the same sort of thing that is customarily done with the secular material of the curriculum. That is, religion has been a subject alongside of other subjects, and "learning" it has been parallel to learning any other set of facts or being subjected to any other sort of drill.

This statement applies particularly to study of the Bible. A characteristic assumption has been that a class in the Bible is a class in religion, as though a Chinese or Indian youth could become acquainted with the meaning of the Christian life by wriggling and sweating over tiresome details of Old Testament literature and alleged history.

Religion is represented, in addition, by a daily service of worship, by more or less personal evangelism, and by rules or other schemes for securing good conduct. It is allowable to surmise that the chief Christianizing influence present in these schools has been nothing that calls itself education, but rather the informally expressed good-will of teachers and of members of teachers' families. I once said to an experienced evangelistic missionary from China, "What is it in the whole practice of missions that most unfailingly gets at the people?" Without a moment's hesitation the answer came back, "The missionary's own love for people." With this line of undoubted efficiency granted, however, a question remains about the efficiency of school worship conducted by these same persons.

Attendance at worship has been, until very recently, almost universally required, but to many pupils the requirement, as might be expected, grows irksome as soon as the high-school age is reached, if not before. In such situations the danger is ever-present that the irksomeness of the service will be transferred to the religion that is represented in it. Yet, though "required chapel" is losing something of its former standing, there are missionaries who still maintain that the bodily presence of pupils, and respectful good order guarantee a sufficient result to make the requirement worth while! On the other hand, it should be almost self-evident that, though abolition of the rule would put an end to an obstacle, the problem of a really Christian education would still remain in all its starkness. Even the groundwork of a comprehensive and rational plan would still have to be created.

(2) A second momentous evidence that our problem has not been mastered is the rather general impression among Orientals that mission schools are endeavoring to inculcate an occidental religion. This, after many years of missionary teaching!

It is not necessary to argue with any one who reads these pages that, theoretically, to the extent that we are intelligent Christians, we transcend what is western in our culture, just as we transcend what is eastern in the culture of India, or China, or Japan. Even the ancient pagan did as much who exclaimed, "Nothing that is human is foreign to me!" But missionary teaching has not made this unambiguously clear to our neighbors of the Orient.

The explanation is not far to seek. For mission schools have been obtrusively foreign, for the most part. Foreign architecture, administrative control, costumes, customs, games, sciences, languages, and in China protection by foreign courts and gunboats —how could these fail to give an impression that the religion taught by the missions is a foreign religion, a western importation? It is true that not all missions or missionaries have been alike in this or any other respect; I wish it were possible to signalize the exceptions by name. But their influence has been to a great degree counteracted by such general conditions as I have named.

Another point at which an impression has been inadvertently given that ours is an occidental religion is the treatment accorded to oriental cultures, their religions included. Again we must warn ourselves not to be unfair to the few in what we say about the many. But it is unquestionable that the assumption, "We are here to teach, not to learn; we have the truth and the correct rule of life, which you are to accept whole and entire as we prescribe them," has been sufficiently common to make a profound and painful impression upon the oriental mind.

It is not fate that pursues us here; it is no external obstacle that has prevented us from being good teachers, but rather our own dilatoriness as learners. Fully forty years ago the comparative study of religions had reached such an understanding of the non-Christian faiths that Christian theologians were pointing out the finger of God in them. The inference was at that time clearly drawn that the correct missionary approach is through recognition of common elements in Christianity and other religions, and through the religious fellowship that this makes possible. Further, the policy of devolution, or the development of self-governing native churches, was even then advocated.

But for many years it was my painful lot to observe the workings of a missionary recruiting policy that ignored such considerations. The preparation that was accepted was pitifully inadequate; for any real understanding of non-Christian cultures was not required, and in fact no thorough study of our own religion. Though emphasis was placed upon familiarity with the Bible, the candidate did not need to possess even the rudiments of the biblical knowledge that was current among scholars. College graduates were sought as missionaries, but then, as now, one could acquire a college degree without acquiring religious culture or even elementary religious intelligence. This was so even in denominational colleges. It was inevitable, therefore—and it was not the fault of the young recruits—that they should be unready for leadership at the points where Christian and non-Christian cultures meet.

We are reaping what we have sown. The low standards of religious culture that have prevailed at the home base have been transferred to the mission stations. This is how it has come to pass that missionary practice has supported, if it has not actually created, a sense of white superiority. Even if it were possible to prove that missionaries generally have not had this attitude, the fact still would remain that their school methods, taken in connection with their evangelistic methods, and in connection with the problem of control, were bound to give this impression to native orientals.

Some orientals, of course, as well as many missionaries, have an inkling of the truth. They perceive that the implications of what we profess about God, Christ, and duty are not occidental or foreign; that they utterly condemn commercial exploitation of weaker peoples; that they are the diametrical opposite of nationalism expressed in protection by gunboats, and that they condemn the sense of superiority and unreadiness to learn as un-Christian. The germ of all this has been present in mission schools, but the conditions for any large growth and flowering of it have been lacking. The plight of mission schools, that is, arises from the fact that they have not been Christian enough, and this in turn from the fact that we at the home base have lacked both religious and educational sense.

(3) A third disturbing fact must now be named. In the presence of growing nationalism and national school systems in the Orient, mission teaching is unclear as to its irreducible functions.

This unclarity is interwoven with the whole history of mission schools. For they provide so-called

general education as well as (supposedly) religious
education. Why they do so, and what contributions
to general culture and economic well-being have thus
been made, we cannot stop to inquire; it is enough
that the religious purpose of missions has been intertwined with the policy of teaching the usual elementary, secondary, and college subjects found in
western institutions. Is there, then, a Christian content for these subjects? Or a Christian way of teaching them? Or, is the reason for teaching the so-
called secular subjects a desire to have pupils where
additional influences, called Christian, can play upon
them? Finally, if the secular state should take over
the secular subjects, just what would the missionaries then teach, and how would they teach it? That
is, what system of religious education would they
offer, and could it be harmoniously related to national school systems?

There was a time when Japanese missions, or some
of them, faced a part of this question under conditions of some anxiety. For the famous Imperial Re-
script on Education seemed to say that the one and
exclusive source of moral authority for Japanese is
their Emperor. Happily, it was found that the document is susceptible of an interpretation that does not
make it conflict with Christian discipleship. But the
incident remains noteworthy because it brings us
close to the ultimate question, What moral authority is to be ascribed to the secular arm?

Christian education and state education encounter each other definitely and inevitably at one point
—at least they will do so when both are clear as to
their respective aims—namely, in their respective assumptions concerning right and wrong in the basic
relations of man to man. It is not at all inconceiv-
able that open conflict should occur at this point between modern states and organized Christianity. In

our souls the conflict is already going on. Surely, any education that deserves to be called Christian will pull against the nationalism of which war is a natural expression, and it will pull against the organized economic self-interest that is "the power behind the throne" in the modern nationalist state. Fosdick has declared that the chief rival of the Christian religion is this modern nationalism.

The growth of just this sort of nationalism is nowhere more evident than in the founding of state school systems in the Orient. The temptation is strong to claim for the state exclusive control of education. Therefore these are troublous times for mission schools. State supervision at least appears to be inevitable; doubtless many mission-school functions will pass over to the state schools; what the end will be no one can say. But our position in the matter is weak because that for which we are willing ultimately to stand, that for which our schools will perish if worse comes to worst, is obscure.

The only possible way to clear up the obscurity is to determine the kind of relation between man and man that we must teach if we teach at all.

(4) A fourth item in the plight of mission schools is backwardness in the technic of teaching, particularly in the teaching of religion. That such backwardness is common is admitted on all hands. "Very often," says a friendly commission that investigated Chinese mission schools, "the courses on religion and the Bible were the poorest that were offered." The most loyal friends of missions are quoting this devastating judgment; they say that mission schools fail oftener in religious education than they do in mathematics and science.

What we behold here is a manifestation in classroom detail of the three defects already noted, namely, lack of a genuine curriculum in religion,

lack of a definitely Christian policy in contacts with
non-Christian cultures, and lack of clear consciousness of the irreducible minimum that Christianity
must teach concerning the relations between men.
The effort to utilize the structure of western secular
schools in the teaching of religion in the Orient results, most naturally, in slackness with respect to
both the secular and the religious demands, but the
religious more than the secular. For the whole policy puts religion into a dependent position, running
the risk of making it appear like an educational
parasite. If there is in Christianity any principle
that in and of itself might guide us to educational
processes as well as ends—and I shall endeavor to
show that there is such a principle—mission schools
have not recognized and applied it. On the other
hand, if method in religious education must be derived from non-religious sources, again the mission
schools have lacked pious thoroughness in their
search for this method.

Such is the plight of mission schools and schooling in the Orient, and most of all in China. In other
mission lands conditions are not sufficiently different
to provide guidance in the present crisis. In short,
then, at the point where we should naturally be
acutely certain of what we mean by Christian education—the point where Christianity is most conscious
of contrasting religious cultures—we have been, like
Hamlet, double-minded and irresolute, "unpregnant
of my cause."[1]

[1]For the factual basis of this analysis of the plight of mission
schools and schooling I have relied largely upon statements made
in the interest of missions by missionaries and mission leaders At
no point have I based any judgment upon the words of an un-
friendly critic. The report on "Religious Education" by Drs.
Weigle and Oldham in preparation for the Jerusalem conference
is as mild as sensitive friends of missions could make it, yet it reveals, sometimes by implication, the truly alarming crisis. A circumstantial document is a mimeographed "Digest of Materials

4. The Unsatisfactory State of Protestant Education in the United States

But this double-mindedness and irresolution are not peculiar to our missionary enterprise. I have used this far-away crisis, for the sake, in part, of simplifying and making vivid some home conditions that we are less than half aware of. *De te fabula!* With a few modifications the four points that indicate a crisis in mission education would describe the state of Christian education among Protestants in the United States. Let us review these points as they prick us.

(1) The Protestant churches of the United States never have had an inclusive plan for the development of Christian character.

If they had such a plan it would be manifest in the curriculum of the seminaries that prepare leaders for the churches. But, until very recently only the faintest traces of the problem of Christian education could be discerned in the courses of study for prospective pastors, and even now, after twenty-five

Relating to Religious Education and Its Problems in Japan, Korea, China, Philippine Islands, and the Near East. Prepared by W. L. Sanders," a copy of which I owe to the courtesy of Dr. A. L. Warnshuis, one of the secretaries of the International Missionary Council. Mr. Sanders quotes from a wide range of publications, and from numerous replies to a circular letter to missionaries in the fields just named. Fragments of information were found in many miscellaneous documents contained in the Missions Research Library and put at my disposal by the Librarian, Mr. Charles H. Fahs. Still another source of information is a long succession of missionaries on furlough who have attended my classes in religious education. Among these persons there have been evangelistic missionaries; teachers in mission schools, colleges, and theological seminaries; Christian Association secretaries, and heads of mission schools and training institutions. It has been my custom to invite these students to focus their study upon the educational facts and problems of their respective missions. In addition, I have had many contacts with graduate students who are natives of mission fields, and in some degree a product of mission schools. The result is that facts about the missions have been showered upon me.

years of agitation for real religious education, in
only a seminary or two can one find any considerable
information upon the dynamics of human growth.
Something is being said, to be sure, about the
church's care of the young, but, just as missions
have endeavored to insert Christian education into
a secular-school framework, so the leaders at home
are laboring to develop church schools within an
ecclesiastical framework that is unadapted to them.
Wherever, in theory or in practice, Christian education begins to reveal the depth and the breadth of
its problems, immediately a gap appears between it
and theological ideas and church customs that are
taken for granted. The theological and ecclesiastical mind is not at home in the sphere of education.

If the mind and the heart of the churches were
awake to the necessity of a comprehensive plan for
the formation of character, the conditions of ordina-
tion to the ministry would be different from what
they are, and likewise the conditions of promotion in
the pastorate. But why linger upon the limitations
of our accepted leadership when the educational
practice of the churches is open to inspection? What
we have, almost invariably, is a core of biblical instruction (usually insubstantial) surrounded by a
rather miscellaneous lot of influences supposed to be
upbuilding, such as persuasion or petty preaching
by teachers, mass evangelism, services of worship,
and a few philanthropic and other activities called
"service." The Bible, a vastly complex thing, is at
the centre, and it holds its position there by virtue
of a non-educational tradition, not because the dynamic relations of the different parts of the Scriptures to human character have been tested. An un-
sifted tradition is the main control.

Conditions have improved in recent years, and
they are improving. I should be among the last per-

sons to be unaware of this, or unappreciative of the
changes that I have joined with others in advocat-
ing. The improvement of the curriculum and of
methods of teaching; the development of the experience of worship; service activities and initiative
therein—these are all "to the good." The movement
for week-day schools of religion, likewise, is evidence
of increasing apprehension of the breadth of our
problem. But it is undeniable that obviously needed
reforms have encountered tremendous inertia in both
the leaders and the led; that the level of teaching,
with few exceptions, is low; that as yet we have no
means of making it reasonably probable that the individual pupil will become ready for the life-issues
that are ahead of him, or that any church as a whole
is being trained to recognize or handle the major
problems of the Kingdom of God as they arise.
Though the church school is improving, uncertainty
and unsteadiness as to the main functions of churches
in modern society are growing.

The lack of a comprehensive plan for the development of Christian character is the openly confessed
reason for the present unprecedented enterprise in
curriculum-study and curriculum-construction on
the part of the International Council of Religious
Education. The aim is to devise a plan of education
—not mere instruction—for both Sunday and week-
day use, and to make it fit the ascertained experiences and needs of pupils of the different ages. The
special theories that are in control of this enterprise
will engage our attention in a later chapter. At the
present moment it is sufficient to point out that this
endeavor is without precedent in the entire history
of the Christian churches.

If to all this we add the history of denominational
academies and colleges in this country, the picture
of our Christianity's educational poverty becomes
still more striking. For the pattern of these institu-

tions is not in any fundamental respect different from the pattern of secular schools. Religion is here, but as a kind of "also" that begs not to be forgotten. There are instances, so plentiful that any one familiar with the field could name several offhand, in which the religious activities officially carried on by church institutions have an entirely secondary place in the institutional consciousness of both students and faculty.

The import of all this is not condemnation of any person, institution, or religious body. The purpose is simply to face actualities in order that we may wisely devote ourselves to a task that all of us recognize as fundamental to the churches and to Christianity. If we are "poor, and blind, and naked," the sooner we know it the better.

(2) Corresponding to the problem of relating Christianity to native cultures in mission fields, we have at home the problem of the proper relation between our religion, on the one hand, and on the other hand, modern science and the industrialism that employs the sciences as tools. Two cultures are endeavoring to live side by side in western society—and in our breasts, too. Each assumes to have an independent and self-sufficing life of its own, and each, casting squinting looks at the other, assumes its own superiority, at least at points of conflict.

Modern science, in order to live at all, had to steer a course of its own, independently of the churches. It was forced by ecclesiastical attitudes to be silent and non-committal on many things in order to have freedom to speak upon others. Naturally it allied itself with industrial interests that showed appreciation of its results, and readiness to support research.

The enormous power that industrial purposes have acquired through scientific control of nature and of

man has produced in the beneficiaries thereof a sense
of self-sufficiency that, beginning as an attitude toward the powers of nature, became in a natural way
an attitude toward human relations in industry. It
ends in a sense of moral self-sufficiency that selects
ends as well as means, and, without a sign of mod-
esty, assumes to direct the destinies of nations and
of the world.

The churches have been wary with respect to the
theological implications of the sciences, as if the sciences and our religion were foreigners to each other.
Our religion has been put into the position of cen-
soring science almost precisely as non-Christian religions and cultures have been censored by the missionary mind.

Toward industrialism, however, the churches,
Protestant and Catholic alike, have been unwary,
though here a moral rivalry was springing up that
is far more deadly than any possible conflict between
science and theology.

With regard to this upspringing of a different
and partly rival culture in the western world, Christian education has done next to nothing. It is true,
as it is creditable, that some theological seminaries,
and some of the later church-school curricula, have
made an effort to fuse a Christian with a scientific
view of nature, and also to reveal some of the conditions into which industrialism has plunged us. But
few laymen, at least, have acquired any considerable
insight into the work of the sciences from any teaching that the church has done; and—what is more
serious—most Christians neither know, nor have
means of learning, that some of the basic principles
of industrialism are at variance with the basic principles of Christianity. Let not the home church cast
stones at foreign missions on the ground that they
have fumbled their contacts with other cultures!

(3) The relation of the home churches to national school systems is only a step or two more advanced than that of oriental mission schools. Not only are our working relations not yet stable, but the churches have not settled in their own thinking what are the irreducible functions of Christian education.

The type of nationalism that has been growing in the West for two centuries or more makes extremely important assumptions with respect to state control of the mind and character of growing citizens. Now and then a legal conflict reminds us that great general principles are being contested. It was so, for example, when an Oregon child was taken from his parents by order of court because, obeying his parents' religious scruples, he refused to participate in the school salute to the flag. The fact that the child was after many months restored to his parents, also by order of court, though they did not recede from their conscientious position, is possibly of great historical significance. Certainly the principle involved touches both religion and the civil state acutely. Yet our churches are complacently unconscious, as a rule, of the tremendous consequences of events now taking place, mostly in silence.

Education, which was once and until recently in the hands of the ecclesiastical power, is passing more and more under the control of the secular arm. What, then, is to be reserved to religion? What are the irreducible functions of Christian education? The churches cannot tell you; they have not made up their minds; within Christian instruction you will find next to nothing concerning the ethical character and the ethical limitations of the state. Here again our home situation is closely parallel to that of mission schools in the Orient.

(4) A fourth evidence of the unsatisfactory con-

dition of Christian education in the home land is our general backwardness with respect to school technic. Under this term I include, in addition to instruction (which aims to increase the pupil's knowledge), opening the world of religious appreciations, the induction of self-discipline, the enlargement of purposes, and the development of judgment and intiative.

The best that we can say for ourselves on this count is that we have begun to wake up, that experimentation and testing have started, and that skilful teaching will now be found at a considerable number of isolated points. In the by and large, however, the work is in the hands of incompetent teachers who give to it only the fag ends of their time and energy. This is said, not in a spirit of fault-finding, but of fact-facing in the interest of the cause.

The reasons for this backwardness deserve a moment's thought. They are substantially the same as the reasons for corresponding backwardness in mission schools, namely, the lack of a comprehensive and reasoned curriculum, failure to appreciate the problems involved in the meeting of independent cultures, and failure to find the proper place of religious education in a total educational scheme. In short, not having thought our problem through, our purposes have been only blunt-pointed, and we have contented ourselves with a quality of craftsmanship that is not worthy of our cause.

5. The Possible Self-Discovery of Christianity Through Christian Education

What has been said may seem to imply that if only we kept clearly in mind what our religion is we should perceive what Christian education should be. This is one angle of the truth, but another angle points in the opposite direction. It is true that if we appreciated our religion we should be better teachers, but it is equally true that if we were better teachers we should see more clearly what our religion is and implies.

One reason why this is so is that when we endeavor to think out the meaning of life with children and in terms that are meaningful to them, we have to let go our sophistications and artificial entanglements. Many a religiously thoughtless person has been made thoughtful by facing the question whether or not he wanted his child to be religiously educated, and if so, how. "My husband and I have ceased going to church since we moved to New York City," said one parent, "but now we must see about this." Similarly, any thoughtful teacher is likely to say, or at least to think, "I have assumed this or that heretofore without thinking much about it, but now I must get at the true core of it for the sake of these pupils of mine."

Neither children, nor the problems of character-formation, were before the eyes of the creed makers. Moreover, most of the worship, the government, and the activities and methods of the churches were chosen and fixed without reference to the needs of growing children and young people. Besides, we have been learning much about these needs and about the dynamics of growth that the men who shaped the structure of our religious tradition could not possibly know. Now, when, from the standpoint of the educator who is aware of these things, we look back at the history of our faith, we see what before we did not behold; there occurs a reorganization of ancient values, and possibly the discovery of an unappreciated or inadequately appreciated dynamic. Thus it comes to pass that the question, What is Christian education? cannot be separated from the further in-

quiry, What especially strikes us in the Christian
religion when we view it from its own experience as
teacher?

If any one doubts that this is one effect of taking
our educational function seriously, let him examine
the text-book material that has been issued since,
say, Sunday-school leaders began to consult the writings of Froebel. I do not see how any one can inspect
this material without getting an impression of growing religious warmth and intimacy to life, nor, if
one looks closely, can one fail to perceive that this
growth is correlated with a shifting of emphasis
within our religion itself. A shifting *within* Christianity, not to something outside it.

If, in addition to studying the growth of text-book
material, we inquire of the most skilled teachers
whether or not endeavors to unfold Christianity to
others have any effects upon one's own insight and
Christian experience, again we shall be told of discovery that goes beyond all that the teacher had
learned from his own preceptors.

Facts like these contradict, in an important particular, the prevalent view of what Christian education is and does. The general assumption is that it
merely spreads to others, and applies, what we already know, or what we hold as a conviction or a
standard. But in fact it is in its own right an experiment in being Christian, an experiment through
which the meaning of "Christian" unfolds to us.

It will be impossible, therefore, to develop the
theme of this book, impossible to offer any solution
for the unsolved problem with which this chapter
deals, unless we are willing to see within educational
alternatives some of the deepest religious and ethical
alternatives between which we can be called upon to
choose. Obscurity with respect to what really constitutes Christian education connotes obscurity with

respect to the basic significance of our religion. If the reader will review what has been said about the condition of Christian schools and schooling in mission lands and at home, he will perceive that the underlying defects are religious defects, and that the cure for them depends upon our becoming Christian in a new sense.

CHAPTER II

THE STARTING–POINT OF A SOLUTION

6. *Religion Changes in the Act of Teaching It*

At what point shall we begin the attempt to re-think the nature of Christian education? Perhaps the simplest procedure that moves within the concrete, and does not wander off into abstract definitions, is this: Imagining a teacher and a pupil together, each responding to the other, to ask what this relationship between the two is. What is it to be a teacher, and what is it to be a pupil, where Christian education is going on?

A distinction between the two individuals comes at once to the surface. I do not refer to the fact that usually one is considerably older than the other, for sometimes this age-relation is reversed. The important difference is that, whereas the teacher acts in a representative capacity, speaking for the church, or for God, or for a cause or a curriculum, the pupil represents nobody but himself. Let us examine this contrast and some consequences of it.

The teacher certainly is an agent or an instrument, but is he nothing more than this? Is he a lamp that grows incandescent and warm only when and because some one else presses a button? Is he merely an animated tool? Everybody, Catholic and Protestant alike, will answer that what the teacher himself is, his individual personality, what he is by virtue of his own choices, efforts, and habits, is a vital factor in the teacher-pupil relationship.

For Catholics this answer might conceivably call attention to a rather odd .difference in standpoint

23

within their church. According to the Roman doctrine, in the sacrifice of the mass, which is regarded as the central channel through which the saving grace of God flows into the church, the character of the officiating priest is non-essential. He may be a bad Catholic and a bad man, he may be drunk or trifling at the time, but if he has been properly ordained, and if he says mass according to the prescribed formula, the full value of the sacrifice is realized. On the other hand, a bad Catholic or bad man, or one drunk or trifling at the time, even if he had been ordained, and even if he spoke Catholic doctrine and ideals without a flaw, could not be a good teacher of the Catholic religion. Why this discrepancy between the minimal requirement for mediating God to a congregation and the minimal qualifications of a teacher who is to stand in the presence of a child? I shall leave the answer to any Catholic who may be interested in the question.

Probably Catholics and Protestants would give the same reason for their insistence upon truly Christian character and earnestness in the teacher, namely, that what the teacher is mingles itself inextricably with what he says, so that the response of the pupil is a response to the teacher as well as to the curriculum that he uses, the church that commissions him, and the God on whose behalf the church speaks through him.

In fact, that which we can be most certain of whenever we undertake to teach is some interplay between the teacher and the pupil, with some resulting modification of the pupil's personality. This, indeed, is psychologically inevitable, and it has far-reaching implications.

The first of these implications will now be stated, but others will be postponed for a time. The personality-principle implies that Christian education, as well as the Christian teacher, is not a mere tool or in-

strument of our religion, but the actual fulfilment,
or attempt at fulfilment, of the ends of our religion
in the teacher-and-learner relationship.

Something like this has been said many times, but
whether the full meaning and consequence of it have
been perceived may be doubted. For it signifies that
what is most personal and free in each of the persons
concerned can be educational in the most Christian
sense. The pupil, as we have remarked, speaks for
nobody but himself. The teacher, in turn, though he
is a messenger and transmitter, is such by his own
conviction and voluntary loyalty. This loyalty of his
adds impressiveness to the message and to the authority back of it, making concrete, near, and warm what
otherwise would not seem so close. Moreover, the
teacher adjusts himself to the pupil, varying the
form of words, the emphasis and angle of thought,
and the type of attitude, to suit the age, the experience, and the individuality of the other. Thus, into
the relationship there is injected a meaning to which
the teacher's own individuality clings and must cling,
and likewise a meaning to which the pupil's individuality clings.

Consider, now, that personality is a sensitive,
changing thing, and that no two personalities are
exactly alike. Any two Christians are Christians in
at least slightly different ways, probably in ways that
are not slight. Pupils, likewise, are individual and different from one another; their spiritual responses,
though couched in identical words, are not exactly
the same. Here, then, are two necessarily variable
elements. Though we reduce the variation to the lowest possible point, we do not quite extinguish it.

These variations or shadings in religion, taking
place in the acts of teaching and learning it, have received entirely inadequate consideration. One probable reason is that, like biological variations, they

are usually slight and therefore apparently not important.

In fact, they are not always slight, but even when they are they have a way of accumulating that is not unimportant. Religions can change their complexion almost insensibly along with the other changes in their adherents and pupils. A church population, Protestant or Catholic, that makes the transition from weakness to power, from poverty to wealth, or from crudity to culture, drifts into changed religious attitudes. It does so by accumulating such slight individual variations as have been described.

Christian education participates in these variations not only because the teacher's convictions reflect them, but also because he is, and is known by the pupil to be, a representative of his church. Through the teacher the church as a whole says, "Follow us"; or, if it says, "Follow Jesus," the pupil assumes, in the absence of specific information to the contrary, that following Jesus consists in what his professed disciples do. Thus the prevailing habits of Christians, which are changing habits, supply an interpretative background to anything that teacher or text-book or sermon or the Bible says, and to any worship or other activity that is included in the church programme.

This background-meaning shifts because ideas and conduct shift. General formulas of approval and disapproval may remain the same while particular acts, attitudes, and notions exchange places to any extent in the scale that reaches from what is praised, through what is permitted, to what is condemned. Practices in which the religious society acquiesces become standards, at least standards of the religiously permissible. One can see this from the short history of the motor car, or from the history of race relations during the last hundred years. The atrophy

of a custom—family prayers, for example—is reflected in a changed sense of duty, though there be
no change in the formulas of piety. Even sudden and
profound spiritual displacements can occur, as in the
Great War, without formal acknowledgment. It is
then the emotional situation that does the effective
teaching. The same curriculum material may have
been taught in 1913, 1918, and 1928, but how different the kinds of Christianity that it represented to
the pupil! All this "not-in-the-curriculum" meaning
is mediated to the pupil by the personal presence of
the teacher.

What shall the Christian teacher do about this
kind of inescapable fact? He will, of course, endeavor
to hand on to his pupil the best thing in the religious
inheritance, and over and above what he intention-
ally hands on he will almost automatically transmit
much more. Education always is transmission; no one
need fear that it ever will cease to be this. But the
other factor, likewise inevitable, is minimized by
Catholics and fumbled by Protestants. It is true that
Protestants sentimentalize over the importance of
"the teacher's personality"; they sometimes even substitute winsomeness for sound work within the curriculum. But never, I think, has it been recognized
that precisely in the personal relations between
teacher and pupil the religion of the churches under-
goes modification either slowly or rapidly, and never
has this process of modification been taken purpose-
fully in hand and given deliberate direction.

The concept that now emerges is that of the possibility of a church that, through its educational system, exercises voluntary selection among possible
changes in its religion some of which are bound to
occur. Changes unforeseen and not fully voluntary
will continue to take place—the complexity of the details and the unpredictable factors in personality as-

sure this—but mere drift can be reduced, it can be recognized as such and therefore modified far earlier than is now the case, and there can be conscious and controlled development, growth, in the qualities of our religion.

7. The Christian Teacher's Dilemma

Almost invariably the assumption has prevailed that the work of the Christian teacher is to transmit a religion, and that the contribution of the teacher's personality is simply and solely that of a reinforcement of the transmission-process. We now see that this "simply and solely" is a psychological impossibility. When teachers of religion become psychologically awake and thoroughly realistic, they will perceive that they must take a voluntary attitude toward a flow in religion that cannot in any case be wholly prevented. They will be face to face with a practical dilemma: Shall the personality-factor in teaching be so used as to secure the maximum of conformity and the minimum of change, or so as to produce attitudes of freedom in the presence of conditions that might lead to change? There will dawn upon the mind the possibility of religious creativeness through Christian education, whereupon the relation of transmission to creation within the educative process will have to be worked out.

Practically everything that remains to be said in this volume concerns this practical dilemma and its relation on the one hand to existing defects in religious education, and on the other hand to the achievement of something new and better but still Christian. Therefore some pages will now be devoted to a preliminary illumination of the alternatives between which we shall have to choose.

It is not within our power to determine whether

education shall be both transmission from the past and response to the present—it is bound to be in some measure each of these—but we can select one or the other of them as the primary function, and we can make either of them contributory to the other. Accordingly, the Christian teacher's practical dilemma takes this form: Shall the primary purpose of Christian education be to hand on a religion, or to create a new world?

A dim inkling that education is not mere transmission pervades the schooling of both the state and the church. For no school endeavors to perpetuate, whole and unchanged, any culture whatever. When we teach literature we select the specimens according to our own taste, not according to the taste of our ancestors. When we teach history or biography we ourselves determine what shall be foreground and what background. And when we come to morals, again we select. We do it rather drastically, too, for we never tell the young the whole truth about the conduct of the present adult generation, nor about the standards that it in practice accepts. By maintaining discreet silence concerning parts of our civilization, we hope to save the coming generation from civilization as we ourselves practise it.

Wherever the schools do not avow this policy they come perilously near the edge of duplicity. The schools of the state scarcely ever tell the whole truth about how the government is run and what it has done; instead, they cover up or slur over the blunders and the wrongs committed by our nation, causing pupils to believe that our better national qualities are more commanding than they ever have been. Thus, professing to transmit a political culture, the schools idealize it by a process of selection that really implies condemnation as well as praise, the need of reconstruction as well as of transmission.

An almost identical educational policy prevails in the schools of the church. No Sunday school, church college, or theological seminary paints an impartially realistic picture of the present state of our religion, or—with some exceptions in theological schools—of any past state of it. No church, however holy it thinks itself, goes the whole length of complete self-revelation. When God, incarnated in children, peers about our ecclesiastical garden, every denomination resorts to fig leaves.

This selective function of education, normal and proper though it be, is seldom fully avowed by school administrators; it is seldom thorough, and the implication that education should squarely accept the duty of social criticism and reconstruction is scarcely ever accepted. No, the dominant concern is that the rising generation should not get too far away from precedents, should not become too unlike us.

As it is not within our power to determine whether education shall be both transmission from the past and response to the present, so it is beyond our scope to permit or forbid selection among the possible responses to the present. Selection takes place anyhow, whether consciously or unconsciously, whether by successive yieldings to circumstances or by a continuous plan. The one thing that we can do is to make deliberate choices, and consolidate them into a policy, instead of drifting, or being only partly steered by others, dead or alive, while we vainly imagine that we are wholly guided by them. If we should conclude that our job as teachers is not, first and foremost, to hand on something that already exists, but to enter creatively into the flow of present experience, a part of our problem would then take this form: Is there anything creative in the religion that has been handed down to us, any principle that provides for a self-transcending and self-transforming process within the historic faith itself? If so, this principle might conceivably approve itself as a guide to original, unprescribed, and unprecedented responses to our present world, which is itself unprecedented, and we should then have a creative education that is nevertheless Christian. Let us look at this concept a little more closely.

8. The Concept of a Creative Education That Is Christian

That God is now, as through all history, creating a spiritual or moral order of righteousness and goodwill is a very old item in Christian thinking. At least, words like these are old. But the concept of continuous creation, it appears, has been hard to grasp; the nearest that most minds come to it is the notion of a quantitative increase of something that is qualitatively finished and complete. The growth of the Kingdom of God has been conceived as "more of the same" —more geographic areas covered, more members in the church, more resources at command, more faithfulness in doing duties that the saints long ago performed to the full. Growth, in the sense of qualitative change, the coming into being of something unprecedented and unpredictable from the past, involving possibly the superseding of some ancient good—this notion of the inexhaustible vitality of the divine has not been common.

Oddly enough, however, it has been many times declared that imitation, even of the Master, does not suffice. He was unmarried, and at the crucial period of his life he lived outside of the family; apparently he had no settled place of abode, and it is not clear that he made any economic contribution to his own support. In short, he did not have our particular problems to meet, and to imitate his conduct is no solution

of them. Therefore, instead of imitating him, we are
to adopt his spirit, his ends and principles of action,
and by applying them in our situations develop modes
of conduct of our very own.

The growth of social consciousness and conscience
within the Christian churches during the last thirty
and more years has brought to the surface a most interesting phase of this idea. The Gospels give us no
direct guidance concerning capital and labor, property, the profit-system, corporations, government
ownership, social insurance, international law, and
so on, though these are the sphere of the severest moral
strains of our time. Nevertheless, no one doubts that
in Jesus' approach to life there is something that does
bear upon this whole area of modern social struggle,
and that if we take this approach we shall produce unprecedented modes of social life and unprecedented
good. How our modern mass-life can become Christian we simply do not know and cannot know except
by experimentation; we must create the good life or
we shall miss it. Already we see that the old sorts of
goodness, the Christian life of other generations, are
inadequate and sometimes obstructive, and it dawns
upon us that *we* cannot be Christian unless we take
upon ourselves the burdens and the risks of re-creating in some measure our Christianity itself.

This re-creation, these phases of religious living
that Jesus never thought of, can yet be Christian in
the sense of carrying forward something that Jesus
started or something to which he gave impetus; and
beyond all this is the possibility that something in
his mode of approach to life (as distinct from the
particular things he did, and the particular connections in his thought) is universally valid because it
is the way of perpetual discovery and perpetual creation. It may be—I shall show that this is the fact—
that we cannot maintain vital continuity with Jesus

unless we do take his road of discovery and creation.
It is quite possible—indeed, the preceding chapter
gave examples of this—to attempt a kind of continuity that is self-defeating. The churches have broken away from Jesus time and again at the very
points where they thought they were exalting
him. I do not see how we can ever really outgrow
him; the issue for us is whether we will be creators
with him, evoking the unprecedented by our own
thinking, experimenting, daring, and suffering. Reconstruction, continuous reconstruction, is of the essence of the divine work in and through the human.

Of course we cannot reconstruct anything unless
we are acquainted with it; we cannot take a creative
part in the moral order without intelligence as to its
present and its past. But the focal point of true education is not acquaintance with the past, it is the
building forth of a future different from the present
and from the past. Moreover, creative education implies that the nature and the degree of this difference
are to be determined within and by means of the
educative processes; they cannot be dictated or imposed; they cannot be discovered by exegesis of any
historical document.

This, in a preliminary and schematic way, is what
is meant by creative education that is likewise Christian. Looked at from the standpoint of the learner's
experience, what has been said means that learning
to be a Christian should be, essentially and primarily,
an experience of free creativity. Looked at from the
standpoint of the teacher, it means fellowship of
teacher and pupil in forming and executing purposes that are unprecedented as well as those that
follow precedent. From the standpoint of the church,
it means ecclesiastical self-reconstruction in and
through fresh approaches to the surrounding world.

Of course any such idea of education bristles with

questions, and it is provocative of so many doubts that no one need fear that it will be precipitately adopted. We can afford to examine it in a leisurely spirit. It will be well to look, first of all, at the alternative. How, as a matter of fact, is the transmission-theory of Christian education working? What should we have to give up if we shifted to the theory of creativity? In the next chapter I shall endeavor to present a realistic picture of actual conditions that show in some detail what our alternatives are. After that we shall be ready for exposition of the specific nature of the creative principle, already within our historic religion, that might control Christian education.

CHAPTER III

WHY WE FAIL

9. *The Disparity between Theory and Practice in Christian Education*

The theory that has controlled Christian education almost universally, though not quite so, is that there is a body of most important truth—"saving truth"—which is to be handed on by the church from generation to generation to the end of the world.

This "saving truth" has been variously envisaged. It resides in a set of formulas for belief; or, it is the essence of the Bible history; or, it is a divine drama that is enacted in the life of the Master, and reproduced in the worship of the church; or, it is an inner experience of God that verifies the system of belief. Latterly, with the wide decay of dogma (that is, beliefs authoritatively required), a disposition has appeared to conceive of Christian teaching as handing on the truth in the sense of the true way of life (modes of conduct, worship, motives, appreciations).

Within the resulting variety of handings-on there are differences both as to what is to be handed on, and wherein the handing-on consists. But all of them assume that transmission is the primary function of Christian education. From this, their own standpoint, let us now examine them one by one. This procedure does not imply that one is as good as another; far from it. Let the reader bear this in mind as we now proceed with the question whether Christian education in its common forms is what it thinks itself to be, and accomplishes what it thinks it does.

Some disparity between theory and practice is to be expected upon entirely general grounds such as human fallibility and the enormous complexity of the factors. It is known among yachtsmen that no two boats handle exactly alike even though they are built after the same plans and specifications by the same workmen in the same factory. Even precision machinery and scientific tests do not protect a manufacturer of automobiles from turning out a defective car now and then. How much more should we expect wide variation in the outcome of any scheme of education. It is not of such variations or even failures, however, that I speak. The best teacher of reading might have some incorrigibly illiterate pupils. But suppose we should find a high rate of illiteracy in a population that has had public schools and a compulsory-education law for three generations; surely we could draw an inference concerning the efficiency of the public-school system within this population. Do disparities somewhat similar to these exist in Christian education? Let us see.

(1) Let us assume for the moment that the truths that are "unto salvation" are contained in a set of dogmas, and that Christian education consists in handing them down from one generation to the next. This would make the task of Christian education simpler than any other theory makes it. Yet this task is not being performed in accordance with the theory of it by any communion whatsoever, not even by the Roman Catholic Church.

Even if the Roman priests average high in their grasp of the dogmas in their saving quality (which, in view of the training for the priesthood, seems unlikely[1]), the same is not true of the laity. For more than a quarter of a century Catholic writers have

[1]See the anonymous article, "The Catholic Church and the Modern Mind," *Atlantic Monthly,* January, 1928.

asserted that vitality is lacking in the teaching of
the dogmas. The complaint is of formalism, exter-
nality, words drilled into the memory instead of grasp
or realization. In fact, Catholic authority can be
found for the notion that the exact learning of correct words is the basic requirement in Catholic
method.[1]

Against this formalism, with its deadening effect,
there has been a struggle within the Catholic Educational Association and by various writers of text-
books. The problem has been to make religion concrete, attractive, enjoyable, accepted from the heart
—that is, to produce something very different from
learning and accepting the dogmas. One series of
text-books (MacEachen's), assuming that the real
meaning of the dogmas is that they express divine
love at work for us, first simplifies the formulas, and
then endeavors to invest them with the glow of a
loving response to God. Another series (inaugurated
by the late Dr. Shields), postponing formal statements of doctrine for several grades, inducts the
pupil into love of God by means of analogies drawn
from the warmth of family affection.

If, now, this warming-up process should capture
the minds of pupils, the result would be, not that the
ancient content of the ancient formulas has been assimilated, but that a different, a more humanized
view of God and his dealings with men has arrived!

In fact, a complex of circumstances determines
what the dogmas shall mean to the people at large—
a complex that varies from country to country, from
age to age, and from one local situation to another.
Acquaintance with kings, rulers, and processes of
government; with laws and punishments; with types
of family and community and economic organiza-

[1] See chapter XX of my *Social Theory of Religious Education*
(New York, 1917), especially pp. 300 f.

tion—all this affects the entire range of beliefs concerning God and his government. The general level
of culture affects it; the type of administration in a
given parish affects it, and likewise the organization
of instruction, the personality of the teacher, and his
emphases.

What is uniform in Catholic teaching is words, not
meanings. The formula is handed down, and in the
process the learner acquires a habit of obedience to
the men who at the time are in command of the
church, but the theory of Catholic education is contradicted by the practice.

If it be so in the green tree of whole-hearted Catholic dogmatism, how must it be in the dry tree of
half-hearted Protestant dogmatism? It is not scandalous, but only a natural incident of the attempt
to found continuity upon dogma, that communions
that differ markedly in belief and in the practice of
piety use the same creed; that within each communion the creed that it professes is interpreted or
used in contrary senses, and that the ministers of
each communion, though they have gone farther into
the dogmas than the laity has done nevertheless differ among themselves and from generation to generation. If the Protestant churches should achieve
union upon the basis of a common confession of
faith, it would be common, even at the beginning,
only in the sense of acquiescence in the use of a
single name for that which is not single or uniform,
but various and varying in the living minds concerned. Moreover, the united church would begin the
process of 'interpretation' with the beginning of the
union.

The dogmatic type of Protestant education, un-
able to maintain a real life of its own, has merged
itself, for the most part, in what is called teaching
the Bible. The formal catechism was too dry and life-

less, too much a collocation of words; too frequently
it repelled the learner, and turned him against the
church. Could not the ends of dogmatic teaching be
reached, however, by attaching dogmatic interpretations to the Bible, which is more concrete and juicy?

To what passes this shift in policy has led us in
the practice of it, we shall presently see. That the
shift is a retreat from one of the supposedly central
citadels of Christianity cannot be denied. For unless
the Bible is in and of itself a formulation of dogmas,
study that is primarily directed to it tends to put
dogma in a secondary place in the mind of the
learner. Catholic authorities realize this fully, and
therefore they consciously and of set purpose put
instruction in the Bible into a secondary position.

Without doubt Protestantism's weakened forms of
dogmatic teaching do fix some words in the minds of
many laymen, and they do produce in wide areas a
determination to be loyal to "the faith once delivered"; but this loyalty is chiefly a partisan attachment to a church, or to a party within the
churches; the shibboleths separate men far more
than they separate ideas. The lack of vitality in the
dogmas becomes ironically evident when some un-
questionably orthodox leaders openly support war
without incurring the least suspicion that they do not
really believe in the deity of Jesus Christ!

The hiatus between this theory of Christian education and the actual dynamics of it is so great that
we are justified in declaring that the theory of dogmatic Christian education, Catholic or Protestant,
is illusory.

(2) What, then, of Christian education conceived as the handing-on of saving truths by means
of instruction in the Bible? If this question had been
asked three generations ago, the appropriate reply
would have started out with the then current dis-

putes as to what the Bible really teaches, and the conclusion would have been reached that teaching the Bible is really a process of making and confirming sectaries. To-day the meaning of Bible study is not quite so simple. For ambiguity attaches to both the selection of material and the method of handling it. Some parts of the Scriptures never appear in the Christian education of the masses; some appear rarely; some frequently, some almost continuously. Moreover, within one and the same communion or set of communions the choice shifts from time to time. Clearly, then, this education does not hand on the Bible as the vehicle of saving truth, but rather the varying views of saving truth entertained by those who pick and choose within the biblical literature.

A parallel situation exists in the handling of the material that is selected. Every Protestant teaching body endeavors to extract the spiritual essence from the passages employed or the events recorded therein. But this involves as a constant factor—for we are human—a tendency to find support in the Bible, because of its prestige, for any religious convictions that we strongly hold, whatever their source.

To what extent, moreover, is the history that is supposed to manifest God's dealings with men actually recognized and taught as history? Think of the way the churches have resisted the historical study of the Bible; and think of the inertia that succeeded resistance. Even when historical methods had become firmly lodged in theological seminaries, and the results were current coin among well-educated ministers, the laymen were taught Sunday by Sunday that this or that was true which their own pastors did not regard as true! And when it became inevitable that the laity should be apprised of what was happening in biblical research, the policy was pur-

sued of making the transition with the least possible disturbance of the laity's intellectual and spiritual composure. The result is what might be expected. Along with improved selection of material
has gone compromise of true historical method. In
order to realize how organic this compromise has become in Protestant education, let any one observe
what is treated as actual events in the life of Jesus,
and then compare it with what is historically known.
Any one who has not thought about this matter will
be surprised to find how rare is a teacher or a text-
book that discriminates so that pupils shall do so
among—(a) what is historically known, (b) what
is surmised, or inferred, or chosen as the better hypothesis, and (c) what is attributed to a passage or
event as its spiritual value.

A comment might be added concerning ignorance
of the Scriptures in the very communions that have
assumed that the Bible is the text-book or the source-
book of spiritual truth. But others have so abun-
dantly shown the wide-spread existence of what some
of them call "religious illiteracy" that we need not
pause upon this point. All routes lead to the same
destination, namely, that Christian education, conceived as handing down saving truth in the form of
the Bible, simply does not work.

(3) What, then, of Christian education that cen-
tres in the worship of the church, and that seeks to
make of this worship a mental living over, and thereby a spiritual appropriation, of the divine drama
enacted in the life, death, and resurrection of Jesus?
The focal points in such education are two: Instruction in the Scriptural origins of the church, its history, and its constitution and usages, and participation in the worship and the life of the church. In
one of its forms, this theory makes the sacraments the
channels through which God's saving grace flows,

and then education is directed toward feelingful and habitual participation therein, particularly in the eucharist. Increasing voluntary frequency at the communion is then taken as one of the surest signs of religious growth.

That this sort of education attaches many persons to the church is true, and this attachment not seldom is an inner and devout experience. Here is a measure and a kind of success, but not a kind that proves that the underlying theory has worked. This theory requires that the learner live over certain events that are assumed to have occurred in the life of Jesus. How many of these assumed events did occur as they are described in the material used? The confusion and unintentional evasion that we found in the use of the Scriptures in non-liturgical churches is present in the liturgical congregations also. To what extent, then, is this worship, this sacramental life, dependent upon the historicity of the Gospel narratives? Apparently the dependence is utter. But if so, why does not Christian education in these churches shift its boundaries in response to new historical insight, or even in view of justified historical doubts? On the other hand, if it is proper to supplement history by pious imagination, basing the sacraments and education partly thereupon, how is this exercise of imagination to be guided and tested? The fact is that the liturgical churches as well as the others are mixing up, in religious education, historical and extra-historical elements with no provision for enabling the learners—the laity, at least—to discriminate between the two.

Little time need be spent upon the fact that worship and the sacraments are taken in conflicting senses by different wings within a church; nor in the fact of an historic flow in the meanings that are attached to sacred symbols. These things, which are patent, add, of course, to the considerations already stated. The conclusion to which we come is that here again a theory fails to work. Christian education of this type is something other than it purports and intends to be.

(4) The type of Protestantism that cultivates as the prime essential of Christian life a particular inner realization of God, as in conversion, and then relies upon this experience to verify ancient doctrines, has done little to incorporate this standpoint into Christian education. Instead, the experience in question has been cultivated alongside the teaching-learning situation. To teach Christianity has then meant to instruct in a set of ideas or doctrines, but even the most favorable response to this instruction has not constituted what is recognized as Christian experience. Thus, effort is made to maintain continuity within Christianity by two independent lines of endeavor, instruction and Christian experience. Neither one really grows out of the other or into the other.

Of the suicidal logic of the underlying theory only a word need be said. The instruction is supposed to be based upon a self-sufficient historical authority, yet there is resort to the experience of the Christian as the self-certifying thing. The two authorities are made to appear harmonious partly by refracting history through interpretative lenses, and partly by appropriate picking of the present experiences that are depended upon as evidential. Anything like the experimentation and analysis that alone could establish anything from Christian experience is lacking.

Church practice controlled by this type of theory has been disastrous. Christian experience has refused to be standardized. The attempt to standardize it has plunged multitudes of young people into confusion, and it has separated them from the churches with which they would naturally affiliate. What is perhaps not less unfortunate is the direction taken by many leaders and societies that have attempted to forestall this confusion and negativity. Softening the meaning of old formulas is a main part of the policy, and the result has been that in large areas of our church population there is really no sharp edge at all to the concept "being a Christian." Meantime, religious education in some of its newer forms is feeling around to find where the sharp edges really are. Thus the type of Christian education here under scrutiny breaks down, and new types come to the rescue.

(5) That the hiatus between theory and practice is less extensive where Christian education is conceived as handing on the truth as the true way of life should not be surprising. For entanglements in biblical history, the dogmas, and ecclesiastical forms tend to be reduced, and direct appreciations and choices that the learner can feel as his own tend to become prominent. The work of teaching now becomes more largely that of awakening the learner's powers and getting them into action.

Nevertheless there usually lurks under the surface a not-clearly-expressed premise that introduces into practice what is at least an ambiguity. For "the" way of life usually means a policy and practice that, having been fully realized and formulated elsewhere, are now to be reproduced in us. But this assumed relation of present to past, and of the individual to the mass, brings into question once more the reality and the degree of transmission. A narrow spiritual pragmatism is encouraged. Since "life" is our objective, let us use the Bible, or historical doctrines, so as to "get results"—this is the spirit. But "getting results" may involve us in the sin of trifling with historical questions, or putting aside

profound and time-consuming issues in order to secure immediate movement. Imitation is resorted to
where analysis is required. There may result from
the whole a mechanization of pious habits that corre-
sponds to the intellectual mechanization of the
dogmatist.

These dangers may be illustrated by a specific example. By "the true way of life" is meant, of course,
the way of Jesus. It is sometimes given the inelegant
name of "the Jesus way." But what teacher, following even this theory of Christian education, really
expects the radicalism of Jesus to be reproduced in
the learner? In any case, whatever the teacher hopes
for, what happens is that the learner accommodates
himself more or less to what attracts him in the Gospel plus what attracts him in his ecclesiastical environment. All of us, in fact, because we are individual, modify what we adopt, and because we are social, move with the human stream of our time.

All the main types of Christian education have
now passed before us while we asked concerning each,
Do theory and practice here coincide? All of them
assume that their main function is transmission of a
religious heritage. But not one of them has found
out how this function, in any unqualified sense, can
be performed. There is something in the practice
that is independent of the theory and contradictory
of it. Words are transmitted to some extent; some
outward habits likewise; religious institutions are
kept going, and loyalty to them is evoked; some generalized sentiments and emotions, more or less de-
tached from the life-movement, are repeated, often
with a feeling of affinity with a long past; but round
about all this, and even within it—not seldom by
means of it—something draws or pushes us in directions that the theory does not account for and that
no application of it can prevent. Only in a partial

and ill-defined sense, it now appears, is it possible to transmit our religion by education.

This section has illustrated from educational practice the truth that was expounded in section 6. There we saw the psychological impossibility of preventing changes in religion in and through the teaching-and-learning process. Here we see Christian churches attempting this thing on a large scale, but never achieving it. The transmission theory does not work.

Worse remains behind. Not only does an education that intends to be primarily transmissive fail of its full intent; it also, of its own nature, creates evils for which it is loath to accept responsibility. In the next four sections these evils will be circumstantially set forth.

10. Transmissive Education Hands On Our Faults, But Conceals Them, and by Concealment Adds to Their Prestige

"Transmissive education" is here adopted as a short name for policies and practices that are based upon the assumption that the primary purpose of education, by which its particular processes are to be controlled and judged, is the perpetuation of an already existing culture or some part of it. "Creative education," on the other hand, will be our term for education that places in this position of primacy a purpose to improve or reconstruct a culture or some part of it, and that employs transmission processes—always present anyhow—to this end.

Transmissive education intends, as was indicated in section 7, to hand on what is good in our present culture without perpetuating its defects. Hence it selects for teaching purposes the finer specimens of humanity and its products, representing them as the true reality. Thus: We are neighbors, the true neighbor does so and so, and here are examples of true neighborliness; we are America, the true America does so and so, as these instances show; here is the church, and the church is such and such a fellowship; and here is Christianity, which means thus and so. In each case, that which we approve in a thing is represented as the essence of it. In none of this is there any intention to misrepresent actualities, of course, but only to give force to ideals.

This means, however, selected silences as well as selected material of text-book and of teacher-talk— selected silences that are supposed to block off the channels through which our defects, if we mentioned them, might transmit themselves. But see how this combination of sound and silence works. The school, the text-book, the pulpit does not really block the road between our faults and the mind of the learner. He knows us in a thousand ways that our intended education of him does not control. We may tell him that Christians do not set their hearts upon worldly possessions, but even a child knows that Christians do exactly this. We may illustrate the Christian spirit by picturing a hero, a saint, or Jesus, but the learner, through his myriad contacts with us, naturally assumes that the picture represents something exceptional, remote, not Christianity as a present, going, practical concern.

This mixture, in the learner's mind, of what we offer him as our teaching and what our conduct displays under no such name as "material of instruction" has the following effect: Two mental categories are formed, in one of which he places, with a sentimental approval that is not insincere, the ideal formula or picture, but in the other of which he bestows his understanding of how life actually is lived here and now, together with some sense of participation in it upon its own terms.

He assents, that is to say, to both his teachers,
the one who is called teacher, and the other who is
not. Which of these teachers and teachings will
ordinarily be the more influential with him is scarcely
a problem. Moreover, what often looks like a big,
dark mystery—the enormous moral inefficiencies of
the well-meaning—now begins to clear up. The well-
meaning live in two worlds, both of which they take
at face value, a world of sentiment and a world of
practicality. They can live in these two worlds without hypocrisy because they have been receptive, not
critical, toward both teachers. Transmissive education is the secret.

That our efforts to teach religion are largely
counteracted by the learner's contacts with the life
of our time has been lamented by many, but no likely
remedy is proposed. The reason why we cannot think
of a remedy is that we only half perceive the nature
of the problem. There is also another fact, not yet
mentioned, that is determinative, namely, that our
Christian teaching itself transmits our faults and
gives them prestige.

The mind of the learner cannot be divided into
completely water-tight compartments. Personality is
unitary; it spontaneously seeks, more or less blindly,
to be consistent with itself. Can we at all trace, then,
this consistency-creating process in the mind of the
learner whom we have described? We can, to some
extent. Let us begin with the use of terms—"Christian" for example. This adjective is applied to both
the "ideal essence" of our religion and the unideal
men whom we meet, their unideal piety, and the unideal church which they compose and manage. Some
assimiliation of one of these meanings to the other
is bound to take place unless somehow the contrariety of them is rubbed into the mind. But a rub-
bing-in policy is lacking. Our silence concerning the

defects of Christianity permits the learner's mind,
even when it touches the most vital things of our
faith, to be unwatchful, desultory, and yet receptive.
Under these conditions, the meaning of "Christian"
is of course assimilated to the concrete actualities,
here and now before the mind, that bear this name.
By this process, though you teach ideals without end,
the learner will slump from his ideal sentiments into
conformity with things as they are.

What is more, the social prestige of the church,
its accepted authority as teacher, and the sentiment of the ideal that is fostered by it, all participate in this process of self-unification. Thus it is that
Christian education, by silences imposed by the
transmission theory, in effect sanctions, if it does
not actually sanctify, our common and tolerated
faults. It is, unintentionally, a way of maintaining
the existing low level of religious respectability.

The extent and the force of this silence are little
less than amazing. Every religious communion, local
or denominational, is a scene of contradictions and
conflicts within the moral and spiritual realm. There
are uncertainties as to what is right and best, and
opinions differ; what thinks itself to be idealism
locks horns with what regards itself as practicality;
agitated conscience thrusts at yesterday's goodness,
and prudence and courage debate with each other.
Mistakes are made, many of them. But all this living, breathing actuality, so well adapted to awaken
thought and illuminate the judgment, is outside the
curriculum. The learner gets no training in the analysis of such situations; as a rule he does not know
what happens "on the inside," does not know what
blunders are made, and is not put on guard against
repeating them, and, conversely, he does not understand or appreciate creative acts when they occur.
Every old and obstinate defect in our ecclesiastical

life perpetuates itself generation after generation through pupils who are taught to be loyal without being taught to discriminate. Transmissive education is particularly adept in handing on our sins of omission—and in building tombs for prophets!

11. Transmissive Education Employs Either Force or Evasion in the Interest of Effectiveness

As long as men believed that coercing the body could control the mind, the self-constituted wielders of educational authority, whether in state or in church, used physical force as a means for propagating a culture or a faith. They were logical in doing so. For if we grant the transmissive conception of education, then coercion is good if it really does hammer in the idea, the standard, or the habit that we desire to hand on.

When it was perceived that physical force does not accomplish what was expected of it, resort was had to psychical compulsion or strong pressure. It took three forms: Compulsion by supposedly logical demonstration, habituation through repetition, and restraint through fear. The first, or intellectual compulsion, affected chiefly older pupils, as in colleges and theological seminaries. It was somewhat generally practised by Protestants two generations ago in the teaching of what was called "Christian evidences"; it is a stated practice of Catholics, and apparently it must remain so as long as the basic position of the church is dogmatic and intellectualistic. The second form of psychic compulsion or pressure —habituation by repetition—is represented by the memorization of catechisms; the third form, fear, by warnings against the sinfulness of unbelief, and by sundry well-remembered representations of God and the future life.

Protestant religious education has moved away from the use of both physical and psychical compulsion, but it has unwittingly fallen into the use of evasions. Thus:

(*a*) Appeals are made to the learner's intelligence, by invitations to examine evidence, just as if really free judgment were intended, but if he does not reach the preconceived conclusions of his teacher or of the church, if he balks at accepting what they seek to transmit to him, there follows social displeasure and sometimes a kind of religious outlawing.

(*b*) Attempts are made to induce a favorable judgment upon the Bible, biblical characters, and the church, by stating excellences without mentioning limitations and defects.

(*c*) The Scriptures are commonly used in worship as if all the parts employed were upon the same level of historic fact or spiritual illumination, with the result of confusing actual events with imagined ones, giving the color of finality to the views and peculiarities of biblical writers, and even mixing Christian and sub-Christian motives and standards.

(*d*) What may be called emotional subreption is resorted to, that is, causing the pupil to believe that a doctrine that has been historically associated with an experience that is valuable to him is essentially one with the experience.

(*e*) There is habitual use, especially in worship, of the phrases and the formulæ of obsolete or obsolescent beliefs or attitudes, with no warning that this is the fact.

(*f*) Our faith is stated in the presence of the laity or of the young in terms so general as to conceal issues known by theologians to be there. By the use of euphuistic generalities we may avoid controversy, but we also become characterless.

(*g*) Suggestion is used in such a way as to pro-

mote an institutional loyalty that is narrower than
we should be willing openly to defend. Much talk
about *our* church, coupled with silence about other
bodies of Christians, has remarkable power to keep
the horizon from enlarging.

These evasions do not occur equally everywhere,
but all of them are common and most of them are
almost universal in Protestantism. The explanation
is not that we are human, fallible, and careless. These
evasions flow directly from the assumed necessity of
making the transmission-idea work under modern
conditions. The truth is, of course, that it doesn't
really work; these items are direct evidence of departure from the theory. And the profitableness of
this departure is worse than doubtful. It does make
adherence to a church easier; it may produce lip-
loyalty to ancient creeds, and it may prolong old
usages; but it produces also quiet doubt, dissent, disinterest, and unobtrusive absence. There is increasing comment to the effect that the note of reality
does not ring clearly.

12. Transmissive Education, Its Eyes Fixed Upon Content, Is Slow to Apprehend the Forces at Work

If I assume that I have exactly what you need, I
lack a motive for watching your symptoms. Transmissive education, confident that it has in its keeping
the solution of all spiritual problems, does not feel
that rigorous analysis of changing conditions is of
prime importance to it. The teacher's attention is
naturally upon something that is to be brought out
of the past into the present, not upon the forces at
work in the immediate environment. Here is a material part of the explanation of three deep-seated
defects in the teaching work of the church. They are

frequently recognized and deplored; but what keeps them so alive and respectable?

(*a*) There is something like general recognition of the fact that Protestantism as a whole, in this country at least, is attempting to transmit Christianity through teachers who, as a rule, are incompetent as teachers but competent as Christians. Granted the transmission theory, this is not as illogical as it seems to be. For, when religion is to be delivered in original packages, anybody may be the carrier of it who is loyal to the task. We shall not fully understand the almost universal lack of trained teachers until we perceive that their task has been to hand on something in which they take no creative or responsible part. Assuming that a "message" is what does the essential religious work, we fail to appreciate the dynamics of the human beings immediately in our presence.

Thus it is that Christian missions, until experience brings disillusionment, assume that their essential business is to "declare" the Gospel. Upon this notion was based the former rallying-cry of the Student Volunteers, "The evangelization of the world in this generation." The central act of Christian education, accordingly, was taken to be the presentation of a given ideational content, as the Bible or Christian doctrines. A formal, question-and-answer catechism actually has been taught to African natives, so a missionary to "the dark continent" tells me. This is exceptional, no doubt; nevertheless it is illuminating. It is an extreme case of the same state of mind that assumed that any missionary is competent to teach a Bible class. And indeed, since any missionary is a Christian, it follows—if the "message" is what makes one a Christian—that every missionary carries in himself the instrument for doing the work; all he has to do is to set this instrument going.

This is one root-cause of poor teaching at home as well as in mission fields. It is a habit with us, when we contemplate our untrained teaching force, to say to ourselves, "But these teachers are devoted Christians, and somehow Christianity will flow through them into their pupils." The partial truth that this contains makes the error in it all the more specious. Something of the ideal called Christianity will flow through the teacher, but much else will flow through him at the same time. His method as teacher may even obstruct or conceal what he wants to teach. This is a mere commonplace, of course; nevertheless it never will be duly heeded until education becomes a fresh approach to the dynamics of living rather than the handing-on of a content or a prescription. The solution of the problem of teacher-training awaits the determination of this prior question.

(b) The transmission theory leads directly to a misconception of the nature of technic in teaching. Technic is assumed to be merely instrumental and external to the thing that is to be transmitted, whereas it properly is the sensitive and foresighted response of the teacher to movements of the pupil's personality. Technic, thus understood, is as spiritual as anything in the content of teaching can possibly be. It is spirituality in action here and now. But— and here is the crux of the matter—it makes the pupil and the teacher co-agents with the content in determining what is to be. Because the transmission theory does not and cannot accept the revision of itself that this requires, we see teachers and schools patiently "teaching" Christianity to pupils who at the moment are listless or else engaged in activities that defeat religious ends altogether. A teacher who endeavored to puzzle out an explanation for the irreverence of a group of young people came

to the conclusion that they had learned it in their
Sunday-school.

(c) To the same cause must be attributed the
long fumbling—fortunately, growing less—with the
"application" of the content. It was not chiefly
the Herbartian doctrine of the five steps in teaching that gave this term the meaning that it long had
in both preaching and other forms of teaching. For
transmission, when it definitely formulated itself,
had to state its complete programme in advance of
the acts of teaching and learning. Thus "the application" became a part of the content, and "applying the lesson" consisted in telling pupils or
getting them to tell what our duties are. Not doing
a duty, but naming it; not getting into action, but
transferring still another idea. Teaching, in short,
did not consist in dealing dynamically with the present situation. How it would shock a church, and the
minister himself, it has been remarked, if his people
should start actually to conduct themselves as almost
any sermon advises them to do.

The hiatus between accepted content and accepted
conduct is usually explained by some disrespectful
reference to the human nature of the learner, or to
bad example and influence in his environment. But
these, if they have any such power, should be met by
something at least as dynamic as they. In fact, the
hiatus is a feature of the education itself.

13. Transmissive Education, Thinking to Make Men Obedient to God, Brings Some Men into Subjection to Others

The learner, it is hoped, will become conformed to
the content, and thus to Jesus and God. But the content has been selected and interpreted, and the curriculum organized, not by Jesus nor through infallible inspiration, but by men who are like the learner

himself. The unwisdom as well as the wisdom of these
men goes into their choices and plans, so that the
learner, if he conforms as it is hoped that he will do,
becomes subject to these, his fellows, whether his response to God be great or small.

Transmissive education cannot avoid this compromise, however it struggle to purify itself. Let it assume, if it will, that a divine revelation has been committed to the church; still, however real the revelation may be, somebody's judgment defines its boundaries, its setting in other experiences, its interpretation. The pure "essence" of it never was and never
can be isolated from the rest of experience; it always
bears the finger-prints of those who hand it from one
to another. Always—to change the figure—our vision
of it is through the atmosphere of some period in history, some circle of men.

The authority of the message, therefore, and the
authority of the messenger are not two separable authorities. The Roman Catholics have perceived this,
and they have accepted the consequences of it. They
hold that finality (for the learner) must inhere in the
teacher as well as in the content, and they specifically
provide for it. Their teacher is the Pope, a present,
living, infallible guide, and whosoever, commissioned
by him, is empowered not merely to declare and persuade but also to command.

Protestantism, assuming that the content of instruction can have authority that is independent of
the agent of transmission, confuses the whole teacher-
learner relation. When the teacher leans upon the authority of the Scriptures, he really falls back upon
the unspecified authority of the men whose opinions
gave the Bible its peculiar standing in Protestantism,
upon the opinions of those who more recently have
determined the interpretation, and finally upon the
curriculum-makers and the text-book writers.

The subjection of the laity to the hierarchy in Catholicism is open and above board. The government is an absolute monarchy; it does not pretend to be anything else. There are, however, powers behind the throne. There are reasons why this man rather than another is elected to the papal chair; there are reasons why the Pope chooses this or that man for bishop; promotion within the hierarchy depends upon conditions not stated; the Pope listens to advice, and influences of many sorts play upon him as upon you and me. He does not claim to be infallible in all that he does, in fact; but, since the faithful have no way of dividing between the obligation of absolute obedience and the obligation of respect for the Holy Father, they obey whatever is transmitted through the hierarchy. Thus, even in Catholicism, which is so daringly logical, we have a supposed obedience to God that includes subjection to men in matters in which they do not even claim to be infallible.

The transmission theory of education has no view of authority to offer that will not involve this or some parallel confusion between the commandments of men and the ordinances of God. If we ascribe authority to revelation, we submit to theologians; if we ascribe authority to church, we submit, not to the ideal church, which "never was on land or sea," but to any men who happen to have won control; if we make "Christian experience" our authority, we submit to those who have defined and delimited the terms "Christian" and "experience."

14. The Best Contribution of Transmissive Education Is Its By-products. It is Weakest Where It Thinks It Is Strongest

Ask a thousand men what was the most powerful influence for good that Christian education brought into their lives, and many more than nine hundred will make replies like the following: It was the teacher's own character; it was the genuineness of a parent's religion, or a love that would not let me go; it was a personal touch at a crisis-point in my life; it was a fellowship that kept me straight until good habits were firmly established. Granted that this is not a precise or scientific test, and that our untested judgments concerning the dynamics of our own personality are subject to a very wide margin of error. Nevertheless, the general, almost unanimous swing of men's judgments in this matter is impressive, and it is in line with the most rigidly scientific knowledge of character-dynamics that we have.[1] We are safe in saying that the mainly effective factor in Christian education is 'the Word made flesh'—that is, the human relations that accompany the teaching rather than the content of the teaching.

But these excellent by-products are partly or wholly offset, as we have seen, by a dilution-process that is inherent in transmissive education. It lays its chief stress upon handing down something out of the past, yet of its own nature, as our analysis has shown, it devitalizes this very thing. The great, the overwhelmingly great, defect at this point is failure to employ the enormous potentiality that actually does reside in the message. Let us, then, close this review of why we fail by contemplating the height and the depth of meaning in such ancient words as these:

> Love your neighbor as yourself.
> Love your enemies.
> God is love.
> He that hath done it unto the least of these hath done it unto me.
> He that seeks to save his life shall lose it.
> He that is greatest among you shall be the servant of all.

[1]Hartshorne and May, *Studies in Deceit* (New York, 1928).

Seek first the rule and righteousness of God.

What shall it profit a man if he shall gain the whole world and lose his own life?

It is easier for a camel to pass through the eye of a needle than for a rich man to enter the Kingdom.

Not every one that saith unto me, "Lord, Lord," . . . but he that doeth the will of my Father.

Thou shalt love the Lord, thy God, with all thy heart.

No one, I think, will challenge the following opinion: Most Americans who have received Christian instruction perceive no inconsistency between the principles here enunciated and the philosophy of "preparedness" for war; no inconsistency with our selfish and self-willed nationalism; no inconsistency with our national superiority-complex, nor with our current superiority-complexes with regard to races, classes, and religions; no inconsistency with sex-inequality in the family, the church, and society generally; no inconsistency with an economic system that values profits above personality.

Recently a most eminent American preacher asked a great ecclesiastical assembly this question: "Isn't it time to take Jesus seriously?" When critics asked why it was that the World War could occur in the western world, which already had had the gospel of peace before it for centuries, defenders of the faith were quick to reply, "Christianity never has been tried." Never has been tried! That is, the church of each generation, when it supposed it was transmitting the revelation of God that is in Jesus, actually transmitted its own half-blind and faulty ways.

CHAPTER IV

THE CREATIVE PRINCIPLE IN CHRISTIANITY

15. *The Creative Christian Principle of the Worth of Persons Is In an Undeveloped Condition*

In the value that it attributes to personality, Christianity includes, and always has included, a creative principle.

There is ground for regarding it as "the" creative principle of our religion, whether as Christians we face man-ward or God-ward. If, however, any one should maintain that other factors in our faith have likewise an original and inherent quality of creativeness, there would be no occasion for withstanding him. For we are not here concerned with any general analysis and exposition of our faith. If, without going outside of Christianity, we can ground educational policies upon the assumption that persons have inexhaustible worth, it is enough.

For the same reason, we need not stop to ask whether this principle has been present from the beginning in the full sense in which I shall use it. Some of the prophets of Israel approximated it at least, and Jesus appears explicitly to have attributed inestimable worth to the humblest person. He appears also to have ascribed the same attitude to the Father. Yet the course of this discussion would not be altered in any essential respect if some one should prove that our present concept has grown from humbler beginnings, or that it is the resultant of complex historical forces. If, in addition, the same personality-principle is found to animate any religion or any movement that does not call itself Christian, one might exclaim,

"The more the better!" The one point that is essential for our present purpose is that all Christians who think upon their religion do regard the principle as a prime essential of it. This is Christian in quality if anything is.

The principle of the worth of persons, though ancient and universally professed by us, is nevertheless in an undeveloped condition. By this is meant, not that we fail to practise what we preach—though our slips and evasions are a disgrace to us—but rather that we have not done the thinking and planning that alone can give effect to what we think we believe.

I have called the personality-principle creative and also educational, and in due time I shall indicate the meanings and the grounds of the propositions herein implied. First, however, some elementary distinctions need to be noticed—distinctions that of themselves will make evident that the Christian churches have not yet effectively educated themselves with regard to the meaning of what all of them confess is vital in their faith.

What, then, do Christians mean when they say that they believe in the "infinite worth" of persons? Is the meaning clear in itself, and is it adequate? What the term most often brings to mind is some picture of a human being in distress or danger that some other human being, or God himself, feels so vividly that he flies to the rescue regardless of the cost to himself. The value of another personality is recognized by us, that is to say, in the sympathy that we feel for him. The old hymn in glorification of the cross expresses it thus:

> Was it for crimes that I have done
> He groaned upon the tree?
> Amazing pity! Grace unknown!
> And love beyond degree!

This self-forgetting impulse to relieve the woe of others is rightfully regarded as an evidence of the nobility of man, and it enhances the moral greatness of God in the eyes of every Christian. Nothing that I shall say will detract from the appreciation of it. Nevertheless, it by no means reaches to the full depth or breadth of the concept of the worth of a person. You can pity a man without really respecting him; you can be so overwhelmed by sympathy for a creature in distress that he becomes for you little more than an object of an approved emotion. The reason why, with great frequency, an affectionately protective attitude toward animal pets and even children has no discoverable relation to moral vigor—is often, indeed, a substitute for moral self-discipline—is that the element of respect is absent. Respect is something more, and more discriminating, than any impulse or emotion, however noble.

Jesus pointed toward the principle we are after in the command to love the other as I love myself. This commandment is not fulfilled by having an emotion, whether of sympathy, fondness, or affection; least of all is it fulfilled by pity, which contains within itself a sense of superiority to the one who is pitied. The something more that is required is partly expressed in such terms as respect and reverence for personality. An example of it occurred in a coal-mining community where thousands of persons had been reduced to penury by prolonged labor troubles. The relief work, through which scores of thousands of dollars' worth of supplies had to be distributed, was managed by a priest. But there was no soup-kitchen, no bread-line, for it was determined to prevent the loss of self-respect that follows public exhibitions of one's dependency. Instead, food, shoes, and other supplies were made up into packages, wrapped as if by grocer, market man, or other merchant, and delivered at the family door exactly as if a purchase had been made by the householder. At Christmas each of 7,000 children received a present in his own home. For this priest, relieving distress was not enough; no doing for the neighbor was quite enough; the person who was in want had also to be helped to maintain inner poise and a sense of personal dignity.

Here is reverence for personality in the form of defense and protection, but even this, full of significance as it surely is, does not bring us to the end of the matter. We must go beyond any concept of status, beyond every implication that the object of our regard is static. The self-love that is taken for granted, and then made a norm for love toward the neighbor, is not a standing still; it is not like the veins of a marble statue, however admirable. Least of all is ethical self-love the same as self-fondness or self-pity, both of which are self-corrupting. Active self-affirmation is meant or implied—such aggressive self-affirmation as claims a right to eat as against permission to eat; a right to move about; to experiment, explore, and learn; to enter into co-operative relations with others of like mind; to construct things; to utter one's mind—in short, to grow and to master the conditions of life in a manner that is determined and judged from within. There arises, of course, the exceedingly difficult problem of adjustment among such self-affirming individuals, but the basis of any acceptable adjustment must be the recognition, not the denial, of this principle.

To value personality, then, is to value self-activity in all persons. If persons are of final worth, then every particular instance of self-activity has within it something of unimpeachable validity. To discover just what this unimpeachable something is requires us often to take apart some psychical or social tangle; it requires also disciplined self-knowledge on the part of us, the disentanglers. We have much generalized approval of freedom, but a much diminished appreciation of the actual use of freedom; much glorification of personality, but far less appreciative entering into the particular thoughts and evaluations in which the neighbor's personality realizes itself.

We must come at last to this: Whatever any person prizes has some value for me—enough value to make it possible for me to enter into fellowship with him precisely where he is. Whatever is obnoxious to him contains something that I also disapprove when I understand what it is. There is then no ground left for excommunicating him from my society.

It is a remarkable fact that, the more intimately we know the whole experience of any one who slips into evil, the less are we likely to despise him. According to the Christian principle of personal worth, there is no unforgivable offense. For my neighbor's worth never is totally extinguished in any dark act that he may commit. I can forgive myself for my own folly, likewise, because, however dense my foolishness at the moment of wrong-doing, even then there was something more to me. It is because one's worst moment has something in common with one's best moment that we can enter sympathetically into the evil in ourselves and others, and be forgiving toward it. The spirit of forgiveness is the spirit of fairness to personality.

Ethical love, which is guidance of action by regard for personality, is justice in the ancient Greek sense of assigning to each what is appropriate to him— what in the light of reason belongs to him. That Greek thought assumed the permanence of such classes as slave and free, and thereby grievously blundered as to what belongs to a man as such, does not detract from the nobility of this concept of being just to all men. It is deplorable, however understandable, that Christianity generally conceived justice, not in this distributive sense, but as retributive. This made justice the antithesis of love instead of the fulfilment of love. The consequence was that approval was given to the harshness and personality-depressing quality of pseudo-justice, and at the same time to the softness and personality-disintegrating quality of pseudo-love. Both were attributed to the Divine Being, and both were approved in man. Hence, acting (supposably) as a Christian, one could support laws, penalties, and social conditions that treated personality as naught, and yet take satisfaction in relieving distress at great cost to oneself.

Even in circles that have sloughed off the old theology of retribution, endeavoring to construe the life of both God and man in terms of love, the most common notion of love is that of yielding to another what is not his due. The obverse of this is failure to realize what is his due as a person. By this route liberalism is becoming, if it has not already become, a humanitarianism that softens our manners and makes us kindly without making us sensitive toward the major injustices.

It would be easy to illustrate this conjunction of kindliness with insensitiveness by citing a past that we think we have outgrown. Let us, rather, consider what has happened under our own eyes—whether or not we have seen it. During the last two generations there has taken place a marked amelioration of the harshness of theology, and of the old antagonisms among Christian bodies. Interest in others in the form of missions has enormously expanded, and so has philanthropy of many sorts. Any one who cared to maintain that the Christianity of to-day is more Christian than that of even fifty years ago could make out a pretty good case. Nevertheless, during these years, which constitute the bloom-period of the

industrial system, Christians have been slow to realize that industrialism is a set of personality-forming
forces. The significance of power machinery has been
supposed to reside in the making and distribution of
goods rather than in the making or marring of men.
Here is dulness at the centre of spiritual vision. For
the accepted modes of daily life estrange men from
one another, and they cause this estrangement automatically to mount into class-estrangement and conflict, and into international estrangement and conflict. This is the inherent human reality of the system
that we are working, at the same time that we Christians believe that we believe in the immeasurable
worth of persons as such.

In our period of history, loving one's neighbor is
taken to mean relieving the distress of those who are
most obviously hurt or neglected, giving pacificatory
advice, and resisting individual moral disintegration
—disintegration, for example, through the dishonesty that the system constantly invites. Christianity
undoubtedly is a palliative; but when a religion that
proclaims "the infinite worth of persons" acquiesces
in an economic movement and an organization of society that go straight against this principle, the
question is a fair one whether palliative good-will
does not add respectability to that which is bound,
if it goes on, to destroy this religion, even though
its name and its institutional shells be retained.

It is customary to interpret words like these as if
they referred especially to the deprivations of the
less privileged members of the community. The rich,
it is assumed, are beneficiaries of the system, while
the others are its victims. But this assumption is another sign that we do not think our personality-principle through. For wealth is not merely the possession
of things; it is likewise a relation between persons, a
relation that affects the character of all the persons

involved. This relation is partly expressed if we call it relative independence on the one side as against relative dependence on the other; it is more fully expressed if we say that the possession of wealth connotes arbitrary power of one person over another.

That this is the fact is so obvious that it need not be argued. But we do need to consider the spiritual implications of it. Arbitrary power can be used benevolently, of course, and consequently there are great differences between persons of wealth. Yet benevolence that is arbitrary cannot escape the consequences of its arbitrariness. The possessor of wealth cannot help exercising over others a power to which he himself gives direction to suit himself; mastery and subjection are of the nature of the situation.

The apparent hardness of Jesus' remarks concerning the relation of wealth to spiritual life has led to many attempts at interpretation. Even in the Gospels these attempts have begun. Most of the interpretations tend to soften his words. It is the love of money, not the possession of it, that is injurious, thinks one interpreter. What one does with one's money is the main point, thinks another; also how he gets it, adds a third. Scarcely anybody seems to see that the possession of wealth is a relation between persons, and that this relation is the *locus* of the spiritual problem. The great truth, whether or not Jesus had it fully in mind, is that the exercise of arbitrary power over others is corrupting to the one who exercises it. One cannot be reverent of another personality and arbitrary toward it at the same time; and if a man is not reverent toward personality in others, how can he reverence it in himself? The sense of security, of power, of being able to have one's own way, and of ability to command the services or the acquiescence of others, is most seductive. It gives importance to the desire of the moment; it encourages the conceit of wisdom; it directly prevents the humility in the presence of oneself that, on the one hand, makes repentance for faults easy, and on the other hand inspires belief in the possibility of unprecedented good.

Does any reader judge that our discussion has skidded from the paved highway of education into the ditch of social controversy? Is there any inherent and necessary connection, it will be asked, between education in the great principles of our faith, and the work of applying these principles upon the massive historical scale here suggested? Let us see. The preceding chapters have given us grounds for holding that transmissive Christian education is failing, and must fail. The question, then, is whether there is in Christianity any principle that could re-create Christian education. Suppose we were to assume that to educate, in the Christian sense, is at least this: To awaken personality and to help it to rich self-activity in a society of persons. Surely, this does not seem far-fetched! Yet it brings us straight to the question, What forces are playing upon the learner that either make or mar personality, and to what sort of insights must learners be led if they are permanently to maintain and make effective this self-activity and reciprocity in it?

Thus arises a surmise that the central motive of any education that is adequately and practically Christian—not merely abstractly or sentimentally so—may be identical with the Christian motive for re-creating the social order. Our discussion has yet to consider many items before the full meaning of this surmise can be seen in a single perspective. We must consider how we become persons, in what sense respect for persons is creative, the kind of education that it requires, the placement of this education in the totality-attitude that constitutes faith in God, and much more. If the present section has made clear that the personality-principle is in an undeveloped condition in the Christianity that professes it, we are probably ready for the next step.

16. What Is It To Be a Person?

An idea of what it is to be a person is embedded in what has just been said. But it will be worth while to bring to a focus what has been implied, and in particular to prepare the way for a specific and unambiguous use of the concept in sections that are to follow.

To be a person is to have satisfactions and dissatisfactions that are "one's own" and that are discriminated, compared, and weighed by the one whose "own" they are, and to act in view of this discrimination, comparison, and weighing. This involves having a past, and knowing it as one's own past; having a future in prospect, and making the transition from one to the other by the kind of acts just indicated. When we attribute personality to infants who cannot thus act, we mean that, since it is normal for them to grow into this capacity, we classify them with their elders, and value them accordingly.

In law a person is any being that has rights and duties, and that therefore may sue and be sued; wherefore a corporation is a legal person, though an artificial one. In ethics, a person is one who is responsible—answerable—for the right or wrong quality of his acts, and therefore is capable of being guilty or innocent. Both the legal concept and the ethical one are closely related to the definition just given in that both presume the specified kind of discriminative conduct. What will command our attention, however, is neither the legal nor the ethical reasonings that have sprouted from this source, but the source itself—the discriminating *ownness* of our satisfactions and of our acts.

In this experience of *ownness* the past, the present, and the future are bound together, and standards of value are attached thereto. That is, one's self enters into the flow of events as one determining factor thereof. Now, this self-insertion into the order of things includes a peculiar recognition of one's self-identity. I am myself, this identical person, only through acts (whether continuous or intermittent) that are my very own. Personality is not a static thing that is first here and then, later, noticed. It has its start and its continuing existence in acts that have the quality of self-awareness. This self-recognition, moreover, is also an act of making myself of worth to myself. Self-valuation then becomes involved in all valuations of objects; we value them from a standpoint.

Such self-constituting acts, as often as they occur, are to some extent original; they do not merely repeat something already existing or already done; they are not just echoes of something else; they cannot be wholly construed in terms of anything else; no generalization can fully express them. Self-identity is not the same as the organic or psycho-physical unity that one has from birth and from before birth, nor is it the same as a mass of habits automatically acquired through the repercussions of pleasures and pains. A white rat "learns" through painful electric discharges not to walk further upon a certain route, even though attractive-smelling food be just beyond; yet we have no evidence that this sort of learning includes any reflection upon or critical viewing of the situation, or that any such incident as an original valuing of a self takes place.

Personality connotes, then, something more than interactions between psychical factors, even if the existence of such factors or elements (denied by able psychologists) be granted. There is supervision of what happens, likewise a new organization that is not deducible from the old. Personal action is, indeed, continuous with the functions of the organism, yet not identical with these functions. It is continuous with mechanical changes, yet it is not mechanical, just as the contents of a book are continuous with paper and printer's ink without being either.

An idea seems to be floating around that the concepts "personality" and "mechanism" as applied to our acts are mutually exclusive, and that between them we have only—to use William James's phrase —a forced option. This forced-option view seems to be held, on the one hand, by some who think that scientific procedure requires us to take an exclusively mechanistic view of our conduct, and on the other hand by some who think that religion requires an exclusively personalistic view. I shall not insist upon the correctness of this my interpretation of the two parties, however, for the reason that both employ now the mechanical, now the personal point of view in respect to human actions.

The mechanist, for example, bases his argument upon critical considerations, not upon any mechanical connections within his organism. He does not represent his reasonings as interactions of his brain molecules, nor as ideas of his that have been caused to stick together in this particular sequence. His thoughts are to him not just effects, of which vocal sounds are the last term. When he speaks or writes he represents himself, even though he be a radical behaviorist, as taking data into consideration, organizing them, directing research activities by purposes, and suspending judgment in the interest of an ideal that is not yet actualized—in a word, he represents himself as self-controlled, not as happening to have been "conditioned" in a certain way. He is not, to himself, just an item in a series; to some extent he supervises and directs what occurs as his experience. Moreover, he addresses his remarks to others under the assumption that they are similarly capable of self-control. He expects his words to influence them, not as the white rat is influenced by being fed or "punished" (to use the lingo of the laboratory), but by their own self-checking, twice-thinking, and putting-two-and-two-together. It does not appear to be possible to put into the terms of mechanism such phases of inter-communication as conveying information, convincing another that he has made a wrong inference, and persuading another to change his valuations.

On the other hand, the opponent of the mechanist assumes that what either says will be understood. Though his personality and that of the other are distinct entities, incapable of fusing, and without intuitive insights into each other, yet communication is possible. Meanings are exchanged—meanings that hold firm through a whole speech or a whole book, though in the meantime changes unimaginable in extent have taken place everywhere in the universe. This exchange of meanings, and this steadiness within the universal flow, depend upon the mechanical connectedness of some of these changes. I can speak with my neighbor because I take advantage of, and use for my own purposes, mechanical relations of air waves, light waves, brain molecules, and such mental processes as perception, recall, and emotion. The most radical personalist assumes that personality realizes itself within and by means of mechanisms, and that the concept of mechanism applies to mind as well as to body. If it were not so, there could be no philosophy! Nor could there be any self-direction or freedom; for, since there could be no security for any expectation, no grounds for choice could be discovered.

That the personal and the mechanical can be continuous without being identical, indeed that they can co-exist as co-ordinate phases of the same event, may be illustrated by what is happening in the writing of these words. My fingers find the right keys of the typing machine, to a considerable extent, without any letter-by-letter supervision; the mechanism of habit does the trick. But just now I erased a phrase and wrote in a different one. This sequence was not just a matter of habit; in fact, few of the phrase-sequences, and none of the sentence-sequences that appear in this paragraph are repetitions of anything that I ever said or (as far as I can judge) ever heard or read. I am supervising the activity of my fingers, then; I am selecting, from the beginning to the end of every sentence; a backward-and-forward look controls the present; nevertheless, habit is mechanically controlling my fingers from the beginning to the end of every word written.

Just now I paused in my typing, sat back, and considered what should come next in the development of this theme. Then was repeated mentally, point for point, the coincidence of the mechanical and the personal that has just been described. Association of ideas and the like took the place of the mechanical action of fingers in the writing of letters. Association was checked when it went too far in one direction, whereupon I went back and took a fresh start. The sense of my task (*Aufgabe*) repeatedly shifted the mental movement. A conceived future was a determinant of the present. Yet the mechanical (association, etc.) never was absent for an instant. That is, individual selection and control were present exactly where mechanical action also was present.

What is called, rather unfortunately, "mechanical causation" means that we have our setting in a system that can be counted upon. Its stability does not depend upon any care that we can bestow upon it. On the other hand, intercommunication, though it depends upon this mechanical stability, depends likewise upon a stability that is produced by acts of personal supervision. The reason why a word retains its meaning from the beginning to the end of a sentence, or even through a whole discourse, is not merely that sound-waves, light-waves, etc., are dependable, but also that persons, though they are individual and variable, can nevertheless hold themselves to a point. There is something original, unique, in every person, it is true, and this uniqueness lies not in something that is done and finished, for it is a flowing thing, like time itself. Yet personality is marked, not by scattering but by gathering. It binds together its own past and future; it holds to meanings in the flux of events; by redirecting its experience it creates meanings where otherwise none would have been. Intercommunication depends absolutely upon this sort of stability. It is the distinctive groundwork of science, of art, and of society.

17. How Believing in God Is Related to Valuing Persons

Is the Christian valuation of persons a derivative from the Christian belief in God? Current Christian education seems to assume that it is. How often does one hear the unqualified assertion that the only true basis for morality is religious faith, that the reason for loving man is that God loves him, and that we must first love God before we can set our human relations right.

Yet a very ancient Christian writer of some distinction held that faith in God is dependent upon faith in man. Said he: "He that loveth not his neighbor whom he hath seen cannot love God whom he hath not seen." Here then, is an educational problem of the first quality. Are we following the practically effective order in human motivation when we endeavor first to suffuse the pupil's mind with the thought of God, and then to bring human life within its halo? Somehow, of course, the life of man and the life of God must be brought together in a single thought; otherwise we shall not understand either ourselves or the divine nature; and without doubt the realization of "God-with-us" enriches and re-enforces our purposes. But saying this does not answer our question concerning the order and the method of growth in Christian motives.

In spite of the assertion that the only true force for the proper adjustment of human relations flows from an antecedent faith in God, great emphasis is placed just now upon the doctrine that we apprehend God's love by witnessing love actually operative in the career of Jesus. Some contemporary church leaders stake the entire question of the existence of God upon what appeared in human form then and there. "Concerning God," they say, "I know only as much as I see actualized in the earthly career of the Master." If this be so, the order of apprehension, and doubtless of motive-growth, is from the human to the divine before it can be from the divine to the human.

When men say that true morality must be rooted in religious faith, they probably have in mind a logical relation of ideas rather than the psychological order of mental growth in any of its phases. They mean, no doubt, that if we trace our moral concepts to their basic implications, we shall find them pointing to a moral or divine order of the world. Obviously, this tells us nothing as to how a sense of duty arises, or a conviction that this or that particular act is a duty, or that this or that is the true ideal of life; indeed, it tells us nothing as to how the apprehension of God arises in the race or in an individual. These are questions of dynamic psychology, not of logical relations between ideas.

The history of religion throws a clear light upon one phase of this question. The character ascribed to divine beings (and the character of God is what now concerns us) always and everywhere reflects something that men have observed in one another. The divine being is a chieftain who leads his tribe in war; or he is a king who rules benevolently and judges righteously; or he is a father who pitieth his children; or he is the moral leader and inspirer of men. He is now a hater of his enemies, or a "jealous god" who exacts homage and tithes, or he is just the opposite of these. He is now arbitrary like an oriental despot, and now sensitively fair. Now he is moved by passions, now he is passionless and changeless. It is a perfectly safe assertion that men first attributed ethical love to the divine being after they had experienced it among themselves. Thus the Christian doctrine that the character of God is revealed in the human life of Jesus fits into what we know of the general development of religion.

We of the twentieth century, however, have not seen Jesus. We have heard people talk about him, and we have read a few stories concerning him in the Gospels, but we have no more seen him than we have seen the Father. Thus the old problem recurs. Does the effective order of motivation run from appreciation of Jesus whom we have not seen to appreciation of the neighbor whom we have seen, or is the character of Jesus first made vivid and convincing by what we witness in contemporary human relations?

Here again, an old Christian idea, that of "living epistles, known and read of all men," gives an answer that accords with the psychology of the matter. This is the true "witnessing church." The church cannot do its witnessing in words, however often we repeat them, however faultlessly they frame propositions of history or of theology, and however we perfume them with emotion. For the valuation of persons that we experience in the give-and-take of conduct not only has the prestige of present, concrete actuality, but it also reflects itself backward upon all history. We read the Gospels in the light of our own candles. What touches us in their stories is their obvious life-similitude. We have known "good Samaritans"; prodigal sons, and fathers of prodigals; when skies were blackest some neighbor has had calm confidence in God; we have seen men choose a cross rather than betray a trust. It is such witnessings as these that bring Jesus out of the dim past and make him, as it were, a contemporary.

On the other hand, when a generation is given to exploiting instead of respecting humanity, biography and history turn to the exposition of the mean motives of our predecessors. If our love for men stops with sympathy, and does not go on to justice, Jesus becomes the all-pitying, and the spiritual laws that he uttered lose their sharp edge. When we indulge in prejudice and race discrimination, or make ourselves comfortable in special privileges, it is difficult to catch the purport of his plain words.

These are simple, indisputable facts of our mental dynamics. We begin with one another; with finite, contemporary persons. Here is where we experience the so-called "indwelling Christ" and the "Holy Spirit" who bears witness to Jesus and to God.

The correct policy for Christian education is now indicated; the learner is to be led, through his ac-

quaintance with the "witnessing church" to realize
the presence and the character of God. But have we
a "witnessing church"? That is, a fellowship whose
daily and united effort is to serve persons and to
make all available resources of the world also serve
them, thus testifying in act for Jesus and God. The
teacher of the Christian religion has no such unambiguous "teaching material" at his disposal. The
personality-principle is struggling for recognition
even within the church, and the conduct of Christians is a mixture and a compromise. This is one
reason why, with great unanimity, lesson material is
drawn predominantly from ancient sources, and this
is why it deals with God and Jesus from a generalized,
not to say abstract, standpoint.

How, then, could God be revealed in and through
this inconsistent, faulty life of ours? This question
must be faced without flinching. Either God can be
found here, and the validity of Jesus' attitudes can
be realized through practice of them, or else, in spite
of our unceasing use of ancient sources and idealistic
generalizations, Jesus will fade into a sentiment, and
the worship of God will become little more than
æsthetic enjoyment. The educational problem that
we now find ourselves "up against" is so serious, and
so central, that a chapter must be devoted to it
(Chapter XII).

18. Problematic and Tragic Phases of Personality

Any one who has followed the discussion as far as
this must perceive that the problems of Christian
education are far deeper and more difficult than they
are commonly supposed to be. Transmissive education has the appearance of being easy, though the
appearance is deceptive; but creative education cannot even deceive itself into a feeling of ease. Though

creativity has its own exquisite joy, it carries within itself the burden of the as-yet-unknown, the tantalizing sense of contingency, and, above all, it requires the identification of oneself with both the evil that is and the good that is not yet. With evil, not only because partial goodness is partial badness, and growth in the good is growth out of a present not-good, but also because, on account of our social interconnectedness, the practical, everyday affairs of the most aspiring soul have to be conducted to some extent upon the basis of the present accepted social order. I cannot buy a loaf of bread, or have a sanctuary in which to worship, without involving myself in the imperfections of our self-seeking economic system. There is not one of us who might not well exclaim: "Wretched man that I am! Who shall deliver me?"

To bring these problematical and tragic phases of personality into Christian education will doubtless seem almost scandalous. I can imagine even liberals in educational theory throwing up their hands as they exclaim: "What? Insinuate uncertainties into the mind of the learner? Teach him that there is anything contingent in the outcome of the divine purpose for the world? Make him identify himself with evil?"

I have no disposition to soften the impact of these questions, nor will I conceal my conviction that what is commonly meant by the teaching of ideals is profoundly illusory. Any really effective teaching of ideals will have to be realistic; it will have to show what the actual is, and that we are and must remain part and parcel of it at the same time that we struggle against it. Christian education must not conceal the truth that to be Christian is to embark upon voyages of exploration, with all their uncertainties, dangers, and frequent failures. If a teacher ever regards his work with his pupils as completed, still he will have the wistful realization that they, like the world in which they live, are still in process of creation, with the end not yet in sight.

Not seldom we make tragic failures. Christian thought has not failed to say as much, but usually it has had in mind incorrigibly selfish or sensual individuals who are regarded as outside the faith. To these we must add failures inside the faith—misshapen personalities that sincerely intend to be Christian, and institutions, mass sentiments, and mass conduct that unintentionally blaspheme everything that is sacred in personality. Two examples of this will suffice: First, until very recently a paternal dictatorship within the family was regarded as belonging to the very texture of the moral order; this was the "Christian family," so much lauded by preachers, from Paul to the twentieth century. A second example is war-making. It goes against our grain to admit that Christianity is or ever was a war-maker, but we cannot re-write history in the interest of self-laudation, nor can we of this day forget what our own eyes have seen, our own ears heard. Let us take a close look at this experience of ours, for it reveals one of the ways in which our religious consciousness itself can become a tragic evil.

In an Armistice-Day sermon preached in 1928 the assertion was made that in the event of another war the churches of one of the largest denominations in the United States, with scarcely an exception, will assist in preparing for war as they did in the World War. This implies that it is not the function of the church to say whether or not there shall be war, but to accept any decision to fight that is made by the secular authority at Washington, and thereupon to do whatever religion can do to make the fighting effective. The chief contribution that religion can make is, of course, in the field of morale; it is the application to war of the increment of power that is ours when conscience approves and we feel that God is on our side. It is this peculiar spiritual increment that distinguishes war-making in the church parlor or in the minister's prayer on Sunday morning from war-making in the trenches and in cabinet meetings at the White House. The weapons of the churches' warfare are spiritual, not carnal.

But they kill, just the same. It is perhaps possible to kill without hate, but certainly these spiritual processes strengthen the arm of those who do hate. The government, being secular and not spiritually-minded, will of course work up hate as a psychical adjunct and reinforcement of hostilities. The churches do not exactly countenance this, to be sure, yet in war-time hate and religious devotion fit beautifully together. Between them they can guarantee that practically all parts of the population and all sides of a man's motivation will be stirred. This is why war-leaders at Washington put so high an estimate upon religion in war-time. If, while war is in progress, the churches should devote all their spiritual resources to peace-making, something very important in war-making would be lacking.

The climax of this spiritual war-making is reached when Christian prayer takes part in it. Strength for the hard task, the prolonged strain, the suffering, the sacrifice of substance and of lives, and possible defeats, is increased by communion with God, who is "our refuge and strength, a present help in trouble." Of course the enemy prays as devoutly as we do, but God does not listen to the enemy. As we pour out our souls, full of trouble, consumed with desire, consecrated to the cause, there steals into our hearts the feeling and the certainty that our cause is God's own cause; and this stealing into our hearts brings a steeling of all the muscles of our soul. Of course, it was the declaration of war that set us praying thus—but for it we might not have known which side God is on!

Here prayer, supposedly Christian, wins God to our side instead of winning us to his side. This inversion is made possible by antecedent religious culture—that is, by previous experience of the genuinely moral reinforcement of personality that can be had through communion with God. So sophisticated can the religion of personality become! Savage warriors worship a god who is frankly partial to their own tribe, a warrior-god, who has no distaste for human butchery; consequently they do not have to find exalted justification for any war that they desire to engage in. But we who worship the God of all the earth; we who assume to value persons so highly that even an enemy is to be loved—we, in order to turn our religiousness into strength for combat, must engage in spiritual exercises of an appropriate sort, exercises, in fact, that divide us against ourselves when we know it not.

This self-division does not begin with the declaration of war; it is already present in our habit of compromising with the causes of war. This is the habit of being Christians at too little cost to ourselves. The sum of the matter is that these persons of ours to which we attribute infinite worth are caught in the meshes of history, and in the meshes of their own fallible self-guidance. Uncertainty, contingency, the tragedy of deep oppositions of a self to itself and of our best institutions to themselves— these have to be reckoned with in any Christian education that is to avoid self-deceptive idealization of our religion.

In such a world, our destiny, both here and hereafter, is a matter of hope rather than of demonstration. But of hope that is grounded, not arbitrary. This is not the place for a disquisition upon the immortal hope of Christians, but a brief statement of the positive relation that exists between our valuation of persons and our after-death outlook is in order.

There are two approaches to the problem of the hereafter. One is represented in the various forms in which ghost-beliefs survive among us; the other in concern for the fate of moral values. The former goes back historically to the dreams and hallucinations that led early man to believe that there is a separable soul, and to the shudders that were felt when the "double" of a dead man appeared. This kind of belief in a future life did not arise from appreciation of a value in this life that is worthy of perpetuation. Indeed, spirits were objects to be feared, and extreme measures were taken to prevent them from operating in the world of the living. Of course it was easy, in view of affectionate relations within the family, to transform some of this fear into hope, as has been done in modern spiritism. But the fact remains that the evidence for survival that traditional spiritism offers has next to no relation to the problem of the destiny of moral values.

When concern for such values becomes articulate, an almost wholly new ground of hope appears. Fear of extinction mostly disappears, and with it the quasi-instinctive grasping after straws of evidence for survival. The underlying question now becomes, Is there anything or anybody in the world that is worthy of survival? When an affirmative answer is given, the next question is, How does this worth fare in the world that we already know and are? From the standpoint of the present discussion, the query may be phrased as, Granted that persons as such have worth to which no limit can be assigned, what is the place of persons in the world-system as far as we know it? What do persons seem to be capable of being and doing when they have a chance? In our branch of animate nature, what direction does evolution take? And, in the light of these considerations, how much dare we hope?

This kind of inquiry is like an ellipse; it has two foci. One of them concerns the broader aspects of the world-system as we know it—both the order and method of evolution and the metaphysics of mind and matter. The other has to do with the minute consideration of what happens to and through persons at times of crisis when conditions seem to be unfavorable to the personal mode of life. I shall say only a word upon each of these.

In the next chapter I shall show that the emergence of persons within nature, and the growing moral significance that persons have, is evidence of a cosmic moral choice, or God. That is, personality seems not to be adventitious, but rooted in the depths of reality. If so, the persistence of persons after death would be natural and reasonable.

What concerns our present discussion more intimately is the strength that persons individually show at times of acute crisis. I mean, at times when persons have the greatest occasion for yielding to the non-personal, and for foregoing their self-affirmation. It is true that the record of mankind is mixed; that many individuals lose their grit, that some become craven, that others subordinate the personal to the seductions of instinct. But, on the other hand, there are instances of the opposite sort, galaxy upon galaxy of instances. Extremes of thwarted purpose, defeat, injustice, persecution, suffering of all sorts, have made personality glow and grow instead of being smothered. This is the sort of world in which such things can happen. If, on the one hand, they cry out against the insensitiveness of external nature and even of men, they proclaim, on the other hand, how power-less is mere power when it joins issue with a strong spirit.

Many men have listened for some word from the dead. We need not quarrel with them for doing so, for it would seem to be entirely fitting that if there is fellow-feeling over there it should speak to fellow-feeling here. Investigation in this field is a rational undertaking. Yet, vastly more important for our hopes than any voice from beyond the grave is the demonstration of power to live out the personal life here and now against all obstacles. Such living would be the best evidence that we are not strangers and sojourners but dwellers-at-home in the world-system as a whole.

After centuries of effort to support faith in sur-vival by pointing to the emergence of Jesus' body from the tomb, the way in which he voluntarily went to his death is the more convincing sort of evidence that death does not have the last word. Even if we knew that his body returned to life, and that he spoke to his friends in his natural voice, it would still be true that not the stone-rolled-away but the cross is the true symbol of our hope. For it, not the open tomb, signifies the quality of his life; it sig-nifies, too, that the great victory of personality was already won, whatever became of the body.

The kind of Christian education that all this points to never would meet the reproach of "soft pedagogy"! It would teach the uncertainty of that which really is uncertain, the contingency of that which is contingent, the imperfections of that—es-pecially in our own selves—which is imperfect, and the failures even of our goodness. It would repre-sent the problems of life, not as solved, but as in a process of solution that requires us to take part, and our part would be truthfully presented as venturesome, risky, mountainously difficult. In other words, the Christian life would be pictured as a process in which, though loaded with our finiteness, we nevertheless participate with God in the gradual creation of a moral order, which is a society of persons actively bound together by good will. The satisfactions that it would offer to the learner are those that attend this kind of personal and personalizing process—the seizure of one's own freedom, the joy of creation even through labor and pain, the fellowship of like radical spirits, the moving equilibrium of faith in God, and hope without a line fence.

CHAPTER V

HOW WE BECOME PERSONS

19. *The Emergence of Persons within Impersonal Nature*

The primary purpose of this chapter is not to plunge us into metaphysical problems, but to call attention to facts that we can control. For our perspective is that of education; we are less interested in how we got into being than in what's to be done, now that we have arrived. Nevertheless, the educational horizon-line is continuous with that of metaphysics. Inasmuch as we are parts of the general system called nature, any meaning that our acts may have is likewise one meaning of the system, and conversely any other meaning that the system has is also a meaning for us. Let us, then, glance briefly at the evolution of personality conceived as a cosmic event.

It is known that our race has a limited past, and that the human and personal sprang from that which is not human or personal. What is "back of" an evolutionary process that exhibits a transformation like this is a rational and necessary question the answer of which should be expected to affect our life-policies.

The question is, what effect the rise of the personal may reasonably have upon our view of the totality of which it is a part. No simple and easy solution of this problem is in sight; the universe is burdened with mystery. Nature is a mixture of things or events that do not obviously belong together. That all of them are interconnected, so that this is a cosmos and not a chaos, is suggestive, but it does not of itself imply that there is a corresponding universal meaning or

central point of view from which mind can see that
it really is at home in the universe. When one contemplates the staggering vastness of the stellar systems that new methods of measurement have revealed
to the astronomer, one feels that our solar system with
all that it contains is indescribably little. What is our
history in comparison with the myriads of light-years
in which the astronomer computes sidereal happen-
ings? What is man? Is mind anything more than a
momentary bubble upon a single ripple in the mea-
sureless cosmic ocean? Our forefathers, when they
formulated their ideas of God and of man, did not
have access to data that could show the scope of the
problem. They had not grasped the notion of universal law; they had no inkling of the vastness of the
universe; they knew nothing of organic evolution.

Even upon this little planet of ours, the scope of
the personal appears to be very restricted. Inorganic
processes grind on in apparent disregard of all ascer-
tainable values; so do most organic processes also.
Evolution does not move as a whole toward the personal; its forms do not constitute any single ascend-
ing series. Man is only the tip of one small twig upon
the great tree, so that we cannot say unqualifiedly
that evolution culminates in personality, or that our
personality reflects its meaning upon the whole. Indeed, no notion of culmination appears to be appli-
cable to biologic processes as such.

Not only the vastness and the machine-likeness of
nature, but also particular details compel us to raise
questions. For, now that persons are here, they do not
seem to fare unqualifiedly well. They appear not to be
favorites of nature, at least not unambiguously so.
This remark does not refer to the necessity of struggling with nature if we are to develop our personalities—this may be at bottom beneficent—but to
the handicaps that no struggle of ours can remove.

Christian thought has endeavored to construe all suffering as upbuilding because disciplinary, but it has made only a part of its claim good, and it has left out of the account many deficits that are not to be described as suffering. There are conditions, not created by us, that curtail personality, blurring its mental sight, over- or under-weighting one or another impulsion, and preventing discrimination and genuine self-guidance. One can carry these considerations into many details if one has an inclination to do so. No one knows why degeneracy should occur or be transmitted from parent to child, or why certain germs of disease should have a place in a reasonable universe, or indeed why one mosquito should exist.

Such are the difficulties in the way of a completely personalistic view of the universe. But to treat them as if they were the whole story would be not a whit better than to swallow the theological tradition at a gulp. Indeed, one might go a long way before coming upon a doctrine that selects its data in a more narrowly dogmatic manner than some of the current "naturalistic" theories of man. The old arguments that were supposed to prove the total depravity of man are not more one-sided and short-sighted than new arguments that are supposed to prove that we are nothing but complicated instinct-mechanisms. What is known as naturalism seems to me to draw its conclusions about man, on the whole, from inquiries that do not deal as seriously with the phenomena of personality as with the phenomena of the sub-personal. Over against the difficulties that the last three paragraphs have without reservation acknowledged, should be placed an equally realistic analysis of the experience of being a person. This may not give us a solution for the entire cosmic problem, but it will at least enable us to see more clearly what our problem is, and it may justify a preference for one cosmic hypothesis as against others.

Whatever else nature may be, it includes at some points the personal function of gathering together something of the past and something of the present in the life-current, separating and combining their factors in an actual though non-mechanical way, and giving a preferential position to some factors over others in the further movement of the life-current. Obviously this is not mere elaboration of the impersonal, and obviously it will not be understood by any inspection of its immediate antecedents if these antecedents are strictly and solely impersonal. No amount of poring over events that are devoid of discrimination and valuation will enable us to predict that the next event will include discrimination and valuation.

It should be obvious that the contrast between two such events (non-discrimination followed by discrimination) points to a ground in the system or series as a totality. Something latent, perhaps, in earlier members of the series makes its appearance in man; but latency is at best an obscure notion. At its worst it takes whatever happens to be observed first or most often as primary, more fundamental, more real than the later or more rarely observed. If, following such a lead, we assume that the world system is primarily impersonal and only secondarily personal, do we get anywhere? How could an impersonal flow do the trick? Can a stream dam itself, build a mill-wheel and a mill, and, pouring itself over this wheel, put values where before there was only gravitation?

This figure does not exaggerate the relation between the elements of the problem. The fact is that the human type of living has come into existence through persistent selection of hard lines of action

rather than easy ones. Somehow there has been a
turning upon the stream and a redirecting of parts
of it. Man has taken upon himself the burdensome
restrictions of moral law when the easy and apparently the practicable way would have been to live on
in the instinctive freedom of his animal ancestors.
The fact of self-discipline, individual and reciprocal,
where no apparent compulsion thereto exists, is an
amazing thing.

Fascinating, too, is the phenomenon of ever-re-
peated discontent with achieved good. Not only are
instinctive satisfactions, however abundant and however secure, insufficient for man, but his disciplined
goodness also furnishes no stopping-place for his
spirit. Whenever a status is achieved, there arises a
fresh and original judgment upon it from a standpoint beyond itself. And when this standpoint has
secured assent and begun to control conduct, behold,
it comes under the scrutiny of still another newly
apprehended and difficulty-breeding ideal. Men have
always to repent of their goodness!

We may grow tired of this self-discipline, and we
may resolve that we will return to "nature," but we
never find the way back. We may grow cynical toward goodness because, judged from before, it shows
lagging and compromise, yet cynicism never has the
last word; we believe in our unrealized better selves
more than in our present, realized selves.

Within this repeated selection of the hard line of
action as against the easy one a general direction
is discernible. Once the personal type of action appears within nature, there starts, apparently never
to end, an intensification of the personal aspects of
experience. For example, to see is not enough; we
must discriminate more and yet more within our seeing. To our natural eyes we add those more wonder-
ful instruments, the telescope and the microscope,

and the more satisfaction these instruments bring, the more trouble we take to increase their range and accuracy. To primitive counting upon our fingers, we add computation, and when computation at one level succeeds, we raise the level. The mathematical sciences, at last evolving from within themselves, become a record of the insatiability of the personal.

These typical instances will suffice as an index of the ever-expanding cognitive task that personality imposes upon itself. A parallel development occurs within the æsthetic sphere. Sights and sounds having yielded an enjoyment over and above that of utility, attention is turned to this enjoyment and its sources. Beauty comes to be sought for its own sake; that is, for its immediate value to persons; and art is created simply as an expression of what we are as discriminating enjoyers. Art, in turn, exhibits the same internal restlessness as knowledge, the same self-imposition of new and harder tasks. If art begins by merely reproducing or imitating, it soon forbids itself merely to copy; it must seize the significant in its object or endow it with meaning that it had not. Then reproduction irks the artist; to be himself he must fly into the unexplored, he must create the undreamed-of. Thus, new art springs from old, new tastes are born, and new principles of criticism jostle those of yesterday.

All of this cognitive and æsthetic restlessness is intertwined with the social and ethical phases of personal existence. Here, too, the spur of self-judgment has the effect of bringing the personal into clearer and clearer relief, and thus it makes the task of relating person to person harder and harder. The primitive way of dealing with troublesome persons was to kill them or put them in fear; the primitive way with agreeable persons was to make them one's dependents, if possible, and at least to get some arbitrary hold upon their favors. The displacement of the blood-feud by judicial settlement of quarrels required enormous self-restraint. This is true, even though the change brought many kinds of reward. Similarly, the evolution of organized relations based upon freedom rather than compulsion is at once an evidence that to be adequately personal we must help other persons to adequate life for themselves, and that men are willing to pay heavy costs for this mutual self-realization. Ever the problem and the task are renewed, and always in forms that demand more intense personalization.

This is our destination, even though we hold back as a child who is in danger shrinks from a stranger who comes to rescue him. Even our frantic practical materialism, when we look beneath the surface of it, bears witness to the name of the stranger who is at the door. For the emotions of our commercialism are defensive, and its theory of itself is apologetic. Though it seizes the citadels of power, it is more and more beset by the foe within who is also the friend within.

The fact of a general direction of this sort within the issues that agitate us should give us pause. Humanity's interest in itself has a quality, a character, that we do not imitate or invent. It finds us before we find it. If at last we voluntarily choose the development of persons and of a society of persons as our directing principle, what then happens is that something already there has assimilated us to itself. There is, in short, a general selection within our most creative choices. I choose, but I am *called* to choose this way; my choosing, at the point where it is most appreciative of personality, most broadly and deeply self-assertive, is a yielding. It is a surrender in which nevertheless I achieve freedom.

This general, interfused selection within our particular choices looks as if it were itself a case of choosing—a long-continued self-guidance by a definite plan. In other words, the phenomenon of human personality taken in the large manifests an interfused personality, or God. I know not how else to construe the history of human personality. By ignoring this history, as often happens, one may indeed slip past the problem and then declare that nature shows no signs of the existence of God. But whoever faced this history without perceiving that some sort of divine influence has us in its grip? If one does not go the whole length of ascribing self-hood to the divine being, one nevertheless attributes to it at least an inherent leaning toward righteousness or toward consciousness in us.

This interpretation of the emergence of the personal is only a fragment of a philosophy of nature, of history, and of religion. There remain many fundamental questions that cannot here be as much as stated. All that is affirmed concerning God is that he is immanent in all choices of ours that make us personal and still more personal; that this immanence, having the form of a choice within our choices, is that of a personal being; and that this being, in that he realizes himself by promoting our self-realization in a society of persons, is ethical in the profoundest sense.

We have come upon the concept of continuous ethical creation, in fact. It is customary to think of the rise of the personal out of the impersonal as having occurred once only, and that once in the dim past of the race. In fact, it occurs with every individual. In each of us the self-affirmation that is the basic fact of personal existence started as an overplus in an organism that had had an impersonal existence from the moment of conception. This self-affirmation, as we have seen, is a valuational act and series of acts; here is the birth of preferences in a being that never before had preferred anything. Out of the organism came that which was to turn and make the organism its instrument and servant. Here is creation as fresh and contrasty as the ancient poet's imagined beginning of the cosmos, when "God said, Let there be light! And there was light."

Nor is this a single and isolated event in the life of the individual; it is repeated as often as we act in the personal way. No moment is quite the image of any other; always there is a margin of originality in any person's total reaction to any total present. Thus, continually, out of the unfree clod that is the organism springs the flower that is the free person. The roots of this flower remain in the soil, of course —which is another way of saying what has already been said, that the personal and the mechanical are not separate and successive, but coincident.

It is now time to turn to the conditions that favor or hinder this becoming of persons. Here our immediate problems are psychological and educational rather than metaphysical, yet the facts that are to come before us will gain profounder significance, a wider perspective, if we think them in relation to divine immanence in the sense just explained.

20. We Become Individual by Our Own Acts. What, Then, of Authority?

To the question, How do we become persons? The answer is, By the coincidence, in one and the same series of events, of a cosmic and a finitely individual originality. Looking at the finitely individual side of the matter, we formulate these events in the most general way by saying that one becomes a person by acting in the discriminating manner of persons.

That is, I do not let experience merely come to me or flow through me; I inspect it (ideally, all of it, whencesoever it comes), putting upon it my very "own" stamp of meaning, which involves more or less of assent and dissent, approval and disapproval, and becoming actively "for" and "against." My thinking must be my own thinking, my convictions must be my own, my valuations and choices must be mine. I must neither drift with the current, nor in my spirit yield to compulsion. I may bend my body when the wind blows; I may choose the time and the manner of speech; but my spirit must always stand upright and have sincere and free speech with itself.

We shall presently take note of the fact that this movement from an individual centre never is the action of an isolated power unit. For we are inevitably (and fortunately) under the influence of one another; indeed, one essential to personal growth, as we shall see, is response to what, as a concession to usage, may be called authority. If any one, after reading the next preceding paragraph, should exclaim, "What! Is the learner to be under no authority whatsoever?" the answer would be that authority, in the sense of inescapable mutuality, is as pervasive as individuality itself. But there are authorities and authorities, as there are lords many and gods many, so that selection has to be made between authorities, and for the purposes of education between theories of authority.

Most kinds of authoritative pressure reflect assumptions that cannot be harmonized with the Christian view of the dignity of personality. We saw in section 13 that even when doing a pupil's thinking for him is honestly intended to induce obedience to God, the effect is to bring some men into subjection to others, whereas, what we need to do is to develop free participation with God in ethical creation.

When doing the learner's thinking for him becomes a thoroughly organized system, as in Catholicism, it stratifies society. In this instance it produces, on the one hand, a reverence for the hierarchy that permits the faults of its members to thrive, and on the other hand it treats the masses with a paternalism that, however benevolent be its intention, gives insufficient stimulus for the development of their capacity for self-government. Here the view of the individual is controlled by an antecedent view of authority, whereas theories of authority ought to conform to our valuation of persons.

The growth of personality is checked whenever, instead of the already-described sorting of experiences in "my own" way, I rubber-stamp my name upon that which I have not made my own. The learner must not passively conform; instead, he must be a co-determiner of any authority that he recognizes. This principle, confessedly, makes difficulties for Christian educators, and not least for those who are intensely benevolent-minded. "Good-will surely should have its way," we reason. Yes, but good-will may conceal a subtle conceit of wisdom, or a subtle desire to have one's way, or the kind of un-faith that insists that there must be short-cuts in the spiritual life. Every attempt, moreover, to secure conformity by sugar-coating a truth, or camouflaging a difficulty, or inducing fear, offends against the first and basic law of personal growth.

What, then, is the positive function of authority in the development of the free person? Not at all to determine in advance, apart from his own self-activity, what he shall think or what he shall value, but to stimulate him to take notice of facts, distinctions, and issues that he might overlook, and to make clear —not to make persuasive—the reasonings and valuations of his neighbors and of his predecessors.

Authority in education commonly takes the contrary course. It first "shields" the learner from acquaintance with some type of fact, opinion, or policy, while endeavoring to saturate his mind with the contrary. Then, to the thing that it wants to fasten in the learner's mind it adds pressures of various kinds that are extraneous to the issues involved—such pressures as social approval and disapproval, fears (as of divine displeasure), depreciation of opponents, and the seductiveness of respectability. Two of the commonest, and unconsciously meanest, devices of authoritative teaching are appealing to conscience under the assumption that of course it is on the side of the teacher's view, and inviting the learner to think something through for himself, when in fact the conditions for such thinking have been carefully shut out. Under such auspices there cannot be a thoroughly Christian education, whatever the content of the teaching, and however benevolent the teacher may think himself to be, for the personality of the pupil is not respected, and he is initiated into a policy of not respecting personality in others.

21. The Acts That Individualize Us Are Inter-Individual

That individual discrimination takes place and grows only through the inter-stimulation of individuals by one another is now so well understood that, though its importance is of the greatest, it may here be treated with brevity. The emergence of each self is conditioned upon interplay with selves or with selves-in-the-process-of-becoming. A criss-cross of noticings, with coincident attractions and repulsions; interpretation of the other by attributing to him what happens in me, and converse interpretation of myself by what occurs in the other; a consequent society

of selves, each of which reflects the others and is reflected in them—this is the genetic account in a nut-
shell.

There is no getting behind this mutuality to anything that is independently self-subsisting in particular selves. That I take experience to pieces as my
dog does not; what I notice and what I fail to notice;
what I like or dislike; how I organize my ideas—in
short, the whole meaning of my world, myself included, develops in this self-and-socius way. This does
not, and cannot, imply that each of us is a mere echo
of others, for a "mere echo" theory would not provide for the rise and development of anything that
could be echoed. Society is more than a complex of
reciprocal imitations; rather, it is a mutuality in
which precedents and the unprecedented are everywhere present and interfused.

The originality that preceding sections have attributed to persons has this quality of mutuality.
Whenever a great discovery or a great invention
bursts upon us, study of it shows that it has been led
up to by a previous mass of experience and thought,
some of which is retained within what is new. Every
religious prophet calls upon us to fulfil or carry forward something already here, usually something ru-
dimental and therefore old in our experience of one
another.

Now and again one fancies that one can so divest
oneself of the entire finite world (one's own past,
one's social and institutional connections and the
whole of history) that at last, as a mere individual,
one is absolutely alone with God. But invariably the
idea of God that is here employed, and the ideas of
life's meaning that emerge from this communion,
show indubitable traces of one's past and of one's social connections. Something original may come into
being by this endeavor to free oneself from all prece-

dents; indeed, the wonder is that more theological and ethical originality does not result.[1] The fact seems to be that if we want to cultivate originality in pupils—and this is essential to an educational policy that is based upon the value of persons—we must listen to one another, we must know precedents from their own point of view, we must appreciate history. Every advance that the learner makes will be an advance of society-in-the-learner.

22. The Becoming of a Person Never Is Finished

This means two things that are complementary to each other. On the one hand, if this proposition is true, it is of a kind to puncture all self-sufficiency, whether of an individual or of a church. "Not as though I had already attained." The "my very own" or the "our very own" never can properly be taken as a mere possession, or as a resting place, or as a norm. It is more like the air upon which an airplane supports itself while passing through it. Whenever a church takes what it already is as normal for to-morrow, it smothers or fails to notice and weigh spiritual growth. "Growth in grace" and a static church are incompatible with each other.

On the other hand, the truth that personality is process rather than status is fitted to lift up the bowed head of any one who thinks that his day is over and he is done for. Thus the same truth humbles us when we become proud and self-sufficient, and yet makes us self-confident when we are tempted to despair of our capacities. It puts down the mighty from their seats, and exalts them of low degree.

---

[1] I deliberately refrain from applying the term "mystical" to these attempts of individuals to be alone with God. My reason is that this term is used in so many different senses that it is no longer a guide-post to any single idea whatever. Recently a philosopher of religion has given it one more meaning, namely, the transition-experience between one organized mode of life and another that is about to take its place.

That this is indeed a truth appears from many angles. Though our mental plasticity probably declines with changes that occur in the brain as it grows old, no one has been able to find the dead-line for self-modification. We definitely know that the tradition that mental fixity rules us from middle age onward, or even from adolescence onward, was based upon the products of a defective educational system and a defective social order. In spite of both these defects there always has been a sprinkling of individuals who to the end of life have kept open "the soul's east window of divine surprise." They have looked for new truth; they have modified their views; they have changed their attitudes; they have repented of their faults; they have expected greater and better things than their own best or the best in the world. And now comes the adult-education movement, with its message that the experience of learning is not a special prerogative of childhood and youth, but the privilege of all. To learn is a part of the dynamics of our original nature.

An amusingly sage observation was made at the convention of church youth held at Evanston a few years ago. The floor, and participation in discussion, were reserved by the young people for themselves, but members of the older generation were permitted to look on from the gallery. With knitted brows these college youth discussed what they would better do with the religion and the churches that older people had bungled so badly. There was a consciousness of being new, different, upheaving. "But," remarked the observer, "the real radicals were in the gallery!" And this observation was partly confirmed by two facts: The young people were as a matter of fact acting under the influence of books and teachings that emanated from the older generation, and yet the assembly showed unmistakable signs of apprehension lest it should go too far—the car of progress did not lack brakes.

Christianity has often demonstrated that the becoming of a person never need come to a standstill. Many an old and mature Christian has the habit of discovering new riches in the old faith, and new applications of it in the practical affairs of life. Here in the Occident the advice to search the Scriptures, and the appeal to reason in sermons, have stimulated many a person no longer young to think a new thought as his own. Such new thoughts may be narrow or erroneous because of uncritical presuppositions and method, but even then the joy of movement is beautiful even though it be also pathetic. In many a mission field men and women who had already accepted a certain status in life as final have been led to reconsider, make new decisions, and hope. The Salvation Army shouts that "A man may be down, but he's never out!" Personal and mass evangelism has so often proved that even hardened spirits can come to themselves—that is, become freshly personal— that we are not justified in saying that character ever becomes fixed.

This is one of the angles from which to judge Christian education. What an anomaly it is to assume that the climax of learning is inability to learn, and that the summit of self-activity is self-imitation. Especially anomalous is this assumption within a religion that values personality as a finality, and that represents God as the Spirit or the Logos, moving everywhere and always as a stimulus in the minds of men.

CHAPTER VI

HOW WE BECOME PERSONS

(Continued)

23. *Personality Can Grow, or Its Growth Can Be Arrested, through the Mastery of Nature*

The becoming of a person, I have said, is never finished. It may now be added that there is no end to the kinds of experience that can contribute to the growth of personality. On the other hand, growth can be arrested in and through any kind of experience. The educational problem, accordingly, is that of determining how to deal with the vicissitudes of life so that growth and not arrest shall occur. We may begin the discussion of this point by reminding ourselves that the personal life has its setting within impersonal nature.

Nature in all its forms is an invitation to act ever more and yet more as a person. It presents unending diversity of stimuli, unending possibilities of weal and of woe, unending problems to be solved, unending dangers to be escaped by headwork, unending opportunities through headwork to increase human power. Not seldom, where formal education is scant, the mere exigencies of nature awaken personality, as, on the other hand, schools grow anemic when they are remote from the tussle with natural forces.

The term "nature" is here used for convenience (likewise in accord with one of the meanings sanctioned by usage) to designate the impersonal facts and forces with which persons have to do. Our bodies, first of all; then the immediate conditions of bodily maintenance, growth, and vigor; next, outreaching

areas for exploration and control; finally a totality
or system of nature that confronts the thoughtful
person as the Matterhorn stands over against the
Gorner Grat.

In what persons do with nature they always express themselves. They can also change themselves
thereby, and thus acquire new needs for self-expression. When I secure control of my body, I secure at
the same time control of my instinctive impulses and
the current of ideas. Attention becomes voluntary,
and I, the person, am to some extent reorganized.
Similarly, when I use my body—hands, feet, eyes,
ears—in the procurement of food for to-morrow, or
in finding out and establishing the conditions of to-
morrow's safety and pleasure, I am changed thereby,
possibly enlarged and liberated by the increased and
branching range of interest, discrimination, and self-
guidance.

Let these simple examples serve as an index to the
whole map of human enterprise in the observation,
mastery, and utilization of nature. From culture of
the body to culture of field or vineyard, and on to
the digging of coal, the making of steel, and the
crossing of oceans by airship, we are faced by changes
in ourselves not less striking than the changes in the
materials within which we work, not less striking
than the new landscapes that open to our eyes. The
conquest of nature always does change us in one way
or another; it can change us into more desirable persons.

The ascetic strain that has been in Christianity
from early times includes a determination not to be a
passive recipient of natural goods, and especially not
to be enslaved by the pleasures of instinct. Thus far
asceticism partly grasps the conditions of personal
growth. But because it does not aspire to make nature positively serve and enhance personality, be-

cause it is a withdrawal from opportunities for
growth, this ever-present motif within our religion
has done us an enormous disservice. It could not stop
the functions of the body, nor yet the outgoing, na-
ture-conquering enterprises of men, yet it has had no
principle for spiritualizing them—that is, making
them contribute to the growth of persons. Spirituality, or religious experience, has been habitually conceived of as a separate, self-subsisting thing, apart
from bodily functions, apart from the uses of muscle,
and apart from the aggressive confrontation of the
world by thought.

Even in the sphere of sex, where asceticism has
chiefly wrought, Christianity has not achieved or on
any large scale attempted the real mastery of nature.
Almost its only word to adolescents whose sex-nature
has just awakened has been a set of don'ts. It has in
language glorified the family, but it has for the most
part assumed that instinct is to control mating and
its results. Until conditions not of its own intentional
making forced Christianity to begin to recognize—
it has only just begun to do so—the full significance
of the personality of the wife, it acquiesced in and
blessed suppression of personality through marriage.
Even now, with all its emphasis upon personality, it
is not committed to the deliberate production of superior human beings by selective breeding. It talks
about, but it does not analyze or experiment with, the
possible contributions of sex-experience to the ethical
life. Toward what is commonly called "birth control,"
in the sense of control by other than ascetic practices,
the Catholic Church takes an attitude of sweeping
and vehement opposition. The reasoning put forth
depends for its cogency upon the results of employing contraceptives, yet experiment under ethically
controlled conditions, through which alone ethical
possibilities could be learned, is forbidden to the

faithful, and such experiments made by non-Catholics are ignored.[1] Protestant churches, on the other hand, when they do not echo the Catholic, are mum. That is to say, they have no guidance to offer at a point where personality-forming forces are at a maximum!

Because the churches have not undertaken to master nature at this point in the sense of utilizing the sex function as a means of heightening personality and enriching personal fellowship and co-operation, but rather in the sense of protecting us from nature, they are almost completely helpless in the presence of a rising generation that thinks without embarrassment in the terms of cause and effect. The pity is that so few young people have learned to look for the deepest effects of all, the influence of different sorts of sex experience upon the personality. Causes and effects are thought of as isolated items, whereas it seems unlikely that sex intimacy, even such intimacy as "petting," much more that of coitus, can be practiced without profoundly affecting the general tone

[1]The Catholic policy justifies procreation without regard to the quality of the offspring or the effect upon the mother. To what extremes this *laissez-faire* system can lead is shown by a case that recently came under my notice. Medico-social workers asked the aid of a priest in planning for a family, already large, that was being increased about once a year by the birth of a defective. The mother was grovellingly insane; the father a habitual drunkard. The church, as represented by this priest, would not lift a finger to check this spawning. Here a theory of the value of life is twisted into what amounts to disrespect for personality. What this theory is, at least as one eminent ecclesiastic has expounded it, may be briefly summarized in the statement that by giving human existence to unborn souls we make it possible for them to become objects of the redemption through Christ. The more babies, whatever their quality, the more God is glorified. One gasps at a redemptive love that requires idiots for its objects! How would such love differ from the maternal instinct in pre-human species?

Between the Catholic view of procreation and a view that has been traditional among Mormons there is remarkable similarity. For large families, and formerly plural wives, are by this Mormon theory encouraged in the supposed interest of souls clamoring to be born in order that they may come into the goodly fellowship of the church and the future bliss of the faithful.

of the individuals concerned. While the young people increasingly know the facts upon which a narrow
sex-policy of a specious sort could be built, the
churches are in the embarrassing situation of not
knowing the facts upon which an ethically constructive policy could be recommended.

When we come to the mastering of nature in the
sense of economic resources, again the ascetic strain
in Christianity works toward our undoing. For men
must subdue and domesticate wild animals and
plants; must plant, and reap, and manufacture—
they must do this, that is, in the interest of their own
increasing well-being. This is one aspect of becoming
increasingly human. Here, obviously, is a most appropriate sphere for promoting the spiritual or personal life. But behold what happened in the name of
religion. First of all, the spiritual was interpreted as
something that happens inside the church or inside
the soul when it withdraws from labor and betakes
itself to prayer. Consequently, though economic activities were acquiesced in, they were thought of as
related to the body rather than the soul, and religion
was thought of as related to them only in the way of
preventing evils of one sort or another. That economic production might be a chief sphere for the
growth of personality has not even yet dawned upon
the Christian church. The obverse of this is that the
economic order assumes to have laws of its own that
are independent of the laws of spiritual life, and a
scale of values that is independent of the scale in which
the Kingdom of God comes first. A set of standards
for saints and for our religious moments, and a different set for the masses and for our secular activities,
in fact a contradictory set—this is what our religion
itself has betrayed us into.

Christian morality of the Puritan type, it is true,
did undertake to bring religion and some aspects of

business together into a single plan. "Diligence in business" was looked upon as part of the Christian's vocation, and industriousness, economy, and thrift were exalted above shiftlessness toward work and frivolity in the use of money. Though this life-policy contributed to a certain sturdiness or solidity of character, there were two fatal gaps in it. First, whereas diligence in mastering nature's resources might enlarge and liberalize the personality, the Puritan type of diligence did not provide for this enlargement. Sturdiness was gained by pinching human interests, not by setting them free. Against this the spirit of our time has rightly rebelled, whether or not it has seen the way to something better. The second gap in the Puritan attempt to connect religion and business is its tacit assumption that the laborers are to achieve character by submitting to conditions of employment that they have had no hand in making, whereas employers are to achieve character by not submitting to anything of the kind. If religious experience included a sense of humor, what holy mirth might not this spiritual naïveté awaken! And if we have any just inkling of how we become persons, how tragically self-defeating such Christianity as this must be seen to be.

It is scarcely too much to say that the greatest enemy of Christianity has been nursed within the household of the faith, and fed and exercised until it has grown to gigantic stature. Mastering nature means for Christians and non-Christians a non-spiritual getting control of something out there. Power over material things connotes ability to get what one happens to want, not ability to improve our wants, not an enlargement-experience for all concerned. And power is attractive, naturally and properly so. Christian ethics should be a stimulus to power-acquisition on the part of employer and laborer alike, but our tradition does not encourage the laborer to seek power, and as for the employer and capitalist, the virtues that are demanded of him are little more than palliatives for the use of power acquired extra-ethically. Weak palliatives, of necessity; for, persons being forgotten in the excitement of the struggle to master nature, things fill the horizon, and, once possessed, they become coin in the pocket of desire. Thus we may grow large in the technic of power-acquisition, yet suffer arrest of our wants. Mastery of things, instead of freeing us from our smaller selves, may make us—it often does make us—slaves to our occupation and victims of our economic system. It raises "the standard of living," but this phrase, in its current use, has only the faintest reference (if any at all) to kinds of personality; it refers, rather, to things purchased. "Things are in the saddle, and they ride men." At last, great accumulations actually inspire awe, and this awe paints a halo about the possessor, however unlovely his personality may be, and however much depression of the personality of others may be represented in his pile.

The depression of other personalities is, in fact, inherent and necessary in this sort of "mastery of nature." The size of the task requires, increasingly so, the massing of human energies and the directing of a multitude of minds as well as hands toward a common focus; the directing of these minds, not by their own thinking, not by the give-and-take that promotes personality, but by a power external to themselves that keeps them at work whether their work has inherent meaning for them or not. We simply cannot separate the a-moral seeking of power over nature from the anti-moral seeking of power over the minds of our fellows.

24. Personality Can Grow, or Its Growth Can Be Arrested, through Play, and through the Life of Appreciation

The play of persons is something more than the friskiness of animals; something more than freshening the body by open air and quickened heart-beat; something more than the immediate pleasure that is attributed to games and contests, the dance, and such pastimes as hunting and fishing; it includes also temporary release from the burden of being a person, but release—paradoxical though this be—by being, for the time, more rather than less a person.

The play spirit is that of care-free, good-humored laughter. In such laughter one rises above one's task, above duty, even. Yet at the same time we can be quicker to discriminate, and we can be more objective-minded, less involved and tangled, than in prosaic labor. In play upon a maturely personal level we behold the actual, know it for what it is, and yet are not subject to it.

Here is the freedom that every person wants, but few can define. It can go into the activities of feet, as when we "take a walk"; into the management of a horse or of a motor car, as when we "take a ride"; into activities of hands, as when we "make things" for the joy of construction; into activities of eye and ear as when we explore nature "for her own sake"; into activities of mind, as when we live over our past without lifting any of its loads, or wrestle with puzzles, or "cap stories," or compose a limerick, or think out a witticism; it becomes one of the richest, most upbuilding of social experiences when individuals get free from one another yet enjoy one another because of what they are here and now and without reference to what they have been or done or to what they may become or do.

Play is not an indulgence that is to be outgrown; it is not a superfluity that I may properly dispense with if I so desire, but a necessity. It is necessary because the conditions of finite existence tend to fasten upon us habits of submission and even of servitude. This tendency must be counteracted, whatever the necessary cost, and through the whole of life. Horace Bushnell made the penetrating remark that when we get to heaven our occupation can be nothing else than play.

The attraction of alcoholic drinks arises from the fact that they reduce inhibitions, and thus produce a sense of adequacy and of freedom. The illusory character of alcoholic playfulness arises from the fact that this narcotic drug reduces the power of discrimination and therefore makes judgment unreliable at the precise moment when it becomes most certain of its own adequacy.

We require kinds of play that give us the sense of emancipation while discrimination is unimpaired or even enhanced. Some experiences that are called play do not emancipate. For example, a football "player" said to me, "This is not play at all, but the hardest kind of work. I do it, not because I like to, but because the sentiment of the college forces me." Other play-experiences are undiscriminating. Many a person assumes—this seems to be common among college students—that the surest way to have fun or a good time is to "let down" toward what is meaningless or even vulgar. This is to forget the pleasure of skill and refinement in play, such satisfaction as awaits a golfer or a tennis player after he has mastered the technic of the game.

Play has a long gamut, then, at one end of which personality is jangled, at the other end of which its notes are those of true joy. Joys are deeper when they are chosen with discriminating taste.

No one need be told that the growth of persons consists in large measure in multiplying and deepening one's appreciations of beauty, of truth, and of goodness. Writer after writer has pointed out that æsthetic contemplation can release us from bondage to commonplace things and to our commonplace self. Now and then the claim is made that it can give us glimpses into a spiritual reality that transcends as well as suffuses the experience of a finite world. However this may be, certainly one must learn to drop off the harness of all strained endeavor, and to permit nature, music, the drama, literature, and the other fine arts to work their work within the mind.

Appreciation of truth, likewise, has repeatedly been interpreted as a sort of coming home after a sojourn in foreign parts. An old saying has it, "My mind to me a kingdom is." Whoever once acquires the habit of enjoying increase of his knowledge just because it is increase of knowledge knows that here is a refuge both from oneself and from the buffets of circumstance. Determination to rise above prejudice and partisanship, to let no fear or other self-interest color one's thinking, and to go thus light-hearted and free-footed after whatever important truth can be learned, produces an elevated self-possession and confidence in the resources of life not unlike that of religious conversion at its best.

Moral sensitiveness, likewise, is essential to personal freedom. No blindness can be worse than the ingrained habit of not noticing the moral quality of events, one's own desires and conduct included. By moral quality is meant any tendency to produce one kind of persons and of personal relationships rather than another. I do not refer to the application of a code, but to judgments of quality, whatever be one's convinced basis of approval and disapproval. There is no worse imprisonment than inability to repent.

On the other hand, there is no emancipation like that of identifying my real interests with the real interests of persons generally.

These few propositions, almost platitudinous ones, concerning the positive place of appreciations in the growth of personality are stated not more for their own sake than for the sake of making vivid the obverse truth that arrest of growth also can occur precisely through these appreciations. Taste in every one of these fields can become a self-involution, or going 'round and 'round within an interest instead of making every interest a door into something beyond itself.

Moralists and religious persons will be quick to assent to this proposition as far as it applies to a narrow æstheticism and to the narrow devotion to science that Charles Darwin so clearly recognized in himself and regretted. But is the same proposition true of our appreciation of goodness? For answer, let us ask whether absorbing moral interest ever is hard and unlovely, or over-scrupulous and feverish; whether it ever freezes the spirit of play, or mismeasures art; whether it ever closes its ears to new information, or ever becomes intolerant of criticism; in short, whether, in the interest of personality, we must not now and then get outside our moral appreciations and judge them in the light of a possibly improved appreciation. What can be more dreary, or more hateful, than goodness?

25. Personality Can Grow, or Its Growth Can Be Arrested through Friendship, Affection, and Loyalty

In friendship, affection, and loyalty to a group, an institution, or a cause, there is opportunity for expansion of selfhood by its free identification with other selves. In so far as reciprocity is experienced therein, these relations are precisely the fundamental ones whereby personality emerges out of the instinctive condition of infancy.

Friendship as the true life of the wise man has been celebrated from of old. But there are unstimulating as well as stimulating friendships. Not seldom this honorific term is applied to mutual support in continuing to be what one already is, or in getting what one merely happens to want.

Latterly, conjugal affection has begun to be considered as commerce between two personalities, with the consequence of assimilating it at its best to friendship, comradeship, and free co-operation of equals. It is only when marriage reaches this level, or at least endeavors to reach it, that it can be unqualifiedly recommended as a true enlargement of life. Something parallel must be said of parental affection, too. It is enlarging when, and only when, it is more than a gush of emotion. A parent who enjoys his child without respecting him is in the way of arresting the growth of both.

There is much undiscriminating praise of loyalty. Is not even a mistaken loyalty better than none at all? it is asked. We may answer, "Yes, but be cautious." It ought to be nearly self-evident that devotion to anything can have the effect of prolonging and confirming its defects as well as its virtues. But supporting defects cannot have a fully wholesome reaction upon the person who does it. My character necessarily partakes of the character of my cause. Now, as a matter of fact, in every historical and finite object of my devotion there are limitations and defects. Therefore, I must be against as well as for it, else I neither fully exercise myself as a person nor stimulate the other persons involved.

Loyalty is particularly likely to cause arrest wherever its object is not obviously personal (as, a church, the state, a party, a college, "the team," in distinction from, say, my family). For here one tends to conceive the object in quasi-personal terms, and then to bestow upon it a regard that might be fitting in friendship or affection, but is self-blinding when it is directed toward institutions. There are plenty of alumni who glow with real emotion toward *alma mater*, the "dear old coll.," and at the same moment give support to what is least manly in college athletics. There are patriots who are as sensitive to the honor of their country ("her" honor) as a doting mother is toward the comfort of her child, yet as insensitive to the demonstrated defects of their country as the same mother may be toward the defects of her offspring. There is a church loyalty that, in the name of the holy, perpetuates what is unholy.

26. Personality Can Grow, or Its Growth Can Be Arrested, through Difficulty, Opposition, Defeat, or Suffering

What each of us does in the presence of adversity depends in part upon his original endowment (native vigor and temperament), but only partly; for, just as our endowment of hearing does not of itself settle our attitude toward symphonies; just as we learn to appreciate compositions for which at first we have no liking; in like manner our first, spontaneous attitudes when "things do not go our way" can be indefinitely modified by practice. According to the kind of practice that takes place in adversity we ourselves either expand or become confirmed in present limitations, or grow narrow.

When I cannot completely have my own way, I can act more, or less, as a person. If, upon encountering a difficulty, I stop in my tracks, or fall back upon my present self and rest there, even though I call this prudence, I betray myself. What I need is a "mode of attack"; I must master the difficulty, or else learn from it how to redirect my unabated energies. I must not permit myself to be put upon the defensive. For personality as such is aggressive, and its problem of growth is to find directions in which aggressiveness can be practised without limit.

When difficulty takes the form of opposition or resistance from others, again the problem is to find a way in which both I and those who are against me can act fully as persons. Quarrelsomeness, obstinacy, conceit, cajolery, putting in fear, calling into play extraneous or unworthy self-interest, argumentativeness, persuasion—to these we resort all too frequently. Not one of them develops personality, which is the main issue in every contest.

There is no adequate resolution of conflict, or of resistance of one to the convictions of another, short of meeting one another as persons, not merely as instruments for enforcing a particular idea or design. Real respect for persons will make us listen to others in the expectation of increasing our own understanding and our own self-balance. Often it will make of me only one witness in a case in which I should like to be legislator, police, prosecuting attorney, judge, and jury, all in one!

In place of argumentativeness, which aims to modify the other without undergoing any modification myself, I require the spirit of conference or discussion. Laughing together, even when we do not agree, is excellent insurance for personality. This does not assume that everybody is equally in the right and equally in the wrong; but it does assume that everybody is always partly right. In no conflict can any of us be wholly right while we deny this; on the other hand, when we recognize it, and accordingly act in the spirit of co-operation, conflict leads to growth of personality.[1]

Religious workers are slow to perceive that overcoming the resistance of another by persuasion establishes an unfortunate relation between the two persons. To persuade another is to do his thinking for him (usually under an implied assumption that he is thinking for himself), and it is to induce acceptance of your outlook by virtue of something other than the truth or value of it, such as fears, hopes, or other extraneous emotions, and social approvals and disapprovals. This superiority-inferiority relation is not an upbuilding kind of intercourse. Its results, moreover, are deceptive. Things appear to be settled when they are not. Christian evangelism always over-rates its results, is beset by persistent illusion, because persuasion, which is the evangelistic method, leaves essential capacities of the convert's personality unawakened at the moment when they seem, both to him and to others, to be most awake.

From a denominational college that is noted for its persistent use of evangelism came a complaint that there was a gap between the self-guided activities of the students and the faculty-guided religious activities. Not that the "campus activities" were inherently antagonistic to religion, but that the readiness of the students here contrasted painfully with their reluctance and passive resistance toward what the faculty regarded as the main concern. What could lessen this resistance? It was necessary to reply that the difficulty was not merely a religious one. In the background was the same difficulty with regard to the curricular work of the college and the whole official conception of what it is to educate. In the foreground

---

[1] I have treated this problem at some length in *The Motives of Men* (New York, 1928), chapter XXVIII, "Release through Co-operative Thinking."

was required attendance at religious exercises, together with the dogmatic teaching of religious beliefs, with its assumption that whoever disagreed with the professors must be to that extent in error. It was suggested that the students needed an experience of entire freedom and self-determination in religious matters; that where such experience is well established, the professors have the best chance for a hearing; but that they should expect, and welcome, unabashed disagreement from any student. As a beginning, a policy was outlined for an open forum on religion, in which professors and students should meet as equals, each individual raising questions and expressing fully his own convictions, no matter how popular or unpopular they might be in any circle.

So much for the educative possibilities in difficulty, conflict, and resistance. But suppose that such troubles culminate in defeat; what then? Well, defeat, whether it occurs through natural obstacles, through opposition from men, or through one's own errors, is both a test of personality and an opportunity for extending its borders. All of us have seen some men grow smaller through failure, and some men larger. When one is downed, one's first problem is whether one's self-respect can stand upright. If it can, the next problem concerns the readjustment of one's plans so that one can actively and outwardly express one's very self in them. "I am captain of my soul" is perhaps a bit flamboyant and somewhat lacking in the humility of a learner, yet it contains a kernel of most important truth. I can get along with little if I have to, and I shall not hang my head because I have less than others. I can get along with ill health if I have to, contracting my activities as my strength contracts, but within this range I can be worth while to myself and to others. Instead of being chagrined and cowed when I find myself in a minority, I can

be stimulated thereby to greater and more discriminating devotion to my cause. If I lose my job, I can
at least endeavor to be worth employing in some hon-
orable occupation. A student was securing a part of
his self-support by taking pay for political activities
that were questionable. In defense of his conduct he
remarked to a professor of economics, "One has to
live, you know." The professor replied, "I deny your
assumption. Nobody has to live!"

How much, indeed, can one not only endure, but
turn to advantage? I know not where the limit is.
The greatest sufferer I have ever met was as poised,
and as serenely self-active, as any person I have
known. He had turned the torture of his body into
a stimulus to new questioning concerning the meaning of life; he thought himself through to a conclusion that gave rational order to his doomed career;
and he had discovered ways to be useful to others,
even in his helplessnes. Not every one has the innate
gift that makes such an abounding triumph possible,
of course, but here is the policy that yields the largest results for anybody. We continually live below
our possible best because we assume that loss is just
loss and nothing else, when often it is opportunity
for some new sort of gain.

Where personality is most valued, there bereavement is most poignant. When fellowship upon the
basis of mutual respect is broken up by death, the
loss is literally irreparable. It is so because each of
the individuals in such a fellowship contributes something that is unique and therefore not replaceable.
What, then, can survivors do with a situation like
this? Christianity, and whatever other religion or
philosophy equally values persons, contain in this
valuation a resource that can turn bereavement into
something different from defeat or mere arrest. I
recall a memorial service for a much-admired, much-

loved, and highly efficient colleague who had been
cut down in the early bloom of her powers. In the
committee that planned the service the remark was
made and assented to, "Let us not indulge our sense
of loss; this wouldn't fit her personality. We must
make the occasion something like her." As a consequence, the service, through active thinking about
her and her cause, became an experience of solemn
and elevated joy, which is not at all inconsistent with
pain. We lived for that hour within the finalities of
life; the finality of death was by no means as
certain.

Much of what is called sorrow is self-pity. It
faces toward oneself instead of reflecting upon the
personality of the other. And self-pity is enervating,
while such reflection is tonic. When I take the objective attitude, bringing to mind the ineradicable
significance of the one who is gone, something of the
potency of his own personality sustains me; it forbids all letting down into self-pity or into pessimism
(which is self-pity writ large), and it even sheds
significance upon a system of nature that otherwise might seem to be merely cruel.

Thus, that which wounds us can make also for
our healing. For verily it is our appreciation of personality in the other that first makes possible articulate sorrow as contrasted with meaningless pain;
but the same appreciation assuages this sorrow in
spite of the inevitable pain of it. It is because
we are persons that we are so vulnerable; it is only
when we reach a profound fellowship of intertwined differences that we first become capable of
being profoundly bereaved. Thus, though the ache
be not removed, bereavement testifies to the real
greatness of life. The universe that makes it possible is a tragic universe, but it is neither tawdry nor
shabby. This is so even if the dead survive nowhere

but in our memory of them, as Maeterlinck's *Blue-bird* assumes. But it would be rash to assume that a universe that can create personality cannot preserve it. What we already are expresses itself consistently when we adopt as a working hypothesis, a guide for exploration and experiment, that personality can fulfil its own inner promise of unlimited growth.

27. Personality Can Grow, or Its Growth Can Be Arrested, through One's Own Sinning

"Surely," it will be said, "there is one kind of loss that is just loss and nothing else. Sin is pure negativity, absolute blackness." Is it not possible, however, that this absoluteness is an opposition between two concepts rather than irreconcilability between two forces, both personal? Is it true that sinning always causes an infinitely high wall to shoot up within the sinner, separating him utterly from himself? Do we not know, rather, that the outcome depends upon whether one takes the evil in oneself "lying down," as the popular phrase has it?

Two papers that were submitted in an examination in logic were so much alike that it was certain that one of the writers had copied from the work of the other. But Professor could not tell whether it was Billy who had cheated, or Arthur. Calling the two to his office, he said, "One of you, but I do not know which one, copied from the other's paper. The one of you who did the copying will, of course, not let me suspect the one who did not. Both of you may go now, but later one of you will come back and tell me about his own wrong-doing."

In a few minutes, Billy reappeared, and he confessed, absolving Arthur of all suspicion. "Billy," said Professor, "what has happened to you?"

"I'll tell you!" was Billy's reply. "I'm receiving

my support from a relative, and I'm making him believe that I'm studying, when I'm not. I've broken down."

Professor responded, "If this had occurred a short time ago, I should have been obliged to report your dishonesty, and you would have been expelled. But the rule has been abrogated, and I am glad. I shall make no report except that you have failed in the course. Billy, this can be the best thing that ever happened to you, for you can make it the starting-point of a new life."

Billy departed from the office, disappeared from the campus, and for years Professor did not know what had become of him. Then came a letter, written upon the stationery of a bank in a distant city:

DEAR PROFESSOR:

Do you remember Billy X, who cheated in your logic examination several years ago? He is the writer of this letter.

I took your advice. I went to . . . University, and graduated there, and now for five years I have been in the employ of this bank. I am holding a position of trust, and I am making good. It all started from that logic exam.

28. Personality Can Grow, or Its Growth Can Be Arrested, Through Worship

Under the term worship may be included all realizations of fellowship with God, regardless of the forms that they take, and whether they occur privately or in an assembly. These forms range all the way from prayers of thankfulness, adoration, repentance, petition, and consecration, to the "practice of the presence of God," which may consist in going about one's daily task with a sense of fulfilling the will of God thereby.

There are many ways in which worship can promote the growth of personality. (1) It can supplant fear, worry, and wearing haste with calm self-possession. (2) By reminding us of central points of view it can promote mental perspective, making great things look great, and small things small. (3) It can include such a facing of our faults as leads to repentance and amendment of conduct. (4) It can intensify our devotion to a cause, and prevent hardships from taking on exaggerated importance. (5) It can save our goodness from over-strenuousness, over-assertiveness, and angularity by making us realize how small we are and how great God is. (6) It can humanize us by fellowship with other worshippers, even those whose worship is much unlike our own, and it can unite a group in support of a cause. (7) It can include a repeated or even a continuous weighing of issues and results, together with sensitiveness to new needs that arise in a changing world.

Generalizing the personality-forming influence of such practices, we may say that worship can gather together what has been and what is, with a view to determining, both individually and socially, what shall be, and that it can do this with the greatest thoroughness, breadth, and poise because it includes a consciousness of doing it with God. Here, then, is a possible climax of self-expression, self-transformation, social unity, and objectivity of mind (the opposite of self-involution). Indeed, where except in worship does personality reach such a climax? For consider that here the personal, most awake, confronts the actualities that may threaten to crush or smother it, and is not crushed or smothered, but stimulated; is not thrown back upon itself, but drawn out to the utmost through the realization of a fellowship that reaches to the utmost.

Put into terms of education, this means that in worship the learner can sharpen and broaden his discrimination in one ethical area after another without end; he can thereby check his faults, and likewise his virtues, which always need revaluation; he can increase his sense of oneness with his fellows; he can broaden his social horizon; he can acquire a habit of rejoicing in the good even when it is costly; and, in his realization of God, he can acquire the spirit of unlimited adventure.

Worship can be all this. Yet one can worship without experiencing as much as one of the things that have been mentioned. Self-pity, and self-indulgence in almost any form, can confirm themselves by dwelling undiscriminatingly upon the thought of God as friend, comforter, and helper. One can repent of faults that are unpleasing, and yet retain those that are most agreeable. The social sense can be intensified at the same time that it is kept narrow, with sectarianism or class discrimination as the result. Instead of learning to rejoice in unpopular goodness even though it bring hardship, one can go in any direction with the worshipping crowd. And faith, instead of inspiring to unlimited adventure, can become the bulwark of an unprogressive society.

At the present moment an extensive movement for the enrichment of worship is going on in the United States. It takes many forms. In denominations that in an earlier age cast liturgies aside, we see again coming into use set prayers and chants, surpliced choirs and processions, ministerial robes and priestly manners. The ancient and the remote are more and more becoming the vehicle for expressing present piety. The altar is returning to churches of non-sacerdotal type, and with it something of the old sacramental attitude and emotional stirring. Symbolical figures in stone, wood, and stained glass are increasing—for the most part conventional figures borrowed from the long past. Church architecture

also leans heavily toward forms that prevailed when
common worship was essentially a sacramental
drama to be gazed at over and over again rather
than a repeatedly fresh thought-attack upon the
problems of a changing life. The same movement,
when it takes hold of persons already accustomed to
fixed liturgies and sacramental attitudes, sends many
of them back toward the Roman Church in search of
a fully satisfying worship.

The current explanations of this movement run to
the effect that we are recovering for religion æsthetic
resources that our fathers mistakenly cast aside;
that mystical realizations, fostered by symbolism and
sacramentalism, are needed as well as the ethical and
practical and purposeful attitudes that the last generation or two has one-sidedly cultivated; that all the
dignity and beauty that we can command are required
for an adequate approach to God, and for a fitting
expression of his presence in the world.

Something of all this is going into the newer
schemes for religious education. Training in worship through the experience of worshipping is the
fundamental idea, and worshipping on the part of
the young is promoted, for the most part, by pro-
viding for it orderly forms, dignified in character,
that look forward to ultimate participation in the
just-described enriched worship of the congregation.

How many of the personality-forming processes
enumerated a little way back are in this "enriched"
worship? How many of the arrest-processes? Any
such question appears to be far from the minds of
those who are in the movement, except some of the
workers in religious education. There is no doubt
that common worship is becoming in many churches
æsthetically pleasing, restful, and elevating. Yet it
has the appearance on the whole of being an indulgence in refined sentiments the most obvious value

of which is a general refreshment of mind. It is a restoration of fatigued powers. But mark! The particular character of a given restoration of our powers is shown by the use to which they are put after being restored. Since the worship in question takes place weekly, we may ask what is the activity or the care that leaves us fatigued every Saturday but finds us fresh every Monday?

This change in worship is being thrust upon us by the increasing mechanization and depersonalization from which our industrial life is sick and starving. We must have relief; and it is natural and proper that we should seek it in religion. Worship should provide restoration for the frayed-out and mechanized spirit—should be, in a sense, recreational, like play. But what if our enriched worship, like golf or a comedy, should strengthen us for "more of the same" in our secular life instead of setting us to re-creating it in the interest of persons?

We have as yet no evidence that our enriched worship makes us more discriminating with respect to the ethical issues of modern life; no evidence that the increasing use of formulas for repentance represents increasing repentance; nor that the social spirit of these worshipping groups is going to dissolve the walls that separate men into sects and classes; nor that the unpopular "better" gains support as against the conventional "good." If any one should assert that this enrichment of worship, though it rightly insists that æsthetic resources should be utilized and that a sense of history is needed, nevertheless is (in its present state) a recreative adjunct of middle-class secular pursuits, I should not know how to refute him, much as I should like to do so.

The conclusion of the matter is that worship can promote either a refined but unprogressive piety (which connotes an arrest of personality), or a piety that, because it awakens personality, accepts the burdens and the joys of moral creativity.

29. These Laws of Life Are Laws for Christian Education

Our discussion in the last half-dozen sections may seem repeatedly to have wandered from Christian education to Christian experience or living taken as a whole. Certainly some experiences that have been mentioned belong to adult years rather than to children and youth, and only now and then have we had in mind such a situation as a teacher and a class. Yet there has been no wandering from our central theme. The laws of life—its perennial issues and possibilities of weal and woe—are also laws of education. For, first of all, education, as we saw a little way back, is for persons as such, not for young persons only. In the second place, the very same laws of growth apply to all ages. In fact, only a few of the specific experiences to which reference has been made are absent even from childhood. Go through the list: Mastery of nature, the body included; play, and appreciation of truth, beauty, and goodness; friendship, affection, and loyalty; difficulty, opposition, defeat, and suffering; sinning; worship—all of them are found in one way or another in all the school ages.

There are two special reasons, moreover, why such a survey as this should be made. To begin with, teachers naturally look for short formulas or for general points of view that can be applied throughout the process of teaching and managing pupils. The result, frequently, is a principle so highly generalized that it fails to give guidance in particulars. For example, if we say that personality grows through social give-and-take, we have not yet discriminated between the different sorts of give-and-take and their respective effects upon personality. We gain something if we go on to say that friendly interactions are more upbuilding than quarrels, but we have not reached the end until we see that even friendship and affection can arrest personality or not according to the way they are handled. What I have endeavored to do is to supplement our usual formal statements about growth by exhibiting typical areas in which such formulas clearly are inadequate, and by showing how personality really grows or is arrested in these areas.

A final reason for this unusual approach to some of the laws of learning is that the analyses of Christian character that usually underlie plans for Christian teaching do not reach the core of the issues that life presents to us. Sometimes qualities of character are at the fore, or traits or virtues; sometimes motives; sometimes types of activity or of conduct, but always something that is unconditionally recommended. If you have this or that, or are this or that, or do this or that, you have arrived. This kind of assumption is held with such confidence by so many educators that to challenge it may be rash. But it is facts such as I have adduced that do the challenging. A pupil can sincerely accept all the advice of his Sunday-school teachers through all the grades, and yet be an arrested personality! And the arrest may be at the precise point where he and his teachers are most sure that he has arrived![1]

---

[1] I shall not leave the matter in this negative form, but in Chapter VIII I shall show some of the positive applications to curriculum-building, etc., of the mode of analysis that I have employed in the present chapter.

CHAPTER VII

SCIENTIFIC METHOD A NECESSARY EXPRESSION OF PERSONALITY

30. Is Religion, As It Claims to Be, an Exercise of Intelligence?

Whatever else religion may be, it is an attempt to make adjustment to things as they really are. At its lowest terms, it is endeavor to be on the safe side; in its higher forms it seeks escape from the false appearance of things, or it resists the supposedly false beguilements of impulse, or it becomes devotion to and self-identification with that which is supposed to have the deepest and widest validity. Every religious man believes himself to be, to the extent that he is religious, a wise man.

Since intelligence is one factor in wisdom, religion always supposes itself to be an exercise of intelligence. It assumes that its priests, prophets, and preachers have delved deeper than the common run of mortals into the mysteries of life, and that its saints have come face to face with realities that the rest of us apprehend only at a distance and perhaps through the reports of others.

Religious education, consequently, includes measures for inducing pupils to employ their capacity for knowing, and for organizing life by means of thought. If, then, we inquire how, as a matter of fact, religious education actually employs intelligence, we do not thereby approach the sacred from outside itself, nor measure religion by non-religious tests. If the result of such an inquiry should prove to be embarrassing, the situation would be simply that of religion being shamed by religion.

The results are, in fact, embarrassing. For the

main tradition of religious education, Christian as well as non-Christian, as far as knowledge and thinking are concerned, is that of exercising intelligence to a very limited degree and then stopping—often not only stopping but blocking the way to further use.

We do not have to search history for illustrations. Roman Catholic teaching is openly committed to prescribing grooves in which the religious intelligence of the pupil shall move. When he is able to define ancient doctrines and usages with exactness, to discriminate them from near-by errors, to defend them against common objections, and to recall the precise duties that the Church imposes upon him, the intellectual part of Catholic teaching is done, as far as the laity is concerned. Within this field such questions as, Is this true? What more is true? and, How much of this is certain, how much probable, and how much problematic? simply do not arise. All vital questions of the soul's welfare are already settled and adequately formulated; the main work of intelligence is finished; henceforth the faithful are to believe and apply, not to think in any creative sense.

If training for the Catholic priesthood is somewhat more exciting than this, the reason is not that the principles of it are different, but that the priest, and especially the theologian, must be ready to explain and defend the faith more completely. For this reason, non-Catholic philosophy and science may be learnedly analyzed, but the ever-present question concerning them is, At what points are they consistent, or inconsistent, with the standards of the faith? Religious intelligence, that is to say, goes 'round and 'round in its own tracks; the mind that might go exploring is tethered in a pasture.

Protestantism, by virtue of the right that it

ative ability. Instead, then, of asking what sorts of truth scientific research has established, let us inquire, rather, When is a man scientific? When we have answered this question we shall be in position to ask what stake, if any, the Christian principle of personality has in science as such.

31. When Is a Man Scientific?

The popular answer is that any one who accepts what science affirms is scientific. There is no little preening of feathers on the part of those who are conscious of being "up to date" in this sense; no little sense of superiority; some brow-beating, too. But, one can accept a science upon authority just as well as a theology; orthodoxy in science is no more costly than orthodoxy in religion. In fact, when a science has become respectable, mere suggestibility in the populace brings it followers.

A man does not become scientific by "accepting" anything. What counts is one's attitude toward evidence rather than one's liking for a conclusion. To the extent that any one understands the grounds of a science, and is able and disposed to weigh evidence in its field, then, he is scientific. *To this extent* he is so; but specialists in the sciences have been known to walk unsteadily at the borders of their specialty, and beyond these borders to stagger. What is found in the narrow area that one has studied is now and then offered as an interpretation of other areas that one has not studied; or, what preoccupies one's mind stands in the way of further research; or, being an authority at one point tempts one to over-value one's wisdom at other points. Almost any academic community knows only too well that in their personal relations men of science can be anything but scientific.

Is then this elusive individual—the man who is truly scientific—to be defined as one who governs his entire conduct solely by what is scientifically known? Alas! "There ain't no sich creetur!" Conduct, in all men whatsoever, is governed by a complex of determinants, of which information is only one. Likes and dislikes of many sorts also play their part, and they always will do so. And this is not because of an infirmity in human nature, but because of its inherent strength and wealth. Imagine what life would be like if personality were only a transition-point between seeing a set of facts and automatically starting an activity. Think of never doing anything because we like to do it! It is the good fortune of men of science that they have many likings besides that for facts and laws, and that it is not always incumbent upon them to prove that their conduct is good from any other point of view than that they and others prefer it.

But not too fast! When we inspect our experience with our preferences one by one we perceive that many of them are vain and doomed to disappointment. This is so because questions of fact always are involved; we get what we want, or fail to get it, by virtue of some relation between our desires and things as they already are. Here is where science has an essential and unique function to perform in the guidance of conduct, though it be not, and cannot be, the sole determiner. Physiology does not prove to me whether or not I should prefer to live, but it does show me what prolongs and what shortens life. Hence it may be the main guide to my diet, my recreations, my residence, even my occupation.

Even here, however, science is master only within limits, for I still have to make up my mind to what degree this "life" of mine is to be construed in terms of years, and to what degree in terms of intensity of approved experiences. Which is better, to vegetate for a hundred years, or to luxuriate for fifty? I have known two brothers, each with a condition of the heart that permitted length of days only upon condition of greatly restricted activity and experience. One of them adopted the policy of living as long as possible, but this doomed him to daily penury of experience, with fear as his constant companion. The other chose to live in a larger sense, come what would. Arranging his affairs as though he expected death to overtake him at any moment, he gave himself to large and varied interests and to new experiences, never boisterously, but always with the consciously accepted possibility of undue excitement or strain, and the snapping of the thread. Thus he lived, not in fear, but zestfully, enjoying the world and his friends, and making them enjoy him, until indeed his chosen mode of living gave birth, out of itself, to death.

What science has to do for us in a case like this, and indeed in all cases, is to get facts before us so that we can make our choices intelligently, knowing what the alternatives really are, and what will be the cost of each. Among the costs must be reckoned, of course, not only the necessary intermediate activities before a desired value can be reached, but also the effects upon other persons and upon one's own personality. It is not really profitable business to gain the whole world at the cost of injustice to others or the shrivelling of one's own soul. Wisdom requires, then, a look ahead in terms of cause-and-effect; but this is possible only when we have taken a cause-and-effect look behind—in other words only through science.

There is much gazing behind and before that is not science. The impulse to do it somehow or other is simply human; it is as old as man and as oft-renewed as infancy. What we endeavor to do when we are scientific-minded is to control this looking behind and before by a definite technic that tends to reduce our errors and increase our predictive power to the utmost. This is the meaning of the oft-repeated statement that science is "organized common sense."

The rehearsal of these things, which have been said so many times before, will not be useless if it helps us forward with our main question, which concerns the relation between the scientific frame of mind and the Christian valuation of personality. We now see that the scientific frame of mind is to be defined, not by exposition of the content of the sciences at any period of their history, but by analysis of the modes of attack upon fact that characterize science as contrasted with uncritical rule-of-thumb. The crux of the matter is scientific method, and the question that concerns us is, What sort of personal attitudes and habits must one have who approaches all facts by this method?

This question relates to the kind of "ownness" that one stamps upon one's experiences. What is called "the scientific temper" is a matter of character in the same sense as generosity or miserliness, ordered industry or slovenly puttering. Let us consider the nature of scientific procedure, then, from this character-angle.

32. What Are the Principles of Scientific Method?

For our present purpose, which has to do with personal attitudes rather than details of technic, the following six propositions will sufficiently indicate the kinds of readiness and the kinds of self-judgment that are involved in strictly scientific procedures:

(1) Scientific method is intellectual co-operation. Every scientific mind submits its processes and its products to other minds for their critical appraisal. A science grows by mutual interchange of information and critical judgment—that is, both by adding to the work of one another, and by subtracting from it. This is not only *a* method of intellectual co-operation, it is the only known method. Here we are on track of one solution for a troublesome problem. To be a person I must act freely as an individual; yet, to be a person I must be responsive to the free acts of others. I must, then, be free and bound at the same time, and somehow these two phases of my experience must be harmonized and synchronized. In scientific procedure at its best this harmonizing and synchronizing actually is achieved; one is highly individual and highly social at the same time and concerning the same matter. Indeed, here is social unity that not only does not repress individuality, but actually stimulates it.

(2) In scientific work there are no foreigners, no social classes, no special privileges, no institutional or hierarchical prerogatives. If you know a fact better than anybody else; if you can refine a procedure; if you can prove that some accepted generalization is defective; if you can make a fresh analysis or broader generalization than one now accepted—if you can do any of these things, your credentials are adequate, and you will be listened to regardless of every other circumstance about you. This is the ideal of science. Of course the ideal can be invaded by anti-scientific impulses, as in the late war; for men are complex, not mere intellect. But what is required when this principle is compromised is simply to be more scientific. Here, of course, emotions of an ethical and religious sort can play into the sciences, reinforcing what they already intend to be. It is a

striking fact, however, that the scientific bond rather
than the religious is the one that was least ruptured
by the Great War, and the one soonest mended.

(3) The spirit of science is eagerness to learn,
not to teach, in the sense of inducing another to conform to what already is in your mind. Only the other
day a man of science told me that in the midst of one
of his class-room demonstrations a student inter-
jected the questions, "Isn't A related to B in such
and such a way, and if so, doesn't so and so follow?"
"Young man," replied the veteran of science, "I have
been specializing and teaching in this field for
twenty years, but you have shown me something
new!" The professor told me this story with glee
and an attitude of triumph, not of chagrin. He was
still a learner because he was a true man of science.

(4) Though the sciences employ every type of
logical procedure, they are particularly reliant upon
observed fact as compared with reliance upon the
self-consistency of a thought structure. This means
caution not only toward speculative philosophy and
theology, but also toward the systematizations of science itself. This requires profound humility; one
must "sit before fact as a little child," as Huxley put
it. But a certain mental toughness results. It is the
toughness both of assertion of fact as fact, and of
caution toward assertiveness even with respect to
facts. And this caution has its own technic, for it requires not only a second look, but also systematized
analytic observation, which often or even generally
proves that things are not what they seem. Hence the
habit of suspending judgment and of resisting suggestion; hence also the penchant for accuracy and
for measurement wherever it is possible. All this
makes intelligence both aggressive and humble.

(5) Scientific method is characterized, likewise,
by the use of hypothesis, experiment, and mathe-

matical analysis for the purpose of extending the range and the fineness of direct observation, and for supplementing it. It is thus, for the most part, that causal relations are ascertained, and that we become certain of the existence of a vast number of things that we have not observed. Mental pictures or formulæ for the invisible or non-observed phases of our world are continually being constructed, reconstructed, destroyed, and replaced. Here is where "scientific imagination" becomes a part of the most rigorous intelligence and objectivity. The experimental attitude, with its free but tested employment of imagination and hypothesis, is extremely interesting as a partial realization of certain possibilities of character. If we make it general, applying it within all the practical, moral, and religious interests of mankind, we undertake not only to "make out" what is about us, but also to "make" what shall be about us, and Margaret Fuller's "I accept the universe," and Carlyle's "Gad, she'd better," are out of place.

(6) The sixth point is implied in each of the preceding five points, but there is reason for stating it by itself. Within the sciences, as far as they are true to their own principles, there is no obligatory proposition, no orthodoxy. Nothing is obligatory except the attitudes here described put into action, together with the improvement of special technics wherever possible. The fellowship of scientific minds does not rest upon common acceptance of any conclusion whatever, but solely upon a common understanding of procedure and common appreciation of the ideals that should control it. This is a counsel of perfection, of course. Workers in the sciences are not always in the listening mood; they do not always escape overfondness for the offspring of their own intellect; waves of interest, and wave-troughs of disinterest in this or that area are mistaken for insight into the

bounds of the actual; and any systematized whole that has worked thus far acquires undue prestige thereby. But all this is a deflection of the would-be scientific mind from its true and intended course; and recovery from the aberration requires nothing but increased fidelity to the recognized principles of method. The plasticity of the intellect when it is most scientific has been marvellously illustrated in our day by what has happened in physics. If anything could become scientifically orthodox, it would be the basic conceptions that physics derived from Newton—notions regarded as essential to the whole structure of the physical and natural sciences. Yet Einstein is listened to, and with remarkable placidity physicists re-examine the foundations upon which they had erected all their towering edifices.

33. These Principles Glorify the Personal and the Social, Not the Impersonal and Mechanical

These six marks of the scientific attitude, taken either in their totality or one by one, are so many accents upon personality, its value and its capacity for achieving its freedom within the system of nature. Whenever the work of science goes on, human spirits lift themselves out of the mere flow of events, and assume a course of their own. The autonomy of the person is manifested in suspension of judgment; in "putting questions to nature," as the method of hypothesis has been called; in initiating learning as against waiting for events to work upon us; in the self-overcoming that submits one's dearest thoughts to the test of observed fact, and in the creative humility that prizes, above all that has been learned, the opportunity to learn still more.

Moreover, scientific method binds one person to another upon the basis of mutual respect. One seeks, not the particular-to-me, but the common-to-all; therefore the seekers, not merely the things sought, have value. Men of science flock together in meetings, and in printed contributions, and their converse, when it fulfils its purpose, is not debate, which seeks victory over other persons, but co-operative thinking toward any conclusion that the evidence warrants. If democracy be conceived as organized respect for one another, then science, as far as it follows its own principles, is democracy in the intellectual sphere; it consists, as far as its special functions are concerned, in loving one's neighbor as oneself.

But this is as much as to say that the scientific movement, of which the fundamental achievement is that it has brought to light a true and effective method for intelligence, is a part of the evolving moral order; it is a part of the moving moral creativity that man shares with God.

Behold, then, the tragic blunder of the churches in their hostility, or suspiciousness, or indifference to it. "He came unto his own, and they who were his own received him not." Instead of asking, Does scientific procedure bring out essential functions of personality? Does it respect personality in others, or despise it? Does it bring men together in mutual respect, or does it segregate them from one another?— instead of asking this, our church forces were and are agitated by the question, "Do the conclusions of the sciences agree with what we already are in the habit of thinking? If not, let us resist the whole movement." As well try to resist God! For this was to resist his creative work in the unfoldment of persons; it was to disobey the first and great commandment that we value personality above everything else. We cannot fulfil the law of love unless we practise the principles of scientific method!

This is not an apotheosis of the content of any sci-

ence, least of all a bowing down to the drifting sentiments, moods, and valuations that may prevail among
men of science in any period or any group. The content of science always reflects, more or less, the limitations of the human, just as all churches and all our
goodness do. Men of science individually and collectively are capable of following fashions of thought,
of yielding to suggestion, of being hasty on the one
hand or dilatory and orthodox on the other. Yet, if
we suspect that revision of a science is needed, we
cannot prescribe in advance a list of necessary amend-
ments; we can only ask that the case be re-opened
and freshly worked through in accordance with its
own canons. When would-be science goes astray, it is
science and science only from which it wanders.

34. Christianity Needs to Assimilate, in Its Own Work, the Scientific Attitude and Method

It follows from what has been said that the principles of scientific method are not only valid, they
are a necessity for spiritual health; they are a part
of pure and undefiled religion. To most religionists
this will seem to be an extravagant statement. They
will think that they have met all reasonable require-
ments when they bid god-speed to anybody who wants
to pursue science. Their spirit is, "Let science go its
way, while we go ours." But this is a two-fold blunder. On the one hand, it invites the sciences to continue and develop their alliance with, and subordina-
tion to, industrialism and nationalism; on the other
hand, it ignores the conditions of effective self-guidance in what are called spiritual matters.

That the principles of science must be incorporated
into our religion and our religious education as a
properly inherent part thereof appears from the following considerations:

(1) Analysis of causal relations is necessary in order to make goodness efficient. We have already found this out with respect to a few of the functions of good men. In the field commonly called "charities," for example, we have begun to see that case-work and other methods of analysis that lead toward prevention as well as relief are essential if good-will is to reach its goal. Christian missions—to their credit be it said—employ scientific medicine as an expression and a method of love. The religious-education movement of to-day is, among other things, a reaching out after scientific insight into pupils' minds and into the effects of this and that kind of pupil-experience. But there are still great areas of church activity and relationship in which we judge our efficiency chiefly by guesses. This is true, for example, of preaching and of worship, upon which enormous labor and funds are expended. It is true of evangelism, the church press, and most of the teaching in church schools. Meantime, only here and there has a field been studied so that church workers can really know what is needed or what accomplished.

Examples could be multiplied indefinitely. Christian education is not in position to tell us *how* to be good except in a few relations. But teaching pupils to be good-in-general is precisely the way to produce an inefficient church and an inefficient Christianity— a religion that knows neither how to be good nor how to repent for not being so.

(2) Scientific method is necessary, not only to give effect to good intentions; it is necessary, likewise, to the discovery of what is good and what bad. Shall we say that some impulses are unqualifiedly good, and therefore to be indulged without limit? Love, for example? But everybody knows how foolish love can be, how self-defeating. What really is a good sort of maternal affection? We find this out by

analysis of causes and effects, not otherwise; and this analysis discloses the fact that maternal affection can be positively bad.

Our common notions of what is good and what bad have come down to us, on the whole, from sources that by no stretch of generosity can we regard as entitled to authority. Taboos, customs, the interest of a ruling class, the prescriptions of priests, erroneous judgments concerning causes and effects—all these have had a part in forming the traditional code. Only a part, of course, for correct observation mingles with wrong inference, and personality-forming valuations with personality-arresting ones. What may be called racial wisdom is there along with racial unwisdom; but which is which can be ascertained only through analysis that traces out the relations of things. As yet we have not learned that good-will is really good only when it wills something that really is worth while, and that anything else that calls itself good-will, however sincerely, is illusive and dangerous. The strictest methods for ascertaining the actual results of conduct must therefore be regarded as an essential constituent of morality.

Christianity has emphasized purity of motive, and it has taught that if a man's motives are good, the man is good. In so far as this means that "out of the heart are the issues of life," and therefore that the ends of life are primary, and rules of conduct only secondary, it is an important truth. But what motives are good, and what shall we understand by motive? If by motive we mean a mere psychical urge taken without regard either to the situations in which it acts or to the effects of its action, then no motive can be in and of itself either good or bad. The significance of any urge can be discerned only by looking beyond it to that toward which it moves, only by noting the kind of events that occur when it is

given scope. On the other hand, if motive means desired result, then purity of motive is no diffuse ami-
ability or undiscriminating adherence to anything,
no mere harmlessness, but rather unification of the
self through definiteness of objective. The pure heart
would then be, not any kind of emptiness, but concen-
tration upon an end without compromise on behalf
of self-interest. The quality of a man, accordingly,
would be identical with the quality of the ends upon
which he concentrates his activities.

That our religion has often conceived of goodness
in terms of subjectivity as against what is sometimes
called external obedience to rules is only a partial
good fortune. When individual goodness means "private goodness," there can be any amount of feebleness and fumbling without condemnation. A man who
is conscious of being able to fulfil himself by some
inner adjustment is not likely to develop a due sense
of responsibility for what happens in the world about
him, the world of which, however, he is one determining part. Private goodness is small-scale goodness. What is called purity of motive, moreover, often
becomes one's excuse for bungling and inefficient acts.
In addition, preaching and teaching continually offer
supposed remedies for the ills of the world without
first making a genuine diagnosis—that is, an analysis that shows where the seat of the evil is; or a
pseudo-diagnosis is made in the form of religious
platitudes. One result is that we are left complacent
toward forces of destruction without any inkling that
our motives at this point are bad; another result is
that we actually resist necessary reforms because we
can be privately good without them, and they dis-
turb our devotions.

We require a technic, then, for finding out what
is good and what bad. Lacking such a technic, we
practise customs that frustrate the life of the spirit

without realizing that to this extent we are bad men; and we even set ourselves up to be physicians of the spirit though we cannot discriminate sickness from health. A theologian of an earlier century remarked that every Christian requires a knowledge of two things: He must know the true God and the true devil! We may paraphrase this keen remark for our own purpose as follows: In order to be truly Christian we must discriminate between the good and the bad objectively; this discrimination requires observation and analysis, and these require scientific method.

(3) Christianity requires scientific method in order to utilize its own past. A part of the reason has just been given, namely, that trained ability to search out the good and the bad in the objective world is necessary. This applies to the present world. But similar ability is required with respect to the past of our religion. I shall take it for granted that in order adequately to understand the present, its needs, and how to meet them, we must consult the records of earlier experience. Nothing is more truly practical than the kind of historic sense that continually pries into the dynamics of human movements, and into the reasons for their successes and failures. But we cannot really know the past unless we employ the critical methods of the historian, methods which, in their own kind of data, are an application of scientific method.

One thinks at once of the handling of biblical material in church schools. Whereas theological specialists search the Scriptures by critical methods, assuming that we canot know the meaning until we know the facts, teaching the laity is for the most part an attempt at edification by means of the Scriptures without bringing the facts to light. Not that there is any intention to conceal the historical settings of biblical gems; rather, a belief that the settings are not important. But the figure of a gem set in material entirely foreign to itself does not apply to the life-movement of history. The meaning is in the movement, not something carried along by it.

The present methods of popular biblical instruction lead laymen to form historical judgments without historical information, and to hang their religion upon dislocated, distorted, and even imaginary facts and events. The resulting confusion operates in two directions: On the one hand, the religious appreciations of to-day reflect themselves backward, putting meanings into the Bible that are not there while overlooking meanings that are there; and on the other hand these illusory interpretations then reinforce, with pseudo-biblical authority, the positions from which the start was made. This is decidedly not the way to gain understanding of ourselves from the past. Moreover, the lack of historical perspective, the failure to put biblical narratives and ideas into their literal historical settings, easily permits, or even causes, the temporal and defective in them to be taken as eternal and normative. In a religion that already is old, we cannot have spiritual clarity unless we employ critical methods in the study of its history.

We are in danger, in fact, of having two kinds of religion side by side—an esoteric one for scholars and an exoteric one for the people. On a Saturday evening the remark was made that Jesus had a deep appreciation of domestic life. An eminent New-Testament scholar replied that Jesus did not have any such appreciation of the family; he regarded it as unimportant in view of the near approach of the apocalypse and the new age, when existing modes of life should pass away. But the next morning, Sunday, this eminent New-Testament scholar preached a sermon on the all-sufficiency of Jesus as our guide!

(4) Scientific method is required by any religion that aspires to be universal—scientific method in dealing both with other religions and with itself. There are several reasons why this is so. An obvious one is that the meeting of any two religions awakens questioning and compels thinking. If a unified fellowship is to result, it must be, among other things, a fellowship of intelligence, free and open-eyed. But the principles of scientific method are the principles of a universal fellowship of intelligence, and no others are known or imaginable.

A particular reason why Christianity's aspiration to become universal will require her to assume the scientific attitude is that her own faults and deficiencies are bound to come to light—are even now doing so (as the Jerusalem Conference confessed). The peering eyes of Orientals of other faiths are at this moment turned toward various facts of a disturbing nature—facts never mentioned in the missionary's message. We must join these Orientals in weighing our own past and present, and we must not be behind them in the objectively critical methods that we employ. The spirit and method of apologetics will not do—that is, assuming in advance how our questions are to be answered. The same scrutiny that we give to non-Christian religions must be applied to our own spiritual heritage and to our present practices, relations, and entanglements. The function of inquiry, and of intercourse with persons of other faiths, is not to demonstrate the finality or superiority or even the virtues of our faith. It is to create then and there a fellowship of intelligence applied to the common problems of life and the various efforts to solve them. If our missions had practised this scientific approach with respect to the Bible, Christian doctrine, Christian history, denominationalism, and our entanglements with western industrialism and nationalism, some of the most serious difficulties that missions and mission schools are now facing would have been avoided. The apologetic attitude of jealousy for our religion creates, of course, a correspondingly defensive attitude in other religionists. Our religion then becomes identified with our anxiety for it, and the vulnerable points in our present and our past become a misleading index of the whole.

(5) Another reason why scientific method must be assimilated into Christianity is that innumerable facts of nature make a difference to religion.

Our religion always has been interested in the processes of nature. A list of them would be long, for it would include many items of a physiological sort (for example, the relation of moderation in eating to spiritual states of mind, the control of sex-functions, the effects of alcoholic stimulants, the healing of disease, the methods and the effects of asceticism); psychical processes (for example, dreams, visions, auditions, and trances; how religious inspiration differs from ordinary states; how temptations arise and are overcome; the tendencies of "the natural man"; the religious nature of man; the stages of the mystical way, and much more); and cosmic processes and relations (for example, the method and the order of creation; the interpretation of natural law; the nature of matter; the significance of beauty and sublimity in nature).

Some method of approach to such facts and questions we are bound to have. We cannot study the Bible intelligently without having an attitude and a policy in these matters, for cosmological ideas, and notions of particular events and processes in the natural world, are interwoven with whatever the Scriptures have to tell us. The history of Christian thought, and to an extent the history of ecclesiastical practices, likewise, confront us with conceptions of nature to which we have to say either "Yes" or "No." Fundamentalism even erects into articles of faith its chosen views in the field of biology. In all these matters the question for intelligence, and for the intelligent conscience, is, How can we find out what is true? How get beyond contentiousness over opinions?

The answer already is before us; we do not need to argue it. But we need to take account of the difference it makes whether, as religionists, we merely tolerate the scientific approach, or rather adopt it for ourselves and make it a part of our piety. If we do not employ the scientific approach, we employ some other, and, whether we realize what happens or not, it becomes one of the sacred things of our faith. And the result is a divided self. For we cannot repudiate the sciences altogether, nor fail to make our obeisance to the principles of scientific method. They are principles of intelligence as such, of personality as such. It will be hard for any religion to kick against this goad, but some will do it for a time, and they will be —well, kickers. Other types of religion will endeavor to be liberal toward science, but at the same time they will attempt to squeeze religious juice from facts without really knowing them. The worst thing about this is not even the ignorance that it fosters, but rather the muddy quality of the religious juice that is thus extracted. It has to be muddy because it is derived from a compromise of personality with itself.

At the beginning of this chapter we noted that religion is an exercise of intelligence. From this it follows that the method of intelligence properly is a method of religion. The principles of scientific method we perceived to be inherent in intelligence as such, therefore necessary to the expression of personality, and consequently a particularly vital part of a religion that emphasizes the worth of persons. In the present section we have called upon ourselves, so to say, to utilize in our religious life and work the scientific attitude and procedure, which rightfully belong to us. We find, in fact, that our purposes must largely fail to reach their goal unless they have scientific guidance thereto; that we cannot even make our will good unless we have scientific help in defining our alternatives; that historic continuity and growth of our religion from within itself depend upon the scientific approach to our past and its documents; that we cannot expand into a universal religion except upon the basis of a fellowship of intelligence, which must be scientific; and that the necessary interest of our religion in nature can fulfil itself religiously only through scientific attitudes.

Christianity's concern for the spiritual, which can mean nothing more nor less than the personal, has seemed to many to be a reason for shyness toward the scientific method; but instead of being a reason for shyness it is a compelling reason for making scientific attitudes a part of the Christian consciousness itself.

35. Does the State, through Its Schools, Practise the Principles of Scientific Method More Thoroughly Than Do the Churches through the Church Schools?

The purport of this question is as follows: Many persons, in print and in speech, have held up to our gaze the readiness of the state schools, as contrasted with the unreadiness of the church schools, to make positive use of scientific knowledge and scientific method. The plight of adolescents who upon going to the high school or the college awaken with a shock to the disparity between what they find there and what they found in the Sunday school has been again and again exposed as a warning to the churches. And with entire justice. This disparity concerns both the content of teaching and the method of the mind. Either by positive assertion, or by silence in the presence•of pre-scientific views embodied in the Bible and in tradition, the church schools often make themselves guilty· of transmitting as truth what contemporary learning declares to be untrue. Further, the teaching-and-learning practices of these schools permit the growth of mental habits that are condemned as soon as one enters a laboratory or a course in one of the sciences. On the basis of facts of this kind the inference is not seldom drawn that the state schools are unqualifiedly committed to scientific procedure as the true method of the intellect. Is this true? Or, on the contrary, do state schools have their own ways of compromising, just as the church schools have theirs?

This question is not prompted by the fact that three of our states—a number that may be increased before this book is off the press—forbid the teaching of biology as biologists understand it, but by conditions that are systemic and by most citizens accepted as normal and proper. At points where the traditions, the vested interests, the commitments, and the pride of an institution or of a society are touched, is the practice of state schools markedly different from that of church schools?

Is the attitude of our state schools toward our national state scientific or emotional? Does the teaching of history weigh our national conduct in an even balance, or is history turned into propaganda? How much difference is there between the methods of suggestion used here and those used in churches, and in which is the use of suggestion more common?

Or,.turn to the good-neighbor problem. The state

as well as the church professes to teach pupils to adjust human relations in the spirit of good-will. But does the state employ scientific processes to determine and to demonstrate where our good-will is efficient and where it is inefficient? How does the state school determine what is good and what bad—by following the words of tradition, or by objective analysis that shows just what are the alternatives for choice?

It is clear that the schools of the state are ahead of the church in respect to fidelity to the natural and physical sciences, but no such superiority is in evidence where the more touchy points of individual and institutional self-interest are in question. Conditions vary from community to community in both sorts of schooling, so that generalizations should be made with great caution. I prefer to avoid them altogether until they can be justified by the presentation of specific data. But the following statement is safely within the truth: More information, and more sharp putting of issues, concerning human conduct in relation to poverty and wealth, labor and capital, the profit-motive, property, race prejudice and injustice, the exploitation of weaker peoples, and the real causes of war, can be had in the material that is now provided for religious education in the churches than in that which is provided for civic education through the public schools.

CHAPTER VIII

HOW CHRISTIAN EDUCATION MIGHT BE MADE MORE CREATIVE

36. *The Point of Departure Is the Inherent Radicalism of Christianity*

Christianity, considered as a particular, historical religion, is under fire the world around—such a fire as no other religion ever was subjected to, nor our own religion before our day. Why should this be so?

There are several striking features, and some unique ones, in this criticism and in the responses to it. Christianity has long been accustomed to defending itself against objections, but not these objections. For the main ground of attack has shifted from metaphysics, and even from the history of our religious origins, to the dynamics of social living. The gravamen of the indictment is that organized Christianity does not exhibit the moral power that its theory of itself calls for.

This transfer of the issue to observable ethical facts renders inapplicable and useless the whole defensive paraphernalia that nineteen centuries have elaborated. It is true that the Roman Church still officially clings to the old proofs of divine origin and authority, still practises the old argumentative ways of putting objectors into a corner, but this is now an exercise of the orthodox mind within itself, not the method whereby the forces of the world are met. These forces are applying tests of their own, tests so easily understandable and so obviously appropriate, that the critical world now includes the common man as well as the scholar.

Not least noteworthy is the fact that much of the criticism arises within organized Christianity itself, and that this self-criticism is as circumstantial and as drastic as any. Here is confession, openly made, that in important respects our religion is upon the wrong track. What is not less remarkable is that nobody, except those who have obligated themselves to defend a theory of infallible or quasi-infallible church authority, denies that this is true.

Our religion is, in fact, the most vulnerable thing in the world. The reason is the simple one that it harbors within its vitals an inexhaustible radicalism that always implicitly points beyond every human achievement, and when it is made explicit calls even our religion itself to repentance. What has happened in our day is that the implicit radicalism of our faith has become the main explicit ground for judging us who profess it. Do *you* love God with all your heart, and your neighbor as yourself? Is organized Christianity, in even one denomination, ready to go the whole length with the principles that it proclaims? The world around us, both occidental and oriental, says that we have not done it.

What stuns us in this accusation is the truth that is in it, not the error nor the exaggerations; and we are confused, not so much because we have been "found out," not so much by the strength of any hostility, as by the consciousness that we really do not know how to fulfil the obligations that we as Christians have assumed.

Our state of confusion might of itself suggest that our immediate need is education in the meaning and the practice of this radical principle that so disturbs us. That this is the next step for Christian education will become a rational certainty as soon as we realize that the inherent radicalism of Christianity, all of it, is traceable to the personality-principle that we profess. In these current criticisms, this principle is knocking at the door of our minds. It demands to be thought through; it calls for skill instead of sentimental fumbling; and it summons to a costly consecration.

Our point of departure for creative education is not to be understood, however, as any abstract principle or formula. For the personality-principle is at work already in its own inherently radical manner, demonstrating itself in the concrete. The habit of going far back in history for a vindication of the church has betrayed us into under-emphasis upon signs of present vitality. Indeed, how could any set of past facts prove to us that we ourselves are now alive? But the fact that in our own days we have broken the shell of supposedly Christian habits, not only without ceasing to be Christian, but by becoming more Christian, does prove it. Here is re-creation from within. This is so important for our plans of religious education that we may well take time to glance at several instances of this living self-mastery.

Since the middle of the last century, Protestantism, in spite of much hesitation, has done more difficult shifting of position in response to new knowledge and new conditions than any other old institution. Think of what it had to meet all at once—biblical criticism; the theory of evolution; the machine age; and the new and independent humanitarianism. Biblical criticism undermined the historical foundation upon which Christianity had relied; the theory of evolution destroyed the accepted view of man and of God's relation to the world; the machine age, disrupting old habits and old relations between men, made our inherited standards of conduct insufficient and largely inapplicable; the new humanitarianism organized good-will independently of the churches and of church doctrine, and employed science as one of its instruments. All this at once! The Protestant organizations have floundered and blundered in their efforts to meet this situation, or to avoid meeting it; yet the changes in their thinking, their message, their usages, their methods of work, and their approach to the general life are more massive than anything that other institutions that have a history—say, the colleges and the political state—can show.

This is not the common opinion, it must be admitted. Higher education and the state are regarded as certainly more "up to date" than the churches; and, indeed, if being up to date means drifting with the currents that have newly set our way, then the common opinion is correct. But it is not true that the new situation in which humanity is placed, and the new difficulties of personal and social self-realization in a machine age, have been faced by the dominating leaders in either civil government or higher education. In the ruling notions of what higher education is and how it is to be done there is more inertia than in the prevailing notions of what religion is and how its work is to be done. No one who critically observes from the inside both academic education and religious education can fail to see that the greater plasticity is on the side of religion. As to the modern state, though it employs the natural and physical sciences in various departments of activity, yet at its core, which concerns the purposes and ends of government, it uncritically takes over the economic philosophy of the least progressive class of citizens.

There is no reason for denying, but every reason for recognizing, that the churches also have drifted and evaded and clung to vested interests. But it would be folly in them and a calamity for society if they should bury in a napkin the fact that something that is constitutional in them rebukes and checks these very faults, and more than this, provides for everlasting change without loss of identity. There is no other institution in our society of which this can be said. The crisis just outlined—biblical criticism, and the rest—has brought about a shifting of position, but a shifting that is the achievement of clearer insight of Christianity into itself, and adjustive action from within, not by way of surrender. Let us glance at the facts that bear out this statement.

The biblical criticism that took away the old foundations is now used as a means of illuminating and making inescapable the oldest issues and life-principles that Christianity recognizes as its own. The oldest is the newest, the most alive, the least mechanical and institutionally fossilized. The Bible itself means more, not less, and there is new zest in the study of it. The secret of all this is that the personal within the Scriptures has been rescued from the old de-personalizing mode of interpretation. The traditional method of dealing with the biblical history made it one long-drawn-out dramatic performance in which each character spoke his piece as it was prepared for him by a celestial playwright, or by a collaborating playwright called Satan. Not seldom this supposed drama was more like a marionette play than a stage play with live actors. The effect of abandoning all this forced and mechanical interpretation, and of beholding biblical characters in their whole individuality, is to make it less easy for the user of the Bible to dodge the personal issues that are a base-line concern of our religion, and have been from the beginning.

A parallel effect is observable wherever the churches have assimilated the theory of evolution. No longer able to define and evaluate man by the almost mechanical-manufacture scheme of special creation, nor to conceive his salvation as apart from entwining natural causes, they have been forced to think of him in terms of his special functions, to accent his freedom and creativeness, and to have new concern for the present, finite conditions that affect his welfare and his character. Similarly, the inclusion of all religions within the concept of human evolution has sharpened the question of the functions actually performed by religion in general and by our own religion in particular. The consequence is a shift in the centre of gravity of all our thinking about our religion toward its significance for personality and for the organization of persons in society.

Toward the personal, likewise, moves the reconstruction of standards of conduct that new conditions have forced upon our reluctant consciences. The old question whether sabbaths and other rules are made for men, or men for them, has been up again and again, and always our experience had edged us closer and closer to Jesus' answer. The obligations that we recognize as Christian are increasingly humane, as they are more difficult than those of which our fathers were conscious.

The new humanitarianism, to an appreciable extent, is a derivative from the sympathy with suffering that is traditional in Christianity; but it has broadened this sympathy, brought about community co-operation in it, systematized the expressions of it, and applied methods of science to the discovery of the causes and the cures of distress. Moreover, though it started from facts of distress, it has gone on beyond measures of relief to positive ideals of social as well as individual health and welfare. The former ecclesiastical functions of "charity" in its various branches have in large measure passed over to the state or to voluntary agencies outside the sanctuary.

The effects of this independent or secular humanitarianism upon Christianity are complicated, and they are not always easy to trace. Now and then religion has warned us against forgetting the person in the mechanisms of systematic and large-scale charity. Sometimes the churches seem to feel a stimulus to "doing our part" either by supporting non-ecclesiastical welfare work or by engaging in welfare work of the churches' own. Possibly some persons have been led to think that being very religious is not so much a matter of human relations as it is devotion to relatively passive and contemplative worship. But, overtopping these fragmentary results are two effects, one already well under way, the other already more than peeping over the horizon.

In the presence of the humanitarian movement, with its practical demonstration of belief in man, the churches have been led to consider afresh what they, too, desire for men in this life. Whenever this question is raised—and it constantly is raised almost everywhere—it pushes into the background the old dogmatic system, and it discredits the old ethical formalism that was an appendage of it. Into the foreground now come ancient texts about what the Lord requires of us, about visiting widows and orphans, about Good Samaritans, and so on, and these are stressed as expressions of the essence of Christian piety. Then, almost before we know it, we begin to think the principle in these texts in terms not merely of individual well-being, but of an all-inclusive society.

Before we have conceived the ends of piety in terms of such a society very long, over the horizon comes an appalling Presence. It is Justice, claiming her own, which is none other than the organization of society as a whole, its economic activities included, as a means and a process for the self-realization of persons. Here the upspringing of the modern humanitarian movement eventuates in calling the churches back to something in their very constitution that is radical to the last degree just because it is friendly and human to the last degree.

Over against the dilatoriness of much ecclesiastical officialdom in the presence of the gigantic personality-depressing forces of our present society must be reckoned the fact that in recent years there has appeared a swarm of churchmen and churchwomen who make an irrepressibly realistic showing of the relation between our ancient faith and modern conditions of life. Within the Christian fellowship of to-day there are also groups and societies, as well as individuals, that have loosed their mooring cables from the wharves of conventional piety, and sailed out of the harbor. In spite of shots from the harbor's forts, and in spite of storms outside, they experience a zest that they would not exchange for all the comforts that a less venturesome faith can offer. Gradually the stay-at-homes begin to realize that an issue has been raised that will not down. The total amount of plain speaking from the pulpit on behalf of the justice that is necessary to the fulfilling of the law of love already is great, though the instances of it be scattered—speaking that is plain enough to be risky. Indeed, when was there more boldness in the pulpit than now? Even ecclesiastical bodies, in spite of their barometric sensitiveness toward approaching storms, have spoken prophetic words.

Already the spread of this re-birth experience within Christianity has begun to make social reactionaries anxious; they are by no means sure that the *status quo* can permanently count upon the backing of religion. There is apprehension concerning the "judgment" of ministers of the Gospel when they deal with social conditions from the standpoint of Jesus! There are self-defeating demands that ministers and churches attend to "spiritual" matters and let the social organization alone. More than one organized agency has been out gunning for socially radical preachers and seminary professors. But the awakening spreads even by means of the tactics of its opponents.

Those who are weary of a platitudinous and sentimental religious education should lift up their eyes to the fact that Christianity carries within itself a never-ending supply of what has been called "spiritual dynamite." It is here in the historical deposit that we have inherited; it is ready for our use whenever we have the grit to handle it. Now and then we see it "going off." These "goings-off," together with experiments in "setting it off," provide for Christian education teaching material of the very best sort. It is of the best sort because: (*a*) It is present in our environment, is concrete, and is interest-exciting. (*b*) It involves problems that come home to everybody. (*c*) It requires sharp definition of principles and purposes. (*d*) It requires scientific analysis of facts. (*e*) It offers moving examples of fidelity to Christian principle. (*f*) It connects immediate incidents of present life with the whole past of our faith, with the whole of present humanity, and with the whole of its future—it is not boxed-in material, it leads out indefinitely.

37. Our Educational Policies Should Face Toward the Unfinished Tasks of the Kingdom of God

The Kingdom of God, which is here to be thought of as the world of persons bound into one by reciprocal good-will, is less like a finished cathedral than an unfinished one; and it is less like a cathedral, whether complete or incomplete, than it is like a ship at sea. For motion is of the essence of it, motion that comes to rest in one harbor only to set forth again toward another. Moreover, inside the walls of a cathedral one is shielded from the four winds of earth, while all on board a ship must roll and pitch with it whenever any wind is let loose. One might add—at the risk of making a figure of speech "go on all fours"—that the crew of a ship occupies itself with making its craft go in a chosen direction even by means of the winds that buffet.

The face of present Christian education, Protestant as well as Catholic, is toward the majesty and the beauty of a finished cathedral. Here are its lofty arches and spires; they witness to the transcendence of God. Here is the altar; it is the meeting-place of God and man. Yonder are figures of saints and martyrs in whom the pathos of life is caught up into a symphony of praise and triumph. The hush, the subdued light, the multi-colored gleam from a rose window, the bowed figures of worshippers—ah, here is the Kingdom of God upon earth! What we now need to know is how to conduct ourselves in this place. What words are to be used, what thoughts to be pursued, what gifts to be made, what acts to be performed, what virtues to be cultivated?

The reform of religious education that has been going on in our generation seeks to draw men into the cathedral by means of its inherent attractions, not to force men in by fear or by mechanical drill. This has been the service of the theory of interest. Next, the doctrine of growth through activity, and finally the conception of educative activity as at once individual and social, have likewise made us more and more conscious of the people as against the cathedral. At least, we are more conscious of childhood, acting in childhood's way, as against religious structures, whether of belief, or of worship, or of institutional organization and habit.

As yet, however, we have not found out how to carry the experience of interest, free action, and free co-operation straight through from the class of beginners to the general congregation. It would be only an exaggeration of a truth if one should say that progressive religious education is adding a side-vestibule of freedom to a cathedral of conformity. One might point out, too, that the shadow of the great structure falls upon the lesser one.

This inconsistency, and this ultimate inefficiency, arise through a tacit, not fully reasoned out, separation between major and minor, or large-scale and small-scale, interests of our inherited religion. Children are encouraged to think freely and act experimentally in "their own little world," and young people are "given something to do" in the church. By these means growth of selves within a narrow scope is fostered, and this is so much gain upon older customs. But modern religious education has not yet found the sure way of enlarging the scope of this self-activity, nor of transforming the enormous inherited routine of the churches into a free and self-changing activity. No; above the children and young people towers the cathedral, and this means that the major inefficiences of ecclesiasticism cloud the whole of religious education.

The problem that we here encounter is a complicated one theoretically as well as practically. Before we are through with it we shall have to consider whether the limitations of the young on the one side, and of the mature on the other, predestine our most emancipating education to the absurdity of freedom-eventuating-in-conventionality; also whether, in point of fact, the major problems of the Kingdom of God first confront us in adult life rather than all along the way of our growth; and what might happen to a church that took spiritual life to be inherently a process of free growth in any and every direction that wins free approval. But first let us be sure whether or not, as far as it is found to be practicable with the young, the Kingdom of God and the institutions of religion should be represented as a temporal, unfinished process, with all the imperfections that this implies.

Postponing for a moment the question whether anything in our faith is permanent and unchangeable, we may well fix attention upon the simple and certain fact that the Kingdom of God is in an unfinished condition. If we make it appear so to children, we are at least truthful, and our relations with them are to this extent sincere. If religious education is to initiate them into actualities, it can do no less than this.

Further, if we have any hope that our pupils will devote their mature powers through the whole of life to the furtherance of the Kingdom, we must, as a matter of common sense, familiarize them in their growing years with the great cause that is on our hearts. During all their growth they are certain to be solicited by various enterprises that have a life-long perspective. Habits of thought are certain to be formed as to what counts when one is grown up, and as to how men and women make themselves count. If children know that their parents are identified with any struggles for large things—a national cause, a class struggle, a humanitarian enterprise, an economic ambition—how naturally they acquire a desire to have a part, and how rarely are they deterred by discovering that labor and hardship are the price of success. In a parallel way it would be entirely possible to develop aggressive churchmen; in no other way does it appear to be possible.

Our whole system of religious education needs to be turned about so that the type, the tone, and the habit-direction of pupil-experience shall reflect the unfinished state of our enterprise. The resulting education, in one of its aspects, would be like a father who, desiring to transfer his business to his son, goes over with him an inventory of existing assets and liabilities. In another aspect, it would be like a covered-wagon caravan of pioneers on their way to the great Northwest. The children and the young people in such an expedition, whether riding or walking or assisting in the camp work, face, with their elders, toward Oregon, and toward what they will do when they get there. In still a third aspect, this education would be like a family, parents and children, awaiting the advent of another child, and when he arrives devoting themselves to his comfort, welfare, and growth. In its most difficult phase it would resemble the mental struggle of a dairyman who has just discovered that there is tuberculosis in his herd. That is—to say the same thing directly—when Christian education determines its whole complex of policies by contemplating the unfinished tasks of the Kingdom, it will become a process wherein the learner forms judgments of his own concerning the present and the future of our religion and of life; it will turn him away from comfortable conventionality to the excitement and the labor of hard causes; it will unite him with his fellows on the basis of a forward look rather than upon the present basis of backward and inward looks; and it will give him the thrill, during his growing years, of being a co-creator with God.

38. How the Unfinished Task Links the Young with the Old, and the Present with the Past

The bonds that heretofore have kept the immature members of the community in line with the convictions of the mature are in our day greatly weakened. Controlling the young by sheer authority is less and less common, less and less possible. What is more disturbing to many souls is that our accumulated wisdom, even when the young take the trouble to understand it, is less and less imposing in their sight.

The causes of this change are various. One of them is the enormous increase of intercommunication. Schooling, print, the radio-receiver, the moving picture, the theatre, and increased contacts between individuals, cause knowledge, opinion, and feeling to spread, interchange, diversify as never before. The young are living in a larger world, and they have more kinds of ideas that are their own. In this larger world they find much that their mentors withhold from them, much disagreement with what their mentors tell them. No longer can parents, or the school, or the church, or all of these combined, fix the intellectual or the ethical horizon of the growing generation.

That this is true with respect to young people is recognized by all who have thought upon the subject, but few of us realize how early in the life of children the discovery of the large world begins— the world that is beyond all intended guidance. There is, in fact, even among elementary-school pupils, not only a vast amount of independent judgment upon the adults whom they know, but also much "worldly wisdom," and some "sophistication." The amount is increasing and, under modern conditions, it must increase. The young simply do not live within the pale of "their own little world." Though, like their elders, they have playmates, intimates, and small-group interests, at the same time they live also in the large world that maturity claims as its own.

A second, closely related reason why we of the older generation are losing our impressiveness with the young is that our blunders and our inefficiencies are coming more and more to their notice. They know more about unsatisfactory conditions in the world than the young of other generations had means of learning, and they cannot, under modern conditions, attribute the evils of life to a mysterious providence. When, then, we endeavor to tell them what's what, they reply (in spirit at least, sometimes in words), "Do you really know? Does your performance show that you are competent to guide us?"

A third factor is the increasing habit, of which the scientific movement is a part-source, of thinking of human affairs in somewhat dynamic, or cause-and-effect terms. "What do we get out of it?" is a frequent question. "What's the real good of it?" is another. "*Why* should we?" is a third and a common one. A thing is judged by its results. We of the older generation are called upon to justify our commands and our advice by a definite showing of the actual outcomes of different sorts of conduct.

The old linkage of the young with their elders is gone, never to return. It cannot return because the conditions that have been named are self-perpetuating. Therefore, instead of bemoaning the increasing independence of the young over against our ideas, wishes, and standards, we would better inquire what interests we adults have, what ends we are devoted to, that the young could reasonably be expected to share. There are such interests. An obvious one is play. Many a parent, and the number is increasing, maintains close comradeship with a child through shared games and sports. Another common interest is the safety and welfare of children. In at least one of our metropolitan areas thousands of boys systematically and efficiently co-operate with their elders in protecting school pupils from the hazards of modern street traffic.

In these instances, let it be noted, fellowship between persons of widely different ages rests upon something, objective to both of them, that elicits mutual activity. What closes the age-gap is not the wisdom that reposes in the minds of the mature, but something that does not repose anywhere; it is an ongoing process, an unfinished enterprise that reveals the elder and the younger to each other.

Not otherwise should we expect the young in the church to be unified with the older element. We see beginnings of such unification in father-and-son and mother-and-daughter banquets, which are substantially play-activities; in the use of religious drama, and in philanthropic and missionary enterprises. We need, in addition, common labor and common thinking on behalf of such wide-horizon enterprises as the reconstruction of the church in the light of its ascertained efficiencies and inefficiencies, the reconstruction of family life, and participation in the struggle for elemental justice in the community, the nation, and the world.

Not otherwise is it with the linkage of the generations taken in the large, or historical sense. Continuity with the past does not depend upon sameness of belief, or of worship, or of ecclesiastical organization; but it does depend upon such conditions as working at the same problem, using a common method of approach to the changing conditions of life, and repeatedly utilizing our inheritance as material for freely-planned new structures. Continuity through creative acts, one unprecedented thing sprouting out of an earlier unprecedented thing, is at least as possible as continuity through an unchanged tradition, and it is less subject to the illusion that takes verbal sameness for spiritual identity.

When we have the habit of facing our unfinished tasks in a creative spirit, whatever real values the past of our faith contains will be conserved. Creation is so difficult for us mortals that it drives us to study; it forces economy upon us; it brings into the foreground of thankfulness everything out of the past that we can use for improving the present. When we are most creative we build upon the past with the clearest consciousness; we come, "not to destroy, but to fulfil."

On the other hand, when we face toward the past, assuming that we are called to reproduce it, we endanger the best things in it. The psychology of this is rather simple. The things of greatest moment in history are those that came to the surface in creative periods or personalities. Accordingly, when we endeavor to reproduce the product of such a time or such a person, our very attitude of imitating, or reproducing, or avoiding novelty separates us from the source of that which we so much value. For the period or the person that we rely upon was not in the reproducing attitude.

The difficulty of the unfinished tasks that lie before us is tempting the organized Christianity of our day to retire into a backward-looking fellowship of worship. I do not say or think that the enrichment of worship that is taking place is simply and solely mental involution or flight from reality, nor that well-planned worship ever could separate itself from its antecedents. But I do say that we are in danger, precisely through the increasing worshipfulness of our worship, of dissociating our elevated sentiments from their proper integration with sturdy and creative purposes; and that being lifted up by contemplation of our ancestry, as are some sons and daughters of the American Revolution, is no guarantee of a right to claim continuity with predecessors who were creative. The fellowship of worship will be the truest link with the past when it most continuously and implacably holds us to the unfinished tasks of the present.

39. It Is the Unfinished Task That Leads to Spiritual Insight

The notion, perennial with teachers of religion and morals, that matured and rounded goodness is what gives us our chief insight into the laws of living, is a perennial fallacy. A paragon of virtue or of heroism is less illuminating in its completeness than at an earlier stage when struggle and uncertainty still were its lot. The issues that were met, the way in which they were met, the effects of this or that conduct and policy—in a word, the ongoings of a person or of a group of persons—are the problem-setting, thought-stimulating, information-giving, and ambition-awakening data. And the point in one's own experience at which insight breaks forth is not the moment of complacency with what is or has been, but some moment of unrest, of incomplete satisfaction.

In the background of this proposition there is no ascetic or pessimistic outlook upon life, but rather the simple principle that the mind works only when it has something to do and accomplish. The stimulus that sets it going is the unfinished, which means at one time simple rawness, at another time an intermediate stage of a purposeful activity, or the rise of a difficulty, or failure, or pain. This is a general law, manifested alike in scientific discovery, mechanical invention, the building of societies, the realizations of duty, and the apprehension of God.

It would be easy to heap up examples of this principle from the history of religion. The prophets, as everybody knows, were awakened to the greatness and the goodness of God, not by the virtues of their time but by its evils and its emergencies. And let us not forget that the prophets conceived their job as helping change an unsatisfactory social condition into a satisfactory one. The insight and the enterprise were one whole.

But we need not betake ourselves to far-away instances. The appealing helplessness of an infant is one of the ever-renewed sources of enlightenment for adults who already think themselves wise. It was, in fact, the infant's need for care that founded the family. Conversely, the illness, misfortune, or old age of a parent often brings to filial affection a rich self-discovery. The meaning of love for neighbor comes home to us when we happen upon some one who needs us. At the present moment the significance of neighborliness is growing larger and clearer through experience of conflict between classes, nations, and races. The endeavor to spread the Christian religion in non-Christian lands is forcing Christianity to a deeper understanding of itself and of the essential meanings of personality. The difficulties encountered have been particularly instructive. Violations of the Constitution of the United States—the First as well as the Eighteenth Amendment—are jogging us out of ignorant complacency concerning the real meaning of freedom and of law, and concerning the real nature of social forces. The present partial estrangement between youth and maturity is working for greater moral intelligence on both sides.

These are not only examples of the principle in question; they are also specimens of material ready at hand for the purposes of Christian education. I purposely put into one paragraph both intimate personal relations and social emergencies of large scope. All progressive teachers of religion already commit themselves in some measure to the evocation of spiritual insight through family and other face-to-face relations. There is lagging, however, with respect to such larger relations and emergencies as have been named, though even children have some awareness of them, and are being in material measure influenced by the attitude of their elders. How long is it going to take Christian teachers to realize that at present the attitudes of men toward the major problems of our religion are being formed mostly by mere drift? The correct policy is to familiarize the learner with the most difficult, costly, risky things that Christianity is anywhere attempting to do, and not to stop with this, but to go on to the defects and unmet emergencies of the churches and of the moral order. This, not spiritual coddling, is the way to develop spiritual insight.

Religious education is, on the whole, neglectful of the factor of insight, neglectful of the significance of it for self-realization, and neglectful of the means and processes whereby it may continuously grow. Because of this neglect and the consequences of it, a few words more may be ventured concerning the "how" of spiritual insight and why we need to reform our ways at this point just now.

Active ethical love is a way of discovery; if discoveries are not being made, this is a sign that our love is languid. Every lover knows that love is also light, but because we do not realize why and how this is so, we take insufficient advantage of the fact. It is not enough that we seem to ourselves to be more "sensible" when we are devoted to others than when we are narrow and self-centred. We need definitely to realize that only upon the basis of out-going good-will can we really get acquainted with one another.

Some of our American forebears summed up their estimate of the aborigines of our country in the aphorism, "A 'good' Indian is a dead Indian." They could give plenty of evidence for this conclusion, for it was drawn from much experience of a fairly uniform character. But William Penn and his Quakers knew better; they *knew* better, they did not merely

guess. They were able to find out the truth because
the good-will with which they met their native neighbors enabled these neighbors to show what an Indian really is or is capable of being. On the other
hand, the whites, whose attitude was that of armed
distrust as a backing for exploitation of the weak
by the strong, drew a veil over their eyes before they
looked.

Yet they thought that they were open-eyed and
wise. There is something almost ironic in the working of selfishness, distrust, and fear. Often, when we
think we are "level-headed," "hard-boiled," or even
scientific concerning human nature, we partly fail
to notice or to understand what is directly before
us, and we partly produce what we are looking for.
Thus we become confirmed in our assumption by
what seems to be evidence, when all the while we
merely go 'round and 'round in a vicious circle of
our own creation. Nations arm themselves in order to
be secure against potential enemies, but by these
"security"-measures they make potential enemies
into actual ones and unmake security. Behind this
kind of statecraft is self-imposed blindness. The reason why diplomacy as we know it cannot quite
achieve peace is that it cannot quite believe that peace
really and truly is practicable, and it cannot believe
this because its own conduct is ungenerous.

Our economic wisdom has the same "beam" in its
eye. It says that the goods that the world needs can
best be produced, "human nature being what it is,"
by letting opposing selfish interests fight it out
among themselves. The consequence is that everybody aims, not to produce goods, but to secure a
favorable position in the melée. The costs of the
fighting are then mistakenly reckoned as costs of
production. Because production is not the direct
aim but a subordinate interest, enormous and costly

inefficiencies likewise are charged to the consumer;
and unparalleled "prosperity" becomes consistent
with widespread unemployment and with incomes
below the minimum of comfort for millions of
workers. Why cannot the masters of such an inefficient system believe in co-operation, and why are
they so solicitous lest the public should take a hand
in production? The obvious reason is mental involution and lack of objectivity. The economic order cannot become objective-minded, seeing its inefficiencies
for what they are, and men for what they are, until,
touched by the spirit of ethical love, it seeks to make
production an enterprise which in both its process
and its products enhances personality.

There is an interesting relation between affection
and ethical love. Thoughtful students of marriage
have long known that conjugal fondness can be enriched and prolonged by community of ethical purpose between husband and wife. But there is a phase
of this truth that seems rarely to have been mentioned, if ever. It is that the attitude and practice
of ethical regard can make visible what otherwise
remains invisible. Romantic affection often thinks it
has found and knows one's true mate when in fact
there has been only an introduction between the two
personalities; acquaintance has only just begun.
Idealization of the loved one may then lead on to
further genuine acquaintance, but unless sober respect for personality mingles with idealizing fondness, the result is likely to be misunderstanding,
failure to see or appeal to the capacities of the other,
and disillusionment. Respect for the other (rather
than worship (which often is little more than the
sheen of self-indulgence), is what keeps affection
fresh. It does so by making the union into an ethical
partnership directed toward objective ends the pursuit of which brings out the latent capacities of both

the co-operators. Life together then escapes the mutual self-involution in which affection is so often suffocated; instead of this, affection thrives because of the continual newness of the two personalities.

Why does the sport of spoofing the clergy never wear out? Because so many of the clergy, becoming institutional-minded, grow dull toward the simply human. They furnish daily evidence that Bergson's theory of laughter is at least partly true—the theory that we laugh when we witness the incongruity of a lapse from the personal into the mechanical. The joke hits not merely the austerely absent-minded dominie of yesterday; not merely the minister who substitutes mechanical pigeon-holing of men for really knowing them; it reaches also those modern, neighborly, genial leaders who sacrifice their fine powers to uncreative routine. They, too, with all their approachableness and even self-forgetting kindness, do not quite get down to bed-rock human reality. If they did get down to it, they would be more keenly aware of the real rawness of what we call civilization; their job as messengers from God would loom larger; they would be more concerned for fundamental justice; and the satirist would lose one of his subjects.

In each of these four instances—statecraft, economic orthodoxy, marriage, and churchcraft—the policy of capitalizing an existing status results in blindness to actualities. Here lies the true interpretation of much that bears the reproach of insincerity. When we compare conduct in these four spheres with professions as to policies and with protestations as to motives, our first impulse is to cry "Hypocrite!" How can a statesman in the same breath renounce war as an instrument of national policy, and yet advocate the building of a competitive navy? How can a captain of industry call himself public-spirited at the same time that he is exploiting the public in the interest of his profit-account? How can self-indulgence glorify itself as conjugal affection, and how can the church call matrimony as such "holy"? How can churchmen offer the prayers that constantly pass their lips, and yet accept, as normal, social conditions that precisely contradict their prayers? The answer in each instance is that "they know not what they do." They know not, because they have not approached their experiences and their tasks from the standpoint of the value of persons. Were they to do this, they would be conscious of an unfinished task of the most stimulating sort, and their eyes would be opened to the actualities of good and evil. What a habitual institutional consciousness can do to intelligence is amazing. A few years ago, one of the ablest university administrators that this country has produced advocated large families and also a scheme of academic appointments, promotions, and salaries that made the support of wife and children impracticable before the age of about thirty-five!

We shall be helped out of our blind alleys, not by accusations of insincerity, which, as we now see, are likely to be unfair, but by securing attention to the missing factor. The usual fighting tactics of accusation and counter-accusation should give place to never-ending presentation and re-presentation of the actual conditions of the men, women, and children whom our conduct affects or might affect, together with inescapably clear analysis of the facts and forces that make for and against their full self-realization. This will reveal our unfinished tasks, and these tasks will become lenses through which we shall see our institutions, routines, customs, pet policies— and ourselves—in their truth.

40. What Is Permanent and Unchanging in Creative Christian Education?

It should be clear already that creative Christian education is not a flighty, arbitrary, or history-spurning thing; that it does not dispense with self-discipline, nor dissolve the bonds that hold men together. On the face of the matter, the personality-principle calls for self-organization, for the integration of selves in society, and for a kind of interrelation between persons that can hold through time. It may be well, however, at this stage of our discussion, to formulate this abiding aspect of free creativity so that teachers may test and guide their work in a definite manner.

Two maxims will sum up the matter: Approach all persons in the spirit of respect or ethical love; approach all facts in the spirit of science. These are two aspects of one principle, however, rather than two principles. For, since the scientific method, as we have seen, is a necessary expression of personality, ethical love, which seeks the self-realization of persons, will directly evoke scientific attitudes and practices in both the lover and the loved.

For teachers of the Christian religion the universal guide and test is, Am I helping my pupils grow in the personal or ethical-love way of dealing both with themselves and with others whose lives they touch? Am I helping them extend this fellowship to others who need it? Am I helping them master the conditions of efficient good-will by using the methods of science with reference to all facts involved, whether facts of history, of external nature, or of the mind of man? Am I helping them to such a deep and satisfying experience of this ethical-love way that they are learning to worship?

This single, yet two-fold, principle will find no occasion to revise itself, no matter what changes in other matters may be required. The particular acts in which we endeavor to love one another will vary with varying conditions and with growing insight; likewise the particular technics by which we learn and teach will grow and proliferate in the future as they have done in the past. We do not know what forms the self-realization of persons might take under circumstances that seem not to be entirely beyond the range of possibility. If we could feed ourselves with synthetic foods, or tap some exhaustless cosmic reservoir of electric power, or "crack the atom," what would daily occupations then be like, and how would the forms of human association be affected? Nobody can tell. But the loving approach to persons, and the scientific approach to facts, would have precisely the sanction that they now have.

This permanent element in Christian education is not a dogma; rather, it supersedes dogmatic authority. It is not a metaphysical proposition, though it may well furnish an impulse and a starting-point for metaphysical inquiry. It does not prescribe any particular act as a duty, though duties enough must sprout from it. It is an attitude or a policy, and in this sense a method, or determinant and test of procedure. Further, as we have just seen, it is what logicians have called a heuristic principle, that is, a way of acting that leads to discoveries. It has indefinite fecundity and creativeness because it makes us active to the limit of our personal capacity without imposing upon us any act whatever.

When we realize that this verily is the permanent source of spiritual fecundity, we shall see how needless are some of our anxieties. Before now some reader has queried—appropriately so—whether faith in the eternal God, and loyalty to Jesus, are not the permanent landmarks of truly Christian education. The answer is two-fold: *First*, this faith and this loyalty cannot be handed down as one hands down to one's children the title to a farm; they must be generated afresh in every individual. Therefore the generative source is the matter of prime concern. *Second*, though faith in God, and loyalty to Jesus, have been, in a formal or verbal sense, permanent in historical Christianity, they have not been unchanging, and they cannot be raised above change. The *quod semper, ubique, ab omnibus* does not exist.

The actual content of the idea of God, that to which emotion and conduct are attached, moves on with history. The other day some one raised the question, "Is Yahweh the God of us Christians?" If you answer "Yes," meaning that the Christian conception of God grew out of the Jewish idea of the divine (rather, ideas), you must also answer "No," because there was an outgrowing as well as a growing out. Similarly, if you ask whether Jesus did not give us a final notion of the divine, a notion never to grow further, the answer is that he has stimulated men to take an attitude toward life that makes changes in our notion of God inevitable. Surely growing conceptions of duty and stationary conceptions of the divine cannot fuse or live together. But our ethical problems do and must undergo transformation; the good man of yesterday, the good Christian of yesterday, does not suffice in the new human relationships of to-day.

It would be easy to show that this flow is present not merely in the lay mind but also in technical theology. No theologian of to-day would aver that the term God means to him precisely the same that the term Father meant to Jesus. Theology, like Christian experience, is a stream with many curves, slower and swifter currents, cross-currents, eddies, tributaries, and evaporation. In fact, the history of Christianity is continuous with the general history of religion, and religion in its world-totality is a various and changing phase of the various and changing conditions of humanity. This proposition is not at all speculative; it is a solid and accepted result of painstaking research.

What, then, of loyalty to Jesus as a permanent and unchanging bond of all Christian education? I have already affirmed that recognition of the worth of persons is the permanent and unchanging thing. Loyalty toward this is loyalty toward that to which Jesus was loyal. This association with him, especially in view of the stimulus and support that it yields to our weakness, might without impropriety be designated as loyalty to him. But clear discrimination is needed here. Is not the personality-principle final for us anyhow, whether Jesus grasped it or not? We hold to it because of its inherent validity, just as he did; it is not secondary to anything or anybody.

Moreover, as in the use of the term God, so in our thought of the historic person Jesus, the meaning changes while the word abides. Our views of Jesus involve judgments of a historical sort; questions of plain fact always are included. What did Jesus actually do, and what were his reasons for doing it? What were his exact words, and exactly what meanings did they have for him? Just what experiences came to him day by day, and how did he meet them? The answers to these questions have changed from age to age, and they are changing now. Many of the facts are so obscure that the most knowing persons in the field of New Testament study do not agree concerning them. At the best, only a few items out of Jesus' total experience are as much as mentioned in the records. Consequently, loyalty to Jesus, if it is not to be a vague and sentimental admiration for unfocalized goodness, must select particular points in his goodness, and attach itself to them. Attach it-

self to them because of what they are. The deepest
devotion to him would be reached if we should discover in him some active, creative, and inexhaustible
spring of the spirit that is also in us.

This deep well we do find in him and in us. It is
ethical love or regard for personality. The cups of
this living water that we pass to one another are the
abiding sacrament of our fellowship. Nothing else
can make us one; nothing else can make of Christianity anything more than a thing of time and change.
Apparently Jesus' own attitude was that of friend
rather than that of master. "I call you not servants."
The loyalty of the Christian, accordingly, is loyalty
not to one person, even Jesus, but to persons.

CHAPTER IX

SOME CURRENT MOVEMENTS AND CONDITIONS ANALYZED

41. How "Problem-and-Project" Teaching Is Related to Creativeness

It is now time to consider the bearing of our discussion upon a number of particular problems and enterprises that are agitating progressive leaders of Christian education. The now-rising generation in the churches has been born into a happily unhappy situation; happy because of the unprecedented amount of thought that Christians are giving to Christian education, unhappy because the farther we Christians go with this thinking the farther away seem the solutions for our problems. I refer, not to our discovery of the mountainous inertia of both ministers and laity; not to the superficiality of much religious education that intends to be progressive; not even to the baffling problem of how to secure trained leadership and trained teachers, but to difficulties that are inherent in the very idea of Christian education.

In the churches, as in public-school quarters, awakened thought concerning the process of teaching has circled about three main ideas—interest, activity, and social participation, all on the part of the pupil—with a fourth idea, character, over-arching all three of them like a cloud. The theory that interest is the main condition of learning has on the whole emptied itself into the theory that activity is the main condition—interested, self-propelling activity. At this point the educative significance of the learner's purposes emerges, his very own present purposes as distinguished from the teacher's aims and from later purposes that it is hoped the learner will acquire. It is the learner's present purposeful activity, the plans that he makes and executes, his own projects—so the theory goes—that most promotes growth. This, in brief, is the project-principle, which is commonly called project-method. It includes the theory of interest, but in and of itself it connects, in a degree that the old theory of interest did not, with the idea of the character. The connection between projects and character is in the factor of purpose, or action as a person. When, now, social participation is added, the process that the teacher is required to further is the achievement of organized individual character and of satisfactory social organization through the performance of acts chosen individually and collectively by the learners themselves. Teaching by projects is at the same time teaching by problems, of course, for purposes are responses to problematic situations; but it is teaching by problems that arise within the learner's own experience, not by those imposed upon him.

It would be carrying coals to Newcastle if I were to describe the extraordinary and delightful vitalizing of the school experience of both teachers and pupils that follows upon the conscious use of this principle. What concerns us now is that teaching here becomes a dealing with persons as such, not with memory or other "faculties" as they are related to a given "material of instruction." All the constructive powers, memory or other, are still called into play, but from a different point of view, and with a different motivation. The pupil now works from within his whole self, getting thereby possession both of himself and of his world. The difference is enormous.

The extent of this difference, and the really radical character of the project-principle, often fail of clear recognition. The term project has been applied to handwork; to almost any busy-ness of pupils; to the working out of an idea derived from a text-book or from a teacher; to the separate units in a completely imposed curriculum of instruction, all of which, taken thus, miss the main point. A pupil's project may require hand-work; it will require busyness at times, reflection at other times; it may get its start from text-book or teacher, and it may include the systematic study of a definite area of human knowledge, but these enter into a true project, not by imitation, mere suggestion, or authority; they are rather ways of working out free purposes, and they are significant and educative for this reason.

Here, for the first time, educational theory provides for real integration of the personality. I, the teacher, cannot integrate the impulses, the values, the choices of a pupil; he must do it himself, or it never will be done. As he can be a person only by self-activity, so he can become a unified person only by self-activity in the organization of self-activities. Yet the whole tradition of religious education runs to the effect that the integrative act is the teacher's.

Here, again for the first time, the theory of teaching gets down to social bed-rock. Human society (whatever be the facts concerning the "social" life of bees) is interaction upon the basis of mutual recognition of persons by one another, self-activity calling, as it were, to self-activity, across the gap that separates individual from individual. Wherever real project-teaching occurs, it breaks through imitation, prevents parasitism, consciously avoids regimentation, and provides a prophylactic against herd-action. For it develops social activity that is still self-activity, which is considered, freely chosen, and self-revising activity. Such teaching develops leadership and followership, both from within, and both regulated by results freely judged by all concerned.

In such teaching there constantly bobs up in the learners something or other that from their own standpoint is new and unprecedented. The same general sort of thing may have happened a thousand times in the experience of others; it may be no surprise to the teacher; but for the pupil it is none the less original. Here are conditions that favor, likewise, the rise of totally unprecedented ideas and plans— that which the teacher could not foresee, even that which never has been since the beginning of the world. Thus experiences of creativity occur, and a habit of being creative can be formed.

Therefore true project-teaching is unfavorable to stand-patism. For the same reason it is unusable by dogmatic schemes of social or moral reform. It is dangerous, too, to anything that has a motive for not being investigated by unsophisticated minds. But it is the indispensable sort of teaching for a society that is to make progress by means of intelligence rather than by means of revolutions.[1] These remarks apply alike to religious and to civil society. They should be peculiarly welcome, and project-teaching should be most at home, in circles that profess the Christian religion, with its radical view of the value of persons.

The problems that the project-principle solves are matched, however, by others that it creates. These other problems all spring from the assumption that the projects of the learners are to be supervised. It is true that some most educative projects arise and run their course in the unsupervised plays of children and youth. Yet no one fancies that teachers and schools can be dispensed with; indeed, the deeper we go into the actualities of purposeful and non-pur-

[1] Cf. Kilpatrick, W. H., *Education for a Changing Civilization* (New York, 1926).

poseful activity, the more certain it becomes that play
itself requires supervision, and, further, that the un-
planned influences of adultdom upon the young must
not be left to run their course by chance.

Here, then, is the conception that we must wrestle
with: Teaching by projects implies, because of the
presence of supervision, that the free self-activity
of the pupil is also somehow the free self-activity of
the teacher and of the society that acts through him.
The teacher does not abnegate his own judgment or
the judgment of society as to the relative values of
different possible projects of pupils; he must, in fact,
steer the pupil toward some sorts and away from
other sorts; and through the entire execution of a
project he must stand by, ready to interject the kind
of help that will make the experience of the pupil
most educative. Moreover, the true teacher sees to it
that projects progress from level to level; they must
be hard enough and illuminating enough to carry the
pupil beyond what he now is. The project-principle,
then, does not mean "hands off." Quite the contrary;
it calls for guidance that is more pervasive (since it
follows the whole course of motivation) than any that
the old education ever attempted.[1]

If we may employ the term curriculum in the sense
of this total factor that is deliberately injected into
the life of the learner from the standpoint of more
mature experience, then we can say that the curricu-
lum-problem is the Great Unknown of current education, both secular and religious. The old curricula
are discredited; the principles upon which they were
constructed are discredited; a whole new school world
has to be created. But we have to decide upon the
kind of school world we desire by first deciding upon
the principles and the grounds of our whole supervision of the young. Thus a prior question for all

[1] A fuller treatment of this aspect of the project principle will
be found in my *Law and Freedom in the School* (Chicago, 1923).

teaching by projects is, What are the superior values that we hope the young will discover by our help? Every curriculum expresses and seeks to make effective some want or wants that the mature feel. But what do we want? What would we like to have the young become? What sort of future society do we assume to be desirable?

Not all who think that they are committed to the project-principle have seen that teaching by problems and projects fits into society only at the points where it, too, proceeds by problems and projects. It would be interesting, with the schools of the state in mind, to ask what problems and projects of the state are in the background of school policies, and also how the public school is related to the elements of the civic consciousness that are anti-project, stand-pat, and reactionary. But our concern is with Christian education, and the point that we now have reached in our consideration of it is this: Since teaching by projects implies control of the teaching-situation by some back-lying general project or projects, a curriculum for the young must be organized upon the basis of Christianity's unsolved problems and unfulfilled tasks.

Another question that must be answered if we are to have a project-curriculum is, Under what conditions do pupils who are of different ages and types of experience recognize as their own the various unsolved problems of Christianity, and accept as their own its unfinished tasks? This question has somewhat the form of an inquiry that was current a quarter of a century ago. At what age, it was asked, is interest in stories natural, or interest in heroes, or the Old Testament, or the New Testament? What is the age of "decision," or of the final adoption of a life-philosophy? The form of our present question is much the same because the problem of adaptation is a permanent one, but the content of the inquiry is radically altered. The difference is almost as great as that between watching a game and being one of the players in it, or as that between lying down to rest and getting up to start on a "hike." Exposing a pupil to a problem that points toward something to be done is very unlike putting before him ideas and ideals to be accepted and applied.

Further, the project-relation between the old and the young is different. It is not that of members of a fraternity to candidates for initiation, but that of the members of a family that is in the act of pitching camp in a new spot. The problems of putting up the tent, collecting fire-wood, building the fire, bringing the water, and preparing the supper, are common ones for parents, older children, and younger children, albeit each works at the particular task for which his experience and his powers fit him. Just so, we must ask which unfinished tasks of the Kingdom of God can best be performed by each type of person, and at the same time we must make sure that all realize the unity, and the direction of movement, of the whole.

To the query with which this section started—how problem-and-project teaching is related to creativeness—the answer is: (a) Such teaching, when it fully follows its own principle, is creative education. The principle may be partly used, often has been partly used, in processes that also partly counteract it. Creative teaching, wherever it exists, is creative because it has the problem-project factor in it. (b) It requires system, organization, continuity—in short, a curriculum—which must itself be a problem-project, and therefore profoundly different from all our inherited curricula. (c) The Christian religion can employ problem-project teaching consistently and effectively only to the extent that Christianity itself is a problem and an unfinished task. (*d*) It unifies the young and the old through present, not merely prospective, co-operation in thinking, choosing, and doing. Therefore it requires plasticity on the part of the old as well as the young, and hence necessitates adult Christian education that has no age-limit.

42. "Life-Situations" as Starting-Point and Terminus of Educative Experience

The movement of thought in the general direction just indicated—or aspects of the movement—have found expression in phrases that are new in pedagogical converse. For example, good teaching must be "pupil-centred" rather than "material-centred." In this popular catch-word we see a great reversal coming to consciousness. We shall do well, however, to observe what stage of the process is here reflected. Shall we say that, whereas the good teacher of yesterday studied content much, and the pupil little, the reconstructed teacher studies the pupil much, and the content little? No, this is not the meaning, for the new education requires better command of material than ever. What, then, is signified by putting the pupil at the "centre"?

Granted that the notion of "pupil-centred" teaching springs out of a real awakening to the dynamics of learning, nevertheless one may well ask, in the first place, whether it represents the "interest" stage or the "project" stage of educational theory. Does it conceive the teacher's task as getting the pupil interested in a content that we desire to transfer to his mind, or does it abandon the whole take-this-prescription notion of what teaching is? If it does abandon this notion, still a question remains. Is the desired pupil-action conceived as "pupil-centred"? If not, why should the teacher's mind be so centred? Does not the teacher desire to help the pupil become

A rather than B? If so, why not say that the teaching is "A *versus* B-centred"?

The term "life-situation" stands for a type of thinking that comes appreciably nearer this "A *versus* B-centred" notion of teaching. For it definitely calls attention to the concrete circumstances within which the pupil is living, the manner in which he is reacting to these circumstances, the difficulties that he is encountering, the mistakes he is making, and the specific sort of help that he needs in order to change his situation and himself in a desirable manner. What the teacher does amounts to inserting into the "life-situation" something that seems likely to improve it through the pupil's own acts. The teacher, acting as an experienced friend, may point out something already there in the situation that the pupil had not noticed; show how others in similar situations have acted, and what the results were; or strengthen one desire as against another by holding attention to it or by subjecting it to some social judgment. Material or content (by which is meant ideas already in the minds of the elders) is now thought of, not as something to be "gotten over" at all costs, but as a source of possible help, to be used or not as occasion seems to require.

Here the mind of teacher and of curriculum-maker goes through three stages: (*a*) Ascertainment of points at which help is needed in specific "life-situations" of pupils. (*b*) Search within our mature experience for something that is likely to help. (*c*) In the light of our knowledge of the pupil, devising a technic whereby he shall freely appropriate the help that we bring him.

The mind of the pupil runs through three corresponding stages: (*a*) I am dissatisfied with this or that in my present experience. (*b*) Hello! here's something that has to do with experiences like mine.

Let's see what it is. It appears to indicate a reasonable way to get along. I'll try it. (c) This new way
of getting along is better than the old way. I'm going
to keep it up.

Here the "life-situation" is, or appears to be, both
the starting-point and the ending-point of the whole
movement. The process can be thought of, moreover,
as mutual throughout—pupil and teacher mutually
dissatisfied, mutually discovering and experimenting,
and finally mutually pleased with the outcome.

One could fill many pages with exposition of the
advance that this theory of Christian teaching makes
beyond what was regarded, even a generation ago,
as daringly progressive. One could expatiate upon
the achievement of a dynamic point of view, for here
everything has to do with movement and change;
upon the way in which the pupil's integral personality comes into the foreground and dominates the view;
upon the new relation between teacher and pupil;
upon the new relation, likewise, between material,
especially biblical material, and the pupil; finally,
upon the endeavor to make the pupil's experience
here and now, and in daily affairs, a religious experience. If I were required to say what seems to me
to be the most remarkable feature of this advance, I
should reply, The religiousness of it.

Naturally, some questions remain; how could it be
otherwise? How unfortunate we shall be when our
stagnating perfection makes further questioning superfluous! What point in our progress, then, has the
"life-situation" theory reached? The answer lies in
the direction of three other inquiries: *First*, what,
after all, is a "life"-situation? *Second*, what functions
can the records and memories of past experience perform in present experience? *Third*, what relation between the two persons, pupil and teacher, does the
"life-situation" theory assume?

In order to save space and the reader's time, I shall here set down bluntly and without supporting evidence a few propositions concerning the dynamic actualities in the present life of any pupil. (*a*) His attitudes upon matters vital to the Christian conception of life are being formed in large part by the seepage into his mind and conduct of adult standards and practices in respect to such matters as sacred and secular, church and non-church, young and old, male and female, employer and employee, poverty and wealth, citizen and alien, my country and others, armies and navies, war and peace, and race-distinctions. Most of the influence that comes to him in this manner he is unaware of; yet it is forming and consolidating the major premises upon which his life-long policies will be based. (*b*) Study by the teacher of "life-situations" in the narrow sense of situations already recognized by the pupil as his own will therefore disclose only in part the sorts of help that he requires. There is ground for thinking that only a minor part of the needed help will be proffered. (*c*) The experiments in controlling his situation that the pupil can now make and finish, even with the help of a teacher, will not of themselves result in either approximately adequate insight or approximately adequate habits. Major elements in his situation are beyond his control. (*d*) He is capable of character-forming interests, attractions, repulsions, and loyalties that far outrun his present capacity for controlling his situation. In such matters as are mentioned under (*a*) he can be led into an acquiescent or a resistant habit of mind, and his emotional attachments to mature men, and groups, and types of success can be formed through his own teacher-assisted moral scrutiny instead of being formed for him by casual influences.

As yet the "life-situation" theory has attended

chiefly to problems within the small world that the pupil already recognizes as his without the teacher's help. But if we are to deal educationally with the whole actuality of pupil situations, we must produce dissatisfactions that do not spontaneously arise; we must accept the responsibility of introducing new strains and difficulties into the learner's experience; we must cause him to wrestle with problems that without our help he might not dream of. Not otherwise can the rising generation be helped to rise above the conventional goodness and the conventional compromises with goodness that characterize the older generation.

Our next question concerns the functions that records and memories of past experience can perform in present experience. *First*, they can provide worthy enjoyment through stories, poems, and the like. Such enjoyment, if it is discriminating, leads to the formation of worthwhile tastes, and the presence of such tastes can turn the scale in many situations. *Second*, the lingering past can reveal something of the contrasts of life, and consequently something of the issues that we need to face. *Third*, the past can yield some dependable data for our thinking upon our problems. The dependability of these data, however, must be established by critical processes in the spirit of science.

Of these three functions, the one that the Bible most effectively fulfils is the second. What is there that cuts deeper into the issues that compete for our souls? Next in importance is its culturally-upbuilding store of literary treasures. They can make a great contribution to the taste-side of character. The least important function of the Scriptures is their contribution of dependable, critically sifted data for the solution of our problems.

Teaching by "life-situations" commonly assumes

that the teacher finds in some material, most often
the Bible, a solution for the pupil's problem, and
then gets the pupil to experiment with this solution.
The assumption is that if the pupil makes this experiment he certainly will find his problem solved.
But the Bible is not a book of solutions; it is a tran-
script from life, with its mixture of conventionality
and aspiration, fact and opinion, the permanent and
the temporary. Neither recipes, nor rules, nor scientific information can be derived directly from it.
Even the Golden Rule is not a rule at all, for it does
not tell us what a wise man would desire that others
should do unto him. The Scriptural incidents and
characters that teachers commonly offer as exhibiting
solutions for the present problems of pupils are commonly trimmed to fit the modern situation. A part of
the story is not told, or something is added, or attention is focussed upon a fragment of it. Meantime, the
great contribution that the Bible might make, the
clarification of issues and the suggesting of problems
not already thought of, is relatively neglected, as is
also the use of this remarkable literature for enjoyment "with no string attached to it." There is positive danger that the "life-situation" approach, as
teachers will attempt to practise it, will first conceive
the pupil's problems in inadequate terms, and then
descend toward biblical cant as a solution for them.

Finally, just how does the "life-situation" idea re-
late the two persons immediately involved, the pupil
and the teacher? As two persons working at one
problem, and this the pupil's. No reverse relation—
the two working at the teacher's problem—is assumed. Thus the tendency is toward isolation of particulars rather than generalization or organization
of them. In many cases, to say the least, to isolate the
pupil's case is to grasp it only in part, and then to
offer only a part-solution. I surmise, though I cannot

prove, that every situation that presents a problem of purposeful pupil-self-control involves also a problem of purposeful self-control on the part of the teacher or of those whom he represents (as, the church, or general society). That this is generally the case within the family is now almost a truism among teachers. The conduct-problem, or the conduct-excellence, in the school leads straight back to relations between parent and child. The question how far this principle holds in other relations between younger and older persons also deserves notice. It deserves, in fact, an investigation that is here out of the question. I can merely allude to a few situations that suggest that we cannot effectively help the pupil to solve his problem until we tackle our own, and indeed until we enlist his help in tackling it.

Consider the following instances in which a need for guidance of the young turns out to be at the same time and at the same point a need for guidance of their official superiors—guidance, too, which the young can help supply: The "movie" problem is at one and the same time concerned with attendance by the young at present shows, and what sort of shows the community is willing to have exhibited. Experience indicates that children can help with the latter part of the problem as truly as adults can help with the former part. The problem of the attitude of boys toward policemen is at the same time the problem of the attitude of policemen toward boys, and the solution has to be reciprocally managed. The fire-drill in schools is a drill for teachers and pupils at the same time and in the same sense. The dietary questions that bristle around the school luncheon require teacher and pupil alike to betake themselves to scientific sources that both might like to ignore. The problem of pupil-honesty in tests and other school work turns out to be a problem of the material of the curriculum, the teaching technic employed, and the personal attitudes of the teacher. The most extensive and persistent misconduct of which I have had direct cognizance in any school (this time a proviate academy) was a correlate of mistakes by the teaching staff. The staff could easily have learned a better way from the students.

If any one should interpose that teachers, policemen, parents, and the adult community generally should correct their faults without waiting for help from the young, the reply would be that, as a matter of fact, they don't do it. They get help from the young, if in no other way, at least by imaginatively listening to them. Listening yields the largest insight, of course, when there is the unobstructed give-and-take of conversation, and adults walk straightest when they know that young eyes are looking on.

Education within the churches offers no exception to this principle. The conduct of classes, departments, assemblies of worship, and numberless philanthropic enterprises has been improved by making the process mutual to teacher and pupils. The content of teaching has been enriched, here and there, in the same way. It is not otherwise with so-called personal problems. Good temper and ill temper; peaceableness and quarrelsomeness; selfishness and co-operation; reverence and irreverence; orderliness and disorderliness; attitudes toward money, property, profits, and wealth; attitudes toward classes and types of men; wholesome and unwholesome sex-attitudes; the type of one's prayers or no-prayers—experience in all these spheres is really mutual, whether we realize it or not, and the guidance and improvement of experience go on most steadily and effectively when both insight into the problem and experiment with solutions are mutual.

The conclusion is that the "life-situation" ap-

proach to the teaching of Christianity is an approach
from the right direction, but that, in its present state,
it does not start far enough back nor go far enough
forward. Not far enough back, in that its conception
of pupil-situations does not sufficiently recognize the
historical and social factors dynamically present
therein; again, not far enough back because it does
not press the prior question concerning the real nature of the biblical literature. Not far enough forward because it does not appreciate the extent to
which the pupil, in the process of learning, can help
his teacher also to learn, the rising generation the
risen one.

43. The Projected International Curriculum of Religious Education

If any one questions whether "the world do move,"
let him contemplate the project that bears the name
International Curriculum of Religious Education.[1]
Let him note that the heretofore conservative forces
of the evangelical denominations, acting through
their central organ, the International Council of Religious Education, have their faces set toward a completely new type of curriculum and of teaching.
"Completely new" is not too strong a characterization, for the Educational Commission that is doing
the work rejects the old material-centred basis of curriculum-construction, and adopts a pupil-centred
basis. The resulting enterprise is one of enormous
complexity and difficulty, and the sweep of it is
enough to take one's breath away. First of all, once
the point of view of the Commission is adopted, there
must be an original investigation of the experiences

[1]For the history of the enterprise and the principles upon which
it is proceeding, see the pamphlet, *The Development of a Curriculum of Religious Education,* by Paul H. Vieth (International
Council of Religious Education, Chicago, 1928).

of the young that form their character—the young of different ages and in different types of environment. This yields the problems to be met. Next comes a search for material, chiefly in the Bible, that is likely to help with these problems. This is followed by the testing of this material and of methods for handling it, in experimental classes. All the wisdom gathered from these sources will then pour itself into plans for the printed guidance of teachers and pupils in schemes of religious education for both Sunday and week-days.

Nothing as drastic as this has been attempted heretofore upon so large a scale. None of the reforms of public education now going forward compares with it in difficulty or in the depth and sweep of its possible consequences. How the enterprise will turn out is, in the nature of the case, still problematic. We do not know what sort of guidance for teachers and pupils will emerge, nor how the constituent denominations will receive what their agents prepare. All that we can be sure of at present is that old things are definitely passing away, that the evangelical denominations are becoming more receptive than they have been heretofore, and that their schemes of religious education are bound to be revised in the general direction, at least, that the Commission has already adopted as its own.

For one thing, the day of uniformity is about over. There will be no rigid mass of material to be conned by all pupils of the same grade the country over. There will be no dating of lessons. Instead, problems will be classified, sources of appropriate material will be indicated, and suggestions for methods and experiments will be made. All of these kinds of help will be so abundant and varied that different sorts of school, class, and individual will be able to select what the immediate situation seems to call for. This change to flexibility in what has been so fixed is like an odd change that has occurred recently in one of the branches of engineering. In view of the breaking of ordinary rigid bridges by earthquakes, Japanese mechanical engineers have devised hinged bridges that, upon occasion of a quake, can yield either sidewise or upward without injury.

That the theory upon which the Commission is proceeding tends to shift the position of evangelical religious education from that of transmissive teaching toward that of creative teaching is clear. What remains to be determined is how far the theory goes in this direction. Even if the Commission wanted to go the whole way, the practicability of doing so at this time would be at least doubtful. Local churches, and whole denominations, will be wary of rapid change, and at best the transformation of rooted and almost hallowed ways will take time. No fault-finding, therefore, is implied in the following remarks concerning the intermixture of divergent and even irreconcilable factors in this theory. The situation calls, rather, for wonder and thankfulness for the progress that already is in evidence.

First, then, how is the "life-situation" or "experience" of the learner conceived? There is room in the framework employed by the Commission for tabulating any sort of experience, any sort of situation. For the classificatory device that has been invented invites a report upon any of 1,452 areas of possible need, with the understanding that indefinite subdivision of these areas may be made. In practice, however, this device will not necessarily assist in finding what we most need to find. Everything will turn, indeed, upon somebody's judgment as to the specific points in pupil-experience at which help is needed, and as to the kind of problem that the need opens up. It is entirely possible that "life-situations" or "experience" (a term much used by the Commission) will be conceived in the narrower way that was discussed in our last section, and that the major moral dynamics with which the Kingdom of God is concerned will be treated, as at present it is treated in most Christian teaching, as an appendix to individual, small-scale piety.

Second, this danger, and some others, are enhanced by the adoption of a list of "Christian character traits" or virtues as an instrument for discovering and analysing situations that require help, for determining detailed objectives, and for the classification of material. There is no sufficient evidence that this list has a genuinely objective basis. It represents the combined judgment of the members of the commission, but no test of the reliability of this judgment is mentioned. If another list were made independently by another group of equally able and informed men, there is no reason to suppose that it would correspond at all closely with this one. There is no apparent basis for the selection of some items and the exclusion of others. The spirit of play, for example, and a sense of humor, which are ignored, might claim a place in Christian character alongside of "health-mindedness," which is included. "Justice" does not appear as a main head; it is tucked away in a long list of synonyms for "honesty," and the interpretation given to it is "fair in disposition or conduct." "Obedience" is in the list, but there is no mention of a trait-name for the outstanding instances in which Christian conduct requires disobedience. "Loyalty" appears, but there is no indication of how a Christian discriminates between loyalties and revises his loyalties, nor is there a trace of the critical caution that should characterize the Christian in the presence of customs and institutions and social pressure. The nearest that the list comes to anything of the kind is in the minor

descriptive item, "the intelligent choice of causes."
In fact, one simply cannot obtain here a clew to the
issues that a Christian needs to face, nor how a Christian can determine which side of these issues is the
right one. There is no apparent reason why the Christian virtues should be just 22 in number; an earlier
list, which has been superseded, had 49. In the list as
given there is, moreover, no end of overlapping; there
is no preventive of lop-sidedness; there is no real anchorage anywhere.

And the worst is not yet. For there is excellent reason for doubting the existence of such traits. Harts-
horne and May's exhaustive tests of deceitful conduct fail to reveal any constant trait in such conduct
or in its opposite. Rather, the act of deceiving or of
abstaining from deception depends upon the kind of
situation that one faces, the kind of activity that one
is engaged in, the degree of the temptation, and so
on.[1] Further evidence against the actuality of these
traits can be found in common observation of human
conduct. It is possible for a man sincerely to attribute to himself, and for his neighbors to attribute
to him, almost any list of virtues at the same time
that his life-policies, the direction of his choices in
concrete situations, are not to be approved. A man
who really believes in his own superiority to his fellows in point of both intelligence and wisdom, and
draws logical inferences therefrom as to what is really
good for him and good for them, could tear down the
Kingdom of God without forfeiting his claim to any
kind of goodness named in the catalogue. But if so,
these kinds of goodness are abstractions, not traits
of persons, not something that one does, or has, or is.
The use of such terms as courage, honesty, and reverence is like the use of dryness, lightness, lonesome-
ness, and preparedness; they are, as it were, pre-

[1] *Studies in Deceit* (New York, 1928).

paratory acts of attention by virtue of which we notice something that otherwise might go unnoticed. When we do take notice, what we find is particular dynamic relations not even indexed in the abstract term. The scheme in question uses these abstractions not merely as preparation of attention for the noticing of typical experiences, but also as "workable units" of Christian character, this character being considered as the objective of religious education. Thus these traits become objectives, and of course they control the analysis of material of instruction. It is not to be assumed that this is the exclusive method that the Commission uses for the discovery of situations and the analysis of material; other more concrete methods are named. But it is fair to predict that, to the extent that the table of "Christian character traits" does guide the building of a curriculum, teachers will once more be set at the old and futile task of promoting abstract virtues instead of trained methods of attack upon concrete situations.

Third, the kind of authority that teachers are to wield in the new scheme remains obscure. The learner is to be assisted "to secure control of his present experience," on the one hand; but, on the other hand, the "Christian outcome" to be aimed at in particular situations is to be determined in advance of all dealing with the situation and without conference with the learner. This leaves altogether too much opportunity for the old notion to creep in of conformity as the end of successful teaching—interested and willing conformity, of course, even "control" of one's own experience, but by an echo-self.

Fourth, this curriculum originates in a body that represents evangelical churches only, other Christian bodies being designedly excluded. Therefore it is proper and important to inquire how the Commission is handling the ideas that give to evangelical orthodoxy its distinctive character. Is a specifically evangelical curriculum coming to the birth?

It would be exceedingly interesting to see how any denominational exclusiveness could be squeezed into, or sewed onto, the educational theory that controls the Commission's work. As a matter of fact, nothing of the kind appears to have been attempted or to be in prospect. The reason for its non-occurrence is likewise a matter of interest. Some way back we saw that whenever we set out to follow unqualifiedly the Christian principle of personality we always, in some significant respect, outgrow our present religiousness. Christianity is *per se* self-transcending. It must be so because persons are self-transcending. From this law, so exacting yet so fruitful and even beautiful, evangelicalism, let us be thankful, is not exempt. Because the new curriculum starts from the standpoint of persons and their needs, and aims to put persons into control of their own experience, it is too overflowingly Christian to be contained in the old temple vessels!

This situation has not arisen through anybody's theological or ecclesiastical designs; it is due to a living dynamic that does not wait upon our logic. But when our conscious logic lags behind our Christian purposes, a new problem for Christian education is created thereby. Let us see whether this new problem besets the International Curriculum of Religious Education. The Commission first undertakes to define the objective of religious education "from the viewpoint of the evangelical denominations." This objective, broadly stated, is "complete Christian living," which includes, among other things, "personal acceptance of Christ as Saviour," and, "under normal circumstances, membership in a Christian church." We need not dwell upon the use here of "Christian church" instead of "evangelical church"; rather, let us trace the uses made of the notion of accepting

Christ as Saviour; for in this region is the core of evangelical orthodoxy and of the distinctively evangelical type of Christian experience, if there is one.

The question that is here raised does not imply that evangelicalism cannot grow within its traditional boundaries, as by shifting emphasis from one phase of itself to another; nor need it be assumed that all meaning goes out of the old terms if we do not retain the sense given to them by our fathers. If, in the practical working out of educational plans, the objective of "accepting the Saviour" tends to disappear, this does not necessarily mean that everything that was connoted by the inherited phraseology has lost its hold; but it does signify that the old limitations of the personal experience, of the fellowship, and of the orthodoxy, no longer hold.

What, then, does this new-curriculum plan do with "accepting the Saviour"? I have discovered only one place, in addition to the general definition of objective, where either the phrase or the idea is employed. Under the character-trait "faith," acceptance of Christ occurs as one of several explanatory items. But there are 21 other traits that have no obvious relation to it. In the "areas of human experience," under the head, "specialized religious activities," there is no mention of any sort of acceptance or rejection. Most significant of all, the "statement of a theory of the curriculum," though it is an exposition of how religious experience is to be promoted, has nothing to say, after the formal definition of objective, about this central point of what used to be regarded as the most characteristic evangelical experience. Instead, we find that the controlling ideas, as far as Christianity is specifically mentioned are: The Kingdom of God; Jesus' interpretation of life; Christian personality; Christian conduct; Christian community. There is much about whole-hearted activities, intelligent choices, and co-operation, but not a word about orthodox belief or the conversion-experience.

Thus, under the warm rays of discriminating love, orthodoxy evaporates. But let no liberal incontinently rejoice. Is evaporation of ideas, convictions, and modes of self-discovery and self-realization quite the normal thing in a plan of education that aims to develop thoughtful control of experience? What is the effect of the evaporation-process? Is reluctance to avow religious changes where and when they occur upbuilding to personality? Rather, does it not curse "him who gives and him who takes"? Can we not see, almost at a glance, that the policy of reluctance that has been pursued for a generation has produced religious unintelligence in the churches and in the populace, fostered negativity or a-dynamic neutrality, taken the ginger out of church membership, and prevented multitudes of thoughtful individuals from assuming church connections?

Let us glance at a few facts that must have been under the eyes of every one who reads this book. What intelligent church member has not been chagrined to discover what his unchurched neighbors regard as the conditions and obligations of church membership, a member's beliefs particularly? Who that has had touch with modern Bible study does not know that outworn, often grotesque, notions of the Scriptures are preventing them from being used effectively for purposes of right living? Who is unacquainted with the chilling effect upon many discriminating minds of hearing congregations say that they believe old creeds that, in their *prima facie* sense, have become incredible? As for the young people who come into membership in the churches, what does being a member really signify in their experience? Older, rather sharp, meanings have retired into the silence, but no new meanings have been defined with equal sharpness. The result is a tendency, noted in an earlier chapter, toward spiritual respectability instead of spiritual power.

Here is an educational problem. It affects every individual pupil, the church, the popular mind. It does not concern something that is abstractly theoretical and unimportant for conduct, but that which is essential to intelligent personal decision and self-guidance. Yet, up to the present time, there is no sign that the International Curriculum of Religious Education will recognize the problem or endeavor to solve it. Possibly the constituent denominations would not accept a curriculum that undertook to tell the young just how and why the evangelical churches are shifting their views and their habits. But to the extent that the churches take this attitude, they deprive themselves of capacity to teach one of the most glorious things in the Christian religion, its capacity for self-transcendence.

44. The Projected Reform of Mission Schools

The proceedings of the Jerusalem Conference forecast what promises to be a significant advance in Christian education in mission schools.[1] The root-difficulty in these schools, as we have seen, is their failure to see and to practise more than a fractional part of the creative personality-principle of Christianity. The creativeness of the proposed changes in policy and method, consequently, will be great or small according to the thoroughness or lack of it with which this principle is to be followed. New phases of it certainly have taken hold of the leaders who are most in evidence. They desire to be released from the superiority-complex that has lurked in the missionary motive; they endeavor to separate them-

[1] *Reports of the Jerusalem Meeting* (New York, International Missionary Council, 1928), Vol. II, "Religious Education."

selves from entanglements with economic exploitation and gunboat nationalism; they recognize the
Divine Spirit in native religions; they are ready to
confer with the devotees of these religions on the
basis of mutual respect, and they wish to learn as
well as to teach; they are willing to transfer ecclesiastical control to natives who are competent to receive it; they have grown distrustful of required
courses in the Bible and of required religious exercises; they seek to assimilate and to employ in mission schools the great advances in method that have
been achieved through recognition of the principle
that the self-activity of the pupil is what best educates him.

This is a large mass of obedience to principle. It
means no little painful self-criticism and self-reconstruction. Like the young man who had kept the
commandments, the missionary movement might now
ask, "What lack I yet?" Would not the answer have
to be, "Sell all that thou hast; relinquish thy last
claim to dominate the personalities of others; instead, fully enfranchise them, and trust them"?

If one should say, "I do not desire to dominate
them, but I do want the truth of the Gospel to dominate them," still the reply would be, "Do you assume to choose for others what shall dominate them?
And, indeed, are you sure that you have eliminated
all self-will, all self-conceit, all error, from what you
call the truth of the Gospel?"

Every teacher, I suppose, meets the temptation to
identify the authority of the truth with the authority
of himself as teacher of it. The truth may be a bit
of arithmetic, or the accepted pronunciation of a
word, or a biological law, or an event in history, or a
reasonable rule of conduct, or an estimate of a character, or an interpretation of life's meaning; but,
whatever it is, and however much hangs upon the

pupil's assimilation of it, the teacher who interjects his own will or even sound conviction between the truth and the pupil imperils both the pupil and the cause of truth. At times the teacher may well give information that the pupil needs, but the pupil must be put into possession of the tools for acquiring information for himself, and for correcting the teacher's errors. Expression of opinion, and even of strong conviction, is desirable at appropriate times, but only on condition that the pupil receive training in the methods of criticism of just these opinions and convictions. The teacher's task is to bring the pupil face-to-face with facts, and to develop ability to handle them independently; to bring him face-to-face with values and alternatives, and to develop his ability, through free choices and experiments, to make larger choices and experiments.

If there is any exception to this principle it concerns protection of the very young from immediate hazards the nature of which they cannot realize. In respect to the outlooks of science and of religion, no exception whatever can be admitted. Natural science should not be promulgated upon the authority of the teacher or upon the authority of a consensus of biologists. Where the "teaching of evolution" is forbidden, the wise strategy for educators and for friends of science is not to insist that even this well-established truth be authoritatively taught, but rather, first, that training in scientific method be given, and second, that facts, opinions, and conclusions be placed before the learner simply as facts, opinions of so and so, and conclusions of so and so. If this policy were generally pursued, one result would be that the populace as a whole would realize the truth of evolution, but a still more important result would be some ability to weigh evidence in this field, and to recognize isms as isms.

The appositeness of these remarks in the present instance is to be gauged by the degree in which the educational outlook that emerged at Jerusalem disengages the facts and the values of the Gospel history from the authority of the missionary or of the church as teacher of it. Is it, or is it not true, that the missionary movement is committed to teaching as saving truth, most surely to be believed, the convictions and opinions of the missionary forces— to teaching Orientals in this sense rather than in the sense of turning their attention to data, and training them in methods for handling data?

We find competing principles stated as though both of them could guide mission schools and schooling at the same time. On the one hand, it is declared to be anti-educational to attempt to force the pupil into moulds desired by some one else, or to make him merely an instrument for carrying out the purposes of others; and it is said that teachers do this whenever their object is to make proselytes rather than to foster the growth of free, independent personalities. Here the Christian personality-principle speaks. On the other hand, it is said that the central purpose is to declare a message, and that the whole movement stands or falls with the truth of this message, which is the Christian Gospel. What is meant by truth is indicated in part by the affirmation that what gives to Christianity its distinctive character among religions is the unique importance that it attaches to history. The Gospel is a story of something that happened; it has to do with facts that are to be taught; and they are to be so taught that they will promote certain definite beliefs about God and his purpose and human duty and destiny. Here speaks the authority of the teacher, which identifies itself with the authority of the truth, and the purpose to make proselytes is unmistakable.

Even if the missionary teacher should make no mistakes as to historic facts or the interpretation of them, one might yet object to teaching them in the manner here implied. For this manner of teaching does not submit historical evidence and the teacher's interpretation of it to the free scrutiny of the learner; it does not refrain from imposing beliefs and pseudo-knowledge of facts upon uncritical pupils; it does not unequivocally foster the growth of free and independent personalities; it aims at conformity with the teacher's views, and if such conformity is not secured, the teaching is regarded as to this extent a failure.

This renewed assertion that a certain traditional account of the life of Jesus is true to fact comes at a strangely inopportune moment. For students of the Gospel history are multiplying the evidence, by no means new, that the factual basis of the tradition is insecure. Can the leaders of this forward movement in mission practice affirm that they know that the events in question actually did occur? If not, will they teach their opinions as their opinions, and will they make available for the learner the contrary opinions of historians who are at least as knowing? There lodges a remnant of partisanship, an ism, even in this new and in many ways so forward policy. The educational issue for Christian missions is the old one between two conceptions of how to save our life. An ism can for a time have life within its keeping, but it can preserve this life only by ceasing to be an ism.

CHAPTER X

THE CHRISTIAN EDUCATION OF ADULTS

45. The Why of Religious Education for Adults

The stream of experience is one stream; it has for young and old the same sources; it flows in the same direction between the same banks. Therefore the problems of the Kingdom of God are not graded problems, the solutions are not graded, though there be gradation in the sense of division of labor according to capacity, aptitude, and situation. Christian education, accordingly, is or should be one undivided and indivisible whole for young and old. At times we may find it advisable to concentrate attention upon the needs of the young, and to talk of the church school in the conventional sense of "school" as a place for the immature rather than the mature. I have done this myself, believing that the most effective approach to the whole problem is through our interest in the young and our familiarity with existing organizations for teaching. But I am not as sure as I used to be that this yielding to a popular mode of thought is tactically useful.

In any case, there is a great popular self-deception that must be overcome. The almost universal notion that the time for getting our education is childhood and youth, whereas in adult life we settle down to the use of our education for the rest of our days, is a blunder. It is a pernicious error, more deleterious to the spiritual life than much that bears the opprobrium of sinfulness. The reason why it is so pernicious is that it encourages a systematic letting down and checking of the functions that make

us persons. These functions—which for convenience
may be summed up as the free re-direction of experience—when they are performed with fulness and
vigor, include the free reconstruction of ourselves;
in other words, education. There is something more
in this than the unending re-application of what we
have already learned and already become.

The most common notion of the mature Christian
soul makes it resemble a mechanical device that is
used in the orange-packing industry. The oranges
are brought from the orchard to the packing-house
just as they are picked, with larger and smaller
fruit indiscriminately mixed. But each box that is to
be shipped must contain a definite number of oranges
of a standard size, whether 100, 150, 176, or whatever. The sorting of the fruit into these required
sizes is done by a machine that has corresponding
apertures through which the golden globes fall as
they roll down a trough. So the well-trained Christian is supposed to sort out the great and the small,
the good and evil, by repeatedly applying to his experiences some fixed formula or unchanging motive.
Thus the spiritual life becomes mechanized; it is a
psychical sorting-machine that does the same thing
over and over again without growth in itself.

The resulting evil is two-fold: *First*, the sorting is
poorly done, because it does not take account of the
fact that the content of experience changes, and the
alternatives likewise. In the sphere of the spirit any
unchanging sorting apparatus is bound to become
inaccurate and unadjusted to actuality. *Second*,
through the practice of this inaccuracy the personality does not merely stop growing, it degenerates.
For the mechanizing of one's judgments is the mechanizing of one's self; one's misjudgments upon the
values of experience are at the same time misjudgments upon one's own value. Life now becomes self-

defeating just where it believes itself to be most efficient. Though it believes it is simple and consistent, it falls into no end of entanglements, compromises, and pseudo-pieties.

The only way that a person can maintain himself as a person is to keep on growing, and the only way that one can keep on growing is by thinking and doing "something different," by changing yesterday's "standard sizes," all of which amounts to continuously repenting and continuously entering upon new life. And this is what Christian education means, whether for the immature or for the mature. One stream of experience, one unfinished Kingdom of God, one society of unfinished selves, one method of growth.

46. What Is to Become of Preaching?

When adult religious education is mentioned, thought turns at once to preaching as one possible agency of it. But immediately we are in difficulty. Preaching started as a way of declaring a supposedly unchanging message; it understood its function to be that of sorting and transmission; and this conception of its function, becoming a tradition, has governed it even to the present day. The expository sermon that "opens the Scriptures"; the doctrinal sermon that argues about creeds; the metaphysical sermon that founds a doctrine upon the infinities; the evangelistic sermon that aims to bring sinners to repentance; the inspirational sermon that seeks to inject power into ideas—all of them assume that conformity of the hearer to what is transmitted from the past through the preacher is the test of pulpit power. Not quite all sermonizing falls within this description, but most of it does, even in liberal circles; and ministers who have what they regard as

the newest message still regard the successful sermon as the one that secures assent and conformity.
This is not the method of teaching.

We have seen that transmissive Christian education does not really work; how, then, about transmissive preaching? Is it thriving? No one who is
acquainted with the church life of to-day will affirm that it is. In fact, a deep and wide-spread
doubt exists concerning the whole function and
future of the pulpit. We need not here dig into many
of the facts that contribute to this doubt, or into
the various phases of the truly hard situation that
confronts the ministry to-day; for it is clear, upon
the face of the matter, that transmissive preaching
is not better able than transmissive teaching in a
Sunday-school class to carry through the personality-principle of Christianity.

Incidentally, without doubt, preaching of the
standard type has here and there awakened independent reflection; in spite of its method it has
stimulated some hearers to think thoughts of their
own, and it has called a large number of individuals
out of a careless and uncontrolled way of living to a
life of principle. But over against this must be
placed the fostering of partisanships, the institu-
tionalizing of minds, the obstructions that have been
put in the way of real knowledge of the Bible, the
resistance to natural science, the bolstering up of
decadent pieties, the lack of sympathy for unconventional goodness, and the opposition to necessary
reforms. The severity of these words is not intended
for preachers, but for the presupposition that has
ridden them like a hag. It has held them back, generation after generation, from the spiritual creativeness of which they have been capable. And it has de-
ceived them both by making their apparent task
unduly easy and by inducing them to accept low

standards of efficiency. Even inspirational sermons, though they often awaken emotion, rarely get beyond stirring up an interest that, incapable of motion of its own, drops back into the passivity of some routine.

Preaching doesn't have to be like this, and not all of it is like this. Various essays at something fresher have been made, yet few of them have been governed by insight into what is most needed by the people, or by insight into what public speech can do. Most sermons on current events, current books, and current plays, though they undertake to interpret present experience in a free and unhampered way, seem not to go deeply enough into their problems to become creative. Yet there are sermons that quiver with creative energy. They may take their start with something old, or with something new, but always the theme, the meaning, wrestles with the everlasting necessity of re-creating ourselves and our religion. The number of preachers who reach this level, and the response that is made to them, are sufficient to make us hesitate to accept the theory, which is rather wide-spread, that the pulpit is to be completely supplanted by the other, rapidly multiplying, means of communication. It is said that the day for preaching is about over. I readily grant that the day for some kinds of preaching is growing short; the sooner its sun sets, the better. But in a creative religion there is a permanent place for creative sermons. And sermons can become systematically creative if only their proper place in a total scheme of Christian education can be found.

The greater preaching that is already here has qualities that, though they need supplementing, are of permanent educational significance. Let us enumerate them.

(*a*) It takes an objective attitude toward fact

as contrasted with the subjective attitude of all the historical isms. It assumes the methods and the results of scientific inquiry, not only in the realm of external nature, but also in that of history, the Bible, and moral and religious processes.

(b) It exhibits a spiritually sensitive historical consciousness. Spiritually sensitive; that is, the preacher apprehends with clearness and vividness the actualities in the habits and acts of the worthies of the past, and of the unworthies; and thus he grasps the actual dynamics of the Kingdom of God conceived as a historical process. He is more history-minded than are the transmissive sermonizers.

(c) This objectivity, coupled with spiritual sensitiveness, enables the preacher to understand, as the conventional religionist does not, the human types and the moral issues and forces of our own day. His gospel, as a consequence, cuts deeper into the diseased tissue of our civilization, and at the same time has more generous appreciation for all its constructive forces.

(d) For the same reason, this preaching, like that of the prophets of Israel, has a constant outlook toward public questions, and toward all the forces that move and organize men in masses.

(e) This spiritual realism, as it may fairly be called, results in a new alignment of human forces. The remark has repeatedly been made that the old vertical divisions, such as the denominational, are giving way to horizontal stratifications that run through the denominations, so that the alliances of a conservative are with conservatives generally, the alliances of liberals with liberals generally. The religion that is represented by the preachers whom I am describing certainly works against artificiality, certainly appreciates moral forces wherever they are found. The preacher, therefore, now knows himself to be an ally of all—whether in one church or another, or in no church, and whether or not they give a religious name to what is in them—who labor for the enfranchisement of persons.

(*f*) The relation of these preachers to ecclesiastical institutions now becomes intensely interesting. Apologists for ecclesiasticism such men cannot be; they are thorns in the side of it. Yet they believe in the church. They are its keenest critics, yet they criticise in love, and they are sure that what is now required is but to liberate what is already in the ancient structure. It is noteworthy that, as a rule, they are at least tolerated by the churches, and in some instances held in high honor.

(*g*) Coming close, now, to the question whether this preaching is an effective method of teaching, we note, in the first place, that it opens the whole of the religious issue to the whole people, and then relies for results upon the people's use of intelligence in combination with awakened ethical feeling. What is recognized as the greatest preaching of to-day does not endeavor to do people's thinking for them, but to awaken thinking on their part. It does not impose cut-and-dried duties upon them, but makes them sensitive toward ethical actualities, and then relies upon them to find their duties. The definition of alternatives, and the cause-and-effect analysis of competing modes of living, now takes the place of the customary authoritative declaration of the supposed will of God, as it likewise supplants the supposedly demonstrative derivation of duties from dogmatic premises.

Here is the beginning of the dawn for preaching in the modern world. In reality, it is a recovery and a reconstruction of the oldest recognized function of the pulpit. A teaching function it always has assumed to have, and at times and places this function has been foremost in the mind of the preacher. But preachers have not been foremost (with a few exceptions like Bushnell) in discovering how human beings learn, and how to teach effectively. In large sections of Protestantism, the sermon has even forgotten to endeavor to teach, for it has become either argumentative and declamatory, or hortatory and inspirational, or even a sort of genteel entertainment. No wonder that the question is rising, "What does it all amount to? Is it worth its enormous cost?" If this were what we must understand by preaching, it would not be worth its cost, and it would be doomed. The only salvation for the pulpit lies in the further restoration and further reconstruction of its educative function. The question, then, is, What more is necessary than an increase in the number of such creative sermons as I have described?

Let us turn for a moment from these masters of the pulpit to the hundreds of young men who next May will offer themselves as candidates for the "sacred office." The words that now follow I should whisper, if there were means for doing so, into the ears of all these neophytes of the pulpit: "When I see you going about your calling as the official guide of a congregation, often signalizing your status by what is immediately beneath your chin, I often ask myself how it is possible for you to imagine that you are competent to tell the people what they need to be told. If you really believed that a completed message, all exactly formulated, had been put into your keeping by Almighty God for transmission to a congregation that otherwise would not know of it, you could consistently stand and utter that which you had received, keeping yourself out of it. But you do not believe this; you know that every sermon you preach is your expression of yourself. You select the topic, the point of view, the material, the direction of the thought, the application; you determine what each occasion calls for, what the people need, how much they can assimilate, and how best to reach them. You have your own private ways of judging whether each sermon is a good one—rather esoteric ways, one might remark.

"This, you think, is your calling as a preacher. But "how did you get that way?" Where and how did you acquire wisdom so broad and deep, and so much beyond that of other men? And why do you think that your preaching really gets results, or is worthy of your talents? Do you answer that the people listen and pay? Do not deceive yourself. They rest and recreate themselves at the Sunday service, and they pay you your salary because you keep the machinery of the church going, not because they can put their fingers upon benefits received by them or by the community from your pulpit efforts. You are standing in a false light—false to your congregation, false to yourself, false to the cause that you would serve. I do not blame you, for you are the victim of a system, not the inventor of it."

How, then, can preaching be saved? Saved from its present waste of men, time, and money; saved from its present illusory self-involution; saved to the cause that needs leadership as much as it ever needed it? By adopting the principles, and mastering the basic technic, of creative teaching.

To say that the teaching function of the pulpit must be restored does not mean, it cannot in decency mean, the reversion of ministers to the traditional schoolmaster-type—a superior dictating to inferiors, or even a learned one condescending to share his learning with the ignorant. Rather, the whole teaching-and-learning point of view that is embedded in our discussion of problems and projects, "life-situations," and pupil-centred curricula, must be applied

to the congregation as a whole by the congregation
as a whole. Education through self-activity is a law
for the group as it is for the individual. It is a law
for the minister's own growth. The first requirement upon him, then, is that he take his place as a
learner within a group of learners. His place within
his church is not that of a mature member who
guides the immature, for many a layman who "sits
under his preaching" is not behind him in spiritual
self-discipline or insight. Even if the minister were
more learned than any of his parishioners, this
would not define his function as a preacher. Rather,
he is one who attends to specialized parts of an enterprise that belongs to the whole body.

Our basic church need is that the whole constitu-
ency, acting as a self-conscious unit, should acquire
the attitude of a learner. The minister, as one of the
learners, could then escape the incongruities that
were mentioned two and three paragraphs back.
Even a young preacher, not yet experienced in life,
could escape them by special study of the technic of
learning and of teaching. His influence as a teacher
would grow, in large measure, out of the demonstration that he knows how to learn—that is, how, by
the use of intelligence, to change his habits, increase
his efficiency, and become a different self.

The current preaching to which I have paid a
tribute of praise does not, as yet, give adequate attention to the conditions under which a congregation
might reasonably be expected to learn. It will be
necessary to overcome the isolation of the sermon,
and so to modify the plan and method and organization of preaching that it can be woven into a unified and continuous educational whole. To declare
the truth is not enough, no matter how clearly it is
done; nor to gain assent, however intelligent and sincere; nor even to prick the conscience just where it

needs pricking. People will not effectively grasp truth in its dynamic aspect except through projects of their own that involve problems that they feel as their own. The pulpit could do no greater service in the next quarter-century than help congregations find out what they really want that they haven't already. If many of the sermons ended with an unsolved problem, a tantalizing inadequacy, or even with a confession by the preacher of his own reasoned unsureness, the congregation would still listen, and after a time it would demand that the preacher turn to and help the people learn.

Most preaching at present raps like a peddler at the doors of persons who have no purchases to make. There is no desire to learn, no inner preparation for doing their part in learning. This is too one-sided altogether. It forces the minister to make his sermons out of emotionalized notions up in the air. The weekly renewal of this experience of beating the air, and of listening to the beating, is actually regarded as a duty! The preacher puts "applications" into his homilies, of course, but they, too, are ideas to be contemplated, approved, and enjoyed by the hearer as he hears. "A strong sermon," he says; but who really expects laymen to use anybody's sermons as an architectural design for the structures that one builds between Sundays? Some preachers have thought to escape from this futility by making their sermons a set of incitements to specified acts. But at best such preaching merely jogs men from outside, whereas the need is self-active personalities. They will have to have ideas, of course, and they will require help in getting them, but the method of acquiring them must be that of thinking that is one's very own, and that is dynamic. This means action that is at the same time thought, and thought that is at the same time action. The function of the sermon is to promote action that guides and modifies itself by the intelligence of the agent.

Let us suppose, now, that a congregation is to engage in a project that involves a problem that calls for thought that depends upon getting information and making discriminating analysis. Where, in this whole, might preaching help? We must assume that the congregation does not merely listen, but also provides for itself means for conference, discussion, and prayer, through which an explicit group-consciousness and a common purpose can come into being, and that it provides itself with the means—committees, experts, books, documents, financial resources—for working at its problem and executing its purposes. Granted this setting, the answer is that preaching can help all along the line. It might take the initiative, showing how, out of the last project, or out of new events, a fresh project properly buds; it might analyze the new problem; describe precedents; present information scientifically acquired concerning nature, man, or history; report results and judge them by appropriate tests; be eyes and ears for the congregation, to perceive and make vivid the actualities of the whole in terms of persons, not forgetting the outreaching and inreaching and up-pushing aspects of the enterprise.

The content and the method of successive sermons will vary with the varying nature of the congregation's projects, and with the stage that they have reached. On one occasion the preacher will help the people think their way into an historical situation; on another occasion he will help them build some fair city of the imagination. At one time facts will be amassed and described so as to make a situation concrete; at another time there will be rigorous analysis of causes and effects. The need at our feet will have a voice, and the need for God likewise.

Speaking and listening will become continuous, particularly at crisis-points in a project—its uncertainties, difficulties, failures, successes. And always the feel of persons moving—moving into a fuller selfhood, or moving into a thwarted and narrowed selfhood—will pervade the whole. The background of every sermon will be the value of persons, and the creation of more values by persons. Therefore the application to the persons who listen, and likewise to him who speaks, will be everywhere in every discourse; it will not be an appendage. In short, sermonizing will be a co-ordinating factor in a scheme of co-operative projects in which voluntary or thought-guided action builds the Kingdom of God, and in doing so, re-makes the builders themselves.

In order to illustrate the possibilities of preaching in such a setting, suppose we consider a topic that has been preached about innumerable times since these chapters were begun, the so-called Peace Pact. I have applause for ministers who preached in favor of the Pact, and a ? for those who have been silent about it during these days of agitation. The congregations that have sent memorials to Washington have done well. But has the utmost been gotten out of the situation? Let us imagine that, as soon as the Kellogg proposal was offered to the nations, a congregational meeting had been called to determine what should be done about it. Merely to suggest this first step in a congregational project calls up visions of methods for securing information, for understanding conflicting opinions and the reservations made by some of the signatory nations, for studying and reweighing the Monroe Doctrine, and then the Cruiser Bill! One can picture a whole congregation at work upon these problems for weeks and perhaps months. A great opportunity for various sorts of educative pastoral leadership is here; and an open door for

sermons that deepen the problem, place it in its perspective in the Kingdom of God, and make persons
conscious of the personal within the political. In this
situation the preacher will hardly tell his people what
to do; rather, he will help them command their own
powers of insight, choice, and co-operation. The result will be both action on behalf of others and self-
discovery and self-remaking.

This more personal way leads to more rather than
less action, and it has the advantage of preparing the
actors to meet the next issue upon a higher level. A
mere hurrah for the Pact, and telegrams to Washington under the influence of a sermon out of the blue,
could leave a congregation unalert and even ignorant
with respect to a cause of the greatest importance
that is certain to be with us for years to come, and
that is certain to call for action by any alert congregation. The sermon, as long as it remains an isolated thirty minutes a week of being talked to, will
have only spasmodic effects if any at all, and these
not large; but it can have large and connected and
continuous usefulness as one item in a co-operative
plan of action that requires study and self-discipline.
The abiding function of the pulpit is that of teaching in the best sense of this term.

47. When Is a Christian Church Well Organized?

The conception of preaching that has just been
unfolded leads on into a far-from-common notion of
how the work of a church may best be organized. It
is obvious at once that we have come upon a principle
that requires us to provide for continuity, and a specific kind of continuity, between the teaching work of
the pulpit and that of the Sunday school and the
other agencies that work with children and youth.
Continuity of a calamitous kind there always has

been. Continuity through what is weak rather than what is strong in the traditions of preaching. In what is called the teaching of the young, we find text, exegesis, exposition and illustration, application, emotional reinforcement; authority that separates teacher from pupil; dislocation of ideas from their proper relation to action; remoteness from some of the greater life-currents; missing of the creative aspect of personality; insufficient attention to the unfinished aspects of the Kingdom of God.

The desirable continuity between the pulpit-teacher and the other teachers is first of all that of method, all of them being leaders of projects. But, more than this, there should be continuity in the content of the projects, and this continuity should be realized by all the learners of whatever age. The present notion that in the church school you are supposed to learn something, but that, when you listen to sermons you are supposed to—well, what? helps maintain a gap between "church school" and "church" that nobody has shown how to fill upon the present basis. A children's church won't do it, if it educates by projects instead of by imitation, for projects are just the things you don't work at in what is known as "church." Children's sermons won't do it as long as they are story-entertainment, for the sermon for grown-ups is not story-entertainment. Sermons to adults on the subject of religious education will not do it as long as sermons themselves are not parts of co-operative projects.

The concept at which we now arrive is that of a church, made up of older and younger persons, moving forward as a unit by bringing into co-ordinated action the self-transforming forces that reside in the personalities concerned, younger and older, pupils and teachers, congregation and minister. All, that is to say, are to be learners together; the method of their learning is to be the same, and the problems upon which they labor are to be continuous with one another and often identical.

This brings us "smack up against" the question whether the true basis for the entire organization of a local religious society, or of a denomination, or of a federation of denominations, or of a finally unified Christian church, can be found in any concept except that of Christian education. For what is the business of the church? Is it not to promote the spiritual life of men? That is to say, to promote what is most personal in persons? And what is this "promotion" but Christian education? What other aim could the church have that would not deny or compromise Christian principle? To bring all men everywhere to themselves, and in this process to find our own selves by remaking ourselves—this is education, and this is the work of the Kingdom of God.

If we shift to any other basis whatever, some special interest, taking possession of one or another instrumentality of the church, is sure to come between us and our unfinished tasks. Not all special interests are sinister in origin or intent, of course; consequently, when we say that some one is pursuing a special interest that interferes with a better or larger one, we do not impute insincerity to him. Now, the plague of our churches, even churches characterized by earnest devotion, is that their organs and their special methods represent independent or quasi-independent interests instead of the one thing necessary.

We may take ecclesiastical finance as an easy example. At first sight one would say that managing the fiscal side of the church is simply attending to a material means for spiritual ends, the ends being over here, the means over there. Hence, the finances of a church are said to be in "good" condition when the needed money is secured and economically spent.

What more does one want? The answer is that bargaining for a church lot, or laying stones upon one another that we may have a place of worship, or purchasing electric power and light for it, or setting type for a church paper, is a spiritual experience of one or another sort, and that a part of our job as a church is to see that all the persons here involved grow more spiritual, which is to say personal, through this economic experience. Financial activities are spiritual experiences of high or low order because they are interactions of person with person, interactions in which each person confirms or modifies his ways. Every dollar in a church fund is an outward and visible sign of an inward and spiritual grace, or disgrace.

If, through its business department, a church is not engaged in Christian education, therefore, bringing persons to themselves in and through money matters, there is a central defect in its organization. And the defect is not merely that some part of the proper work is omitted, for neglect at this point reacts upon the central purpose itself, affecting the health of the entire organism. Whatever in economic relations we accept without endeavoring to modify it becomes a part of our valuation of men, not merely of the goods that are bought and sold, nor of the services that are sold for a wage. A "place of worship" is not merely a condition or a means of worship; it is an accomplished fact of worship or anti-worship—as much so as the "amen" with which a service ends. For here, in this physical thing, spirit has met spirit upon the basis of each one's valuation of life. "How much is it worth?" always connotes the question, "What does it mean to us?" and "What, through it, do we mean to each other?" A church that is not using its economic relations as an opportunity for influencing the un-Christian economic principles of society is yield-

ing to them something of the church's avowed faith
in men and in God.

Just so, each department of church activity—worship, preaching, missions, philanthropy, as well as
work with children and youth—should consciously
and of set purpose be a part of an inclusive scheme
of Christian education. Even social enjoyments,
which are an appropriate feature of church fellowship, will be more richly social when, like the camp-
fire converse of canoeists upon a journey, they include a background sense of movement out of a spiritual yesterday toward a spiritual to-morrow. The
"department of education" will disappear, because
all the departments will have education as their central, not incidental, function.[1]

As all roads lead to Rome, so all the conditions of
efficiency in Christian education by the church lead
back to the simplest principles of the Gospel, principles so simple that they are paradoxes. Except the
church deny the self that it already is, it cannot go
on following the Master. Except it lose its life it cannot live its own life. Unless it becomes a humble
learner, it cannot enter the Kingdom of Heaven.

[1]See J. M. Artman and J. A. Jacobs, "Rethinking Organization
for Religious Education," *Religious Education,* December, 1928,
pp. 979–991.
I have shifted my own position upon this question. I used to say
to myself, "What a gain it would be if every denomination and
every local society had a department of education, as the city and
the state have, and would put this department upon a genuinely
professional level." I was thinking more about quality of teaching
than about organizational machinery. But I am convinced that we
are in a position like that of a small child who is beginning to
learn to walk—if we cannot take two steps we cannot walk even
one. That is, unless we proceed to organize the whole church upon
the educational basis, all our efforts to educate the young will be
retarded and largely defeated.

48. The Unsolved Problem of Leadership in Christian Education

The question of how to provide trained leadership for Christian education has been up for lo, these many years, but who can answer it? Concerning it one might exclaim, "Where shall wisdom be found? And where is the place of understanding?" For, though advances of real significance have been made within the last five or six decades in the training of our army of unpaid teachers, in the provision of trained men and women who make the guidance of religious education their life-work, and in the preparation of clergymen for understanding educational processes, the problem travels on ahead of us—indeed, it runs, while we trudge. Above and before us as we trudge glimmers the ideal of a country-wide network of church schools not less thoroughly organized and supervised, and not less skilful in teaching, than the schools of the state. But whence the mechanical equipment? Whence the skilled teachers? Can we bring a force of unpaid, non-professional teachers up to the desired level? If not, how can myriads of really trained teachers be provided? We do well to push forward schemes for lessening the crudeness of our present practices, for we must do the best we can even while we plan to supersede our present best. But will any of these training schemes arrive? May they not all be mere palliatives that slow down our disease without curing it? How will the new International Curriculum of Religious Education fare in the hands of such teachers as we now have?

We do well, likewise, to raise up a force of vocationally trained and paid persons, clerical and lay, for the main positions of leadership. The significance of this movement is, indeed, greater than most persons realize. For the new-type leaders are not restricted in their opportunities for employment to a progressive local church society here and there. Their services are coming into demand also in denominational and inter- or extra-denominational secretaryships, editorships, and the like, and the day is near when professional study of religious education will be regarded as a part of standard preparation for holding such offices. We are approaching a point where, as far as overhead management can accomplish it, changes can be made almost over night in the educational complexion of great bodies.

So far, good; but our progress is into doubts as well as into certainties. How far can the field, the rank and file of the churches, be led to accept what is offered to them from above? And even if they are willing to accept it, can they assimilate it and make it effective? The schools and departments that give professional training in religious education are well aware that this question is staring at them. They are facing, in fact, a practical dilemma: If they accept the current notion of "practical" training, they must be shallow instead of fundamental, but if they open the fundamental educational questions, will not the student become unfitted for service in the churches as they now are?

The recent introduction of departments of religious education into theological seminaries is surely an arresting phenomenon. The *recent* introduction of definite instruction with reference to what every one admits is a, if not the, basic function of the church! One might ask whether this advance movement in the seminaries came about through growth from within (apprehension by theology of what it is and what it is for), or through pressure from without. But it is more profitable to ask whether the presence of a department of religious education implies that the ministers of the future will take up their work under the assumption that education verily is the church's basic function. How many seminaries stand for this conception? And, in case it is not accepted, and made the basis of training for the ministry, what is taken as the main function of the church, and where does religious education then come in?

The question of what should be the difference between preparation for the ministry in general and preparation for leadership in Christian education is a "poser" for theological faculties. On the one hand, anybody can see that a "theological course" does not prepare for educational leadership. On the other hand, preparation for such leadership and this "theological course" cannot both be squeezed into three years. The issue here involved is a fundamental one. It is not solved, it is not even touched, by adding to the theological curriculum a smattering of instruction concerning the church school. A realistic educational approach to the experiences that give worth to persons changes the whole perspective of Christian work, the whole perspective of training for leadership in such work. Either this educational approach is true to facts and to Christian standards of value, or it is not. If it is true to them, it foredooms all sewing of patches upon the old curriculum, for it requires a changed conception of the ministry and of theological seminaries that prepare for the ministry.

The relations between theological training and the training that is given by departments and schools of religious education that start from the educational rather than the theological point of view are in an unsatisfactory condition. There is a tendency to divide church leaders into two categories, those who are supposed to have mastered "content," and those who are supposed to have specialized in applications, processes, or technics. How much "content" a specialist in religious education needs, thus becomes a burning question. A closely related question is, how far the approach to this content is to be controlled by the uses to which it is to be put, and how far by the interests of historical research. It is certain that knowledge of the Bible that is needed for curriculum-building and for supervision of the church school is not provided in the ordinary seminary instruction. On the other hand, seminary standards look frowningly down upon anything different from their own *quod semper*.

The disparity between the two types of training is one reason (there are others) for occasional infelicities in parish organization and administration. Some directors of religious education have found their functions isolated, as if the spiritual life of a church could be mechanically divided like the labor of a factory. Some have even believed that they can fulfil their office by going 'round and 'round in a closed compartment; others have appeared to be presumptuous because they didn't believe it. Some have been required to make bricks without straw, as if spiritual work had no mechanical side. Others have been required to show results within six months, as if not growth, but the shoving around of material masses were the essence of the job. Almost always, for no reason in the world but tradition, the ministry of preaching takes the precedence in every way of the ministry of teaching. Theological training, it appears, confers a prerogative officially to weigh educational processes and products that one has not studied, but training in educational processes confers no like ability to judge preaching and pastoral work —except unofficially and on the quiet. There is unrest among pastors (justified unrest, no doubt) because the performances of persons supposed to be trained in religious education do not fit into pastoral programmes, and there is parallel unrest (no doubt justified unrest) on the part of religious-education workers because the preaching does not fit into educational programmes.

The situation in its totality—the teacher-training movement, vocational training in religious education, and general training for the ministry, all taken together—presents an unmistakable picture of faltering thought. A great idea has begun to take hold of us; it is the most inspiring thought that has fastened itself upon church administration since the beginning of the modern missionary movement. But the idea has us more than we have the idea. We shall not have consistent, harmonious, and efficient leadership training until we have done much more hard thinking, and done it together.

At the present moment this is the substance of our situation: At the top, the training of ministers, and at the bottom, the training of Sunday-school teachers, are controlled by the notion of transmitting something that already is good enough. Between these two stands vocational training for religious education, facing which way? Toward the transmissive ideal, or toward the creative ideal? Some vocational training is rather definitely committed to the inherited view, but not all of it. We are, in fact, developing two types of employed workers, one of which might be called engine-builders, the other explorers. Both have to do with motion, and both have to do with revision; but the one revises processes, the other revises the direction of the journey. The one sort accepts orders, the other interrogates them. Of course these terms apply merely to dominant characteristics and trends; there are all sorts and degrees of mixture. If we ask which of these is getting on the better, the answer must be that, while external appearances give the advantage to the engine-builders, there are internal processes that point in the opposite direction. That the transmissive tendency is recessive one may gather from a number of facts. One of them is the International Curriculum of Religious Education, which springs up within the very garden of conservative evangelicalism. Even among conservatives a theory of teaching (the theory of self-activity and social participation) is gaining acceptance that is undermining the basic assumptions of conservative education. At the same time, the prophetic aspects of the Christian religion are coming toward the foreground. Soares goes as far as to say that our religion has again entered "one of its creative periods."[1] These forces are simply causing the whole standing-ground of transmissive education to disintegrate.

But, wherever Christian education is thus divided in its own mind as to what is Christian; as long as it accepts the personality-principle, yet delays to face the meaning of it, we must look for a divided and ineffective leadership training. Ministers will still be trained to transmit what cannot be transmitted; we shall have, for the Sunday-schools, teacher-training that does not train, and the vocation of religious educator will continue to have one foot on land and one on sea.

No one will claim that any single change can set all things right; yet intelligent, straight-out adherence to Christianity's personality principle as the central and organizing idea of the whole enterprise would work wonders with leadership training. The seminary for the training of ministers (as distinguished from the prosecution of research in religion) would then have as its core a problem in spiritual dynamics—the becoming of persons, the freeing of them, within the rawness of our present civilization. This would make the function of the ministry that of

[1] T. G. Soares, *Religious Education* (Chicago, 1928), p. 63.

education in the strictest sense—education of the
young and of adults as a single, indivisible enterprise. It would obliterate the contest between "content" and "technic" in the training of leaders, for all
would approach both content and technic from the
same point of view. It would provide a basis for uni-
fying the employed workers in a church, for all would
have the same goal, and all would submit to the same
standards and scientific tests. What effect, finally,
would it have upon our vexed "teacher-training"?

Present schemes for making better teachers out of
a mass of laymen whose vocation is not that of teaching are by no means condemned if we say that these
schemes are only a makeshift, that they never can
solve our problem, and that we should plan now for
displacing them. In fact, in the whole long cam-
paign since the beginning of the old Chautauqua
movement, nothing has happened that gives us ground
for thinking that the level of teaching will be raised to
tolerable competence by the teacher-training that is
practised in the Protestant churches. The difficulty
is not chiefly that teachers are unpaid, though financially compensated teaching is taken more seriously
by both the payee and the payer; nor is the main difficulty the part-time, or shreds-of-time, nature of the
work, though the multiplication of full-time workers
would greatly help. There are two still deeper considerations that affect the whole enterprise.

What if thorough training in the learning-and-
teaching process, coupled with competent knowledge
of the Bible and other materials, tended to unfit our
teachers for what is expected of them? And what if
the thing that is expected of them simply cannot be
done anyway? Both these horrifying suggestions are
based upon truth. Thorough training, to begin with,
will surely move in the general direction of the self-
activity principle. You may use as a shibboleth, "pu-

pil-centred," "life-situation," "problem," "project," "freedom," "creativity," or whatever you prefer; you will not go far into the subject before you find yourself committed to the thing toward which these words point. Thus, the study of technic is more than a study of mere technic; it is a study of personality and the laws of its growth, and it develops the kind of respect for the personality of pupils that tends to enfranchise them from all external authority. Further, competent information concerning the Bible and other material unfits one for using them as authority. Consequently, if we should succeed in giving to our teachers a thorough training, we should unfit them for carrying on the transmissive teaching that is demanded of them.

But worse is yet to come. The teacher-training movement is, on the whole, an isolated thing. The church stands looking on and saying to the teaching force, "Now that we have provided training for you, let's see you get results." The pastor is the one most likely to be, in this matter, the voice of the congregation, and, indeed, he is likely to lead the congregation into this deadly attitude. To isolate the process of teaching the young from the process of the church life as a whole amounts in the end to inviting the young to buck the whole church. Sometimes one wishes that they would do it, but they won't. Young minds always find bridges over which they may go back and forth from their own situation to that of some adult group. The thing that is most certain to be learned is the ways of the group. Thus, the whole church teaches, whether it intends to do so or not. It follows that teacher-training, if it is to be practical, if it is to make good teaching really possible, must be part of a general movement in the spiritual life of the congregation.

Thus the teacher-training situation forces us back

to the theological seminary situation, to the need for adult religious education, and to the necessity of organizing the entire church machinery upon an educational basis. There is no panacea for the prevalent poor teaching in the church schools; there is no "method" of teacher-training that will turn the trick in either a short or a long time; there is no way to solve the problem of the church school without solving at the same time the problem of the church.

Does this imply that the present church school is to mark time until a new spiritual conviction takes hold of ministers and members generally? No; for the church school, in spite of its handicaps, may be one of the agents for producing such an awakening. Does it mean that the churches are to wait for the theological seminaries to revise their plan of ministerial training? No; for the churches can help awaken the seminaries from their complacency. Does it mean that the seminaries must wait for the churches to be willing to accept a new type of minister? No; nobody need wait for anybody else to start things going. For we are not dealing with mechanics, but with personality. If we had to deal with mechanical forces, we might conclude that the church as a whole would have to be moved from the outside before anything would happen in any of its parts. But persons are originators, and convictions have power to spread from person to person against all inertia and even against a common will. A minority can be stronger than a majority. God sometimes chooses the weak things of this world to confound the mighty, and by means of that which is not he brings to nought that which is. The main condition of the needed reconstruction is that each one who has caught a glimpse of the truth should stand in his own place, and with the resources at his command, work toward the goal of a church whose whole ongoing in every department shall be education. Let this be done with a stout heart, for rebuffs, mistakes, even failures—since we are dealing with education—can make a contribution to final success.

We do not yet know what our volunteer, unpaid forces are capable of, for we have not tested them under conditions appropriate to such a scheme as this. Nor do we know what sorts of new talent such a scheme would attract toward teaching. We certainly must increase the amount and improve the quality of professional supervision; a large increase in financial costs must be taken for granted; but we must also provide for release of the as yet unused powers of the laity in general. If the method of creation were substituted for the method of transmission, we might find that, because we seek first the Kingdom and righteousness of God, the things that our present poverty so sorely needs have been added unto us.

CHAPTER XI

WHAT CREATIVE CHRISTIAN EDUCATION MIGHT DO TO THE CHURCH

49. It Might Save the Church from Institutionalism by Developing a System of Continuous Self-Criticism

If we could have institutions without institutionalism we could free ourselves from one of the chief causes of spiritual suffocation. Institutions we must have, because the life of persons has to be both social and continuous, and because it has to include doing as well as contemplating. We can exercise our freedom only by putting it into harness, only by partial mechanization of ourselves; but the good harness is the one that frees us, the good mechanism the one that makes our creativity hit the mark. Institutions, however, *qua* institutions, have an inherent gravitation away from creativity toward self-imitation.

The church is a permanent necessity; if what we call churches should disappear, some institution that bears a different name would assume their functions. The supreme function of the church is to claim and secure right of way for whatever we can discern as the supreme truth and the supreme need of selfhood. But churches, in common with all other institutions, acquire a momentum that is repetitious and mechanical rather than personal and creatively variant. Religion comes to mean being loyal and obedient to the partial insight and the institutional creation of yesterday. Precedents, the product of a particular time, place, and state of mind, become controlling assumptions, as though they were the eternal truth, the will of God, or a finished creation.[1]

The spiritual life, then, must be wary of its own organized self. Withdrawal from the institutions of religion may be for some persons under some circumstances essential for the maintenance of one's integrity—oneness with oneself and sincerity toward others—and it may even be the best help that one can give toward making the church spiritually strong. But we shall not fully express ourselves as persons, we shall not be fully emancipated, until we devise an institutional technic that brings three things to expression in the institution itself:

The continuity of the personal self;

The social nature of the personal self, and

The self-transcendence of the personal self.

We have the first and the second of these, after a fashion, in our churches, but we have no recognized or permanent provision for the third. If we had, continual self-transcendence of the church by itself would be taken for granted as much as continuity is now. The lack of this self-transcending factor accounts for the stuffiness of some sorts of ecclesiastical piety and the emotional involution of other types. But the church need not suffocate itself by breathing its own breath over and over; there is nothing in religion that dooms it to this staleness. Nothing, in fact, could be more religious than finding and putting into operation a method for the continuous self-criticism (which means self-testing and judging) of religion and of religious institutions. Such a method

---

[1] In *The Motives of Men* (New York, 1928), Part III, I have shown that institutionalism is one form of a lag that inheres in rationality as such. It is a defect of a virtue. Whether the lag is greater in religion than elsewhere is questionable. If it is, the probable reason is that in religion rationality, attempting to make the most comprehensive assertion of itself, both magnifies its ideal of a satisfied self and intensifies its drag upon the freedom through which alone the self can fully realize itself.

has been outlined in what I have called creative Christian education.

Some will say, "Yes, this criticism is needed, but leave it to the wise ones, those most experienced and mature in religion." That is, do nothing about it until conditions become so intolerable, time after time, that a prophet arises—and is stoned! The question is sometimes asked why we do not have a continuously prophetic ministry, and why theological seminaries convey so little inspiration of this type to aspiring young men. The answer is that, under our present methods, we systematically avoid institutional self-criticism instead of cultivating it. But there is only one way in which we can systematically cultivate it. The institution always will employ its prestige and its power against its critics until the spirit of self-criticism becomes a part of the institutional consciousness as such—a part of the consciousness of laymen as well as of clergymen, of young as well as of old, of pupils in a Sunday-school class as well as of students in a theological seminary. Loving loyalty to our church fellowship does not reach its climax, it cannot do so, through closed eyes, but only through the most searching objectivity. As parental, filial, or conjugal affection is most perfect when it perceives and vicariously shares in all the limitations of the loved one, so our communion with one another in the church family is deepest when together we perceive the unfilled needs of the family, and feel them as our own. This comparison can be carried a step farther. As the surest way to make a man appreciate family affection is to provide a rich experience of it through his growing years, so the effective way, the only effective way, to deal with the institutionalism of the church is to make dealing with it a familiar experience from childhood up, an experience that is at once religious and educational.

50. *It Might Counteract Our Denominational Introversion*

All the Christian communions are denominations or sects in one and the same sense, and all without exception are infected with "ism," though some are more deeply infected than others. In most of the Protestant bodies there is an uneasy awareness of it; something is not altogether right inside. Hence the never-ceasing talk about church union, the holding of conferences to promote it, and the actual fusion of bodies here and there. Every one is sure that the "ism" must be mastered and transcended—at least the other fellow's "ism." It may perhaps have served a temporary need, but only as do our first teeth, which must be shed and replaced by permanent ones.

All is not right inside, but just what is this unrightness? This question is almost never raised in the discussions of church union. Instead, each body, or its representatives, ask what is right inside, and worthy of preservation in the united body that is to be. And because a church-union cure is attempted without first making a real diagnosis of denominational disabilities, we never are reasonably sure that the proposed conditions of union, or the conditions of some actual union, do not prolong and give firmer lodgment to the very thing that most interferes with spiritual efficiency in the separate denominations.

There is good reason for surmising that a sense of the weakness of our churches in the presence of modern conditions is one of the potent, though not clearly defined, motives for getting together. If so, it is pertinent to ask whether unification, as we now contemplate it, is anything more than a bit of defensive strategy, and whether, if it is not much more than this, it can succeed even as defense. In warfare the massing of weak regiments may confer strength, primarily because it concentrates mechanical force, and secondarily because a display of force affects the minds of men. A united church might be impressive by reason of its size, yet this increased impressiveness might not be justified by any increase in spiritual power. In the realm of personality, quality, not mass, is what finally counts. This is why a defeated and crucified man, without a church at his back, can have more influence than all the bishops of all the centuries. Do we really imagine that we of the churches can become spiritually efficient by pooling our spiritual inefficiencies?

Union upon the basis of an agreement concerning "faith and order" would be a pooling of our inefficiencies. For, to speak of "faith" first, we are handling ineffectively the problem of what to believe and how to test our beliefs. Churches clinging to ancient creeds are a monumental sign either that we lack creative thinkers, or, having them, do not make their thought accessible to the people. As a matter of plain fact, one reason why so many of our church members are spiritually logy is that they experience so little intellectual quickening through our church ministrations. Too many problems are already solved, it appears! And who does not know that many, many inquiring minds are repelled from the church because they do not find there, whether it is there or not, any such standards of straightforwardness in thought and speech as they require of themselves.

Some would get over the creedal obstacle to union, and to spiritual life, by assuming that it's not important what a man thinks, provided that his acts are right. But this is too easy by far; it abandons a function instead of fulfilling it. What we need is purposeful activity, but purposing includes discriminating thought. It is important both that we think, and that we guide our thinking by fruitful method. The more deeply we think, the better. In the atmosphere of creative spiritual life, inquiry thrives, because problems are felt, because precedents are known to be insufficient as guides, because the whole personality is stirred.

If, then, there be any intellectual condition that must be met in order to make church union spiritually fruitful, it is the united recognition of intellectual discovery and creative thinking as a normal part of church life. It is the unfinished intellectual tasks toward which the uniting mind must look, not those that we suppose—perhaps mistakenly suppose—are finished. How it would electrify the churches, and revive their energies, if the next world-conference on Christian union should declare, "It is incumbent upon us as Christians to employ the scientific method with respect to all the facts of religion."

"And order." Orders in the ministry may well occupy the thought of our conferences on Christian unity, provided that a dynamic point of view be maintained. A beginning might be made by recognizing the enormous economic waste that is entailed by present practices with respect to the clerical calling, and the spiritual significance of this waste might be brought into the open. We might remind ourselves that the whole of every salary paid to a clergyman represents the sweat of toilers. The sacredness of labor attaches to every dollar, whether it be contributed from wealth or from penury. That we are financially able to support scores of thousands of ministers without inquiring too closely into the contribution they make to the world is not a good reason for doing so. No one who is acquainted with conditions in the churches is likely to claim that the ministry is a skilled profession, or that there is any general practice of discriminating between skill and the lack of it. Nor will any one say that functions to be performed are definite and economically organized, or that there is any sufficient provision for getting square pegs into square holes, and round pegs into round holes. My own observation of ministers does not give me an impression that many of them are shirkers, or in this sense social parasites, though I have no means of judging how common it is to work hard, and how common to impose upon the indulgent piety of the people. But one does get an impression, partly of power yearning to be used, partly of contented tread-mill faithfulness, partly of a comfortable sense of a not-too-exacting dignity.

By all means let us make sure of right orders in the ministry. Suppose we begin with bishops. How many of them really earn their living? Some do, but not all. How many are leading the church, or en-deavoring to lead the church, out of itself, through the pain of spiritual rebirth, into a better self? Some, but not all. For, while one risks a stoning, and perhaps gets it, because he tries to go the whole way with what all of us profess, another is busy keeping the church, and himself, in the middle of the road, which is always spiritual evasion. How many are making any inroads whatever into our industrial jun-gle? Some are, but others have not had a dangerous thought since they were consecrated to the holy office. How many bishops are giving to clergy of the other ranks the kind of leadership that makes them do their best, and then makes them improve upon their best? Some are giving such inspiration, but others are lord-ing it over their subordinates upon the strength of nothing but such virtue as flows through ordaining hands. While one of our chief pastors is puzzling his way through a vital problem, or hewing his way through some difficulty at home or on the frontier, another is lending his presence. There are bishops and bishops. By all means, let us have the right or-ders in the ministry!

The purport of this is not that clergymen are in any special degree blameworthy for having the same foibles as other men, but that a system that invites and indulges such foibles, bestows dignity upon them, and pays men salaries for them, needs to take heed to itself. When creativity appears in the highest clerical office, it has to meet not only the ordinary temptations of mortals, but also temptations that inhere in the enterprise of the church as the denominations now conceive it. Only the very exceptional man withstands these temptations. Now, unless we devise some check upon ourselves at these points before we unite the denominations, the result of union will be to enlarge our defect. Imagine what many of our bishops would become if they were to preside over a world-church of the same sort as our present denominations! To get the whole picture, add to the term bishop all the other terms that name the official leaders and dignitaries of the denominations. Do we really desire a union that entails just this?

What, then, is this "ism" that besets denominations? I have called it introversion, meaning, roughly, the habit of interpreting events in terms of one's own inner states instead of interpreting inner states in terms of objective events. It is not quite the same as selfishness, though it easily becomes the bond-slave of self-interest. If a surgeon should glory in an operation, not because the patient was healed, and not because his own reputation or bank account was swelled, but because the operation added prestige to his medical school, we could not call him self-seeking, but we might say that here is institutional introversion. The true meaning of a medical school is more health; the introverted meaning is more medical school. The true meaning of a church is more righteousness in the community; the introverted meaning is more church. We do not successfully resist this by denouncing it as selfishness, for the true meaning and the introverted meaning so mingle that one can always defend one-self by retiring into the better of the two.

The justness of this description will readily be acknowledged by many, perhaps by most; but at the next step in analysis the many halt or begin to limp. Toward what is the introverted mind turned? Toward its own habits and fragmentary self-expressions; toward what is temporal in itself, or even incidental. Institutionalism is corporate mental retardation through self-imitation. It is primarily retardation of intelligence, only secondarily moral retardation; or at least it is a condition that can be overcome only by a quickening of intelligence. What do we see in a given situation? is the question. The denominational mind may be, in a sense, infinitely well-meaning, but it is undiscriminating; it lacks the habit of seeing out of the window; it is spiritually laggard because—well, because of the kind of education that it has received.

Because Christian education has been, on the whole, transmissive rather than creative, it has turned the mind of each denomination upon its own self as a standard for itself. This ingrained habit resists and drags down our aspiration for a wider fellowship, and it makes this aspiration, when it does assert itself, positively dangerous. Dangerous because it leads us toward we know not what except the perpetuation of our weakness. We are so introverted that we have no tests of an out-going sort. We know something about how to conserve and increase the membership of a church, but we know nothing definite concerning the effect of the church upon the world. Here all is guess-work. For aught we know, small religious bodies may be more efficient than large ones. Church union might thin our religion as well as broaden it. Our next step, then, is not union, but such revision and experimentation within denominations as will show what they can and cannot do, and what policies and processes get results. Some kind of fellowship and co-operation upon the large scale we surely must have, but it remains to be proved that the richest fellowship and the most effective work are dependent upon what is currently meant by church union.

The key to the situation is in Christian education. A creative type of it, giving form and effect to our professed principle of personality, and therefore active, out-going, and scientifically objective and fact-loving, is the antidote to our denominational introversion. It is therefore the instrument of the true spiritual unity of Christendom.

Let us not deceive ourselves as to what sort of undertaking real unification is. It is the unification of persons, not the hooking together of ecclesiastical machines. Now, the unification of persons is accomplished only in the sharing of a common purpose, for it is purposeful living that makes us persons. The unfinished task is the true basis of union, not anything that we are or have, nothing that ever was, no truth that is not in and of itself an attack upon the task of creation. The habit of mind, and the kind of religious experience that this implies, can be spread abroad in the denominations by one thing only—a reborn Christian education.

51. It Might Make the Church a Fountain of Social Radicalism

"The axe is now laid at the root of the tree," Jesus is reported to have said. And indeed, he did go to the roots—he was radical, a social radical. The fact that he did not dictate forms of social organization, but went at the heart of the organizing principle itself, makes him more radical than if he had recommended any kind of social or economic machinery. The principle of ethical love is an incitement to perpetual re-examination of the *status quo*. It will not let us be permanently satisfied with any kind of social mechanism that human wit can devise.

If we could persuade ourselves to make a discriminating use of terms in all discussions that touch our vested interests and our social prejudices we should administer to ourselves a wholesome ethical discipline. The adversary of our souls gets control of us with surprisingly simple devices. Consider, for example, how the term "radical" is related to what multitudes of our contemporaries regard as their moral judgment. The term has become a veritable trap. It is used as a characterization of the communist scheme for social change, though this scheme rests upon the oldest and crudest notion of social dynamics, namely, that our relations to one another can be settled by the compulsion of physical force. On the other hand, our capitalistic order is not called radical, though it also increasingly resorts to physical compulsion as a means for deciding human relationships—the compulsion of clubs, guns, evictions, deportations, and jails in labor disputes, and that of cannon and cruisers in commercial rivalries, not to mention tariffs, and legislation on behalf of "prosperity." The materialism of Marxian socialism is radical, but not the corresponding materialism of the profit-system. The Russian Soviet Republic's denial of freedom of speech and of assemblage to minorities is radicalism, but not the suppression of the same liberties in the United States since 1917. Is it not a bit startling that those who invoke guarantees of liberty that were incorporated into our Constitution in 1791 are in reproach dubbed radicals? Pacifists who do their best to keep alive the radicalism of Jesus are accused of radicalism in a contrary sense, for they are said to be under the influence of the Russian materialism that both resorts to war and suppresses dissent by violence!

Evidently our wits have become tangled up with our emotions. If we strongly dislike a proposed change we incontinently call it radical, though it be shallow in its grasp of actualities, or rudimentary in its ethical sense; then, though some troublesome changes are demanded in the spirit of Jesus, and others in a contrary spirit, we lump all together under the same head. The term "radical," which is properly a descriptive adjective, now becomes an opprobrious epithet, and a means of defense against the advance of disagreeable duties. The current antagonism to radicalism as a whole is a kicking against the goads of a deep ethical radicalism as well as opposition to what is unethical. It would be interesting to know by what classificatory device Saul of Tarsus justified his zeal against the Christians.

For the church to disclaim the charge of harboring radicalism is to act foolishly. To the extent that any church is Christian, it does harbor social radicalism, and cultivates it, for it is inherent in our assumption of the worth of persons. Put into practice in our economic-political relationships, it will "put down the mighty from their seats, and exalt them of low degree." The Christian church, *qua* Christian, is at issue with basic principles in the existing social order, at issue not merely with its excesses and excrescences, but also with what it regards as of its essence.

Capitalism, made anxious by the unrest that appears here and there in the masses, is looking to the church for moral support. But let the church think twice. Capitalism and communism are in some vital respects at one in their basic morals, for both exploit persons as means to the working through of a system; both rely upon conflict, and upon mastery of some by others; and both rely upon physical force as a final sanction. If the church had to choose between them, the preference should go to the plan that looks toward the wider distribution of educational opportunity, the larger participation of the common man in the determination of the conditions of his life, and the more wide-spread access of men to the physical resources that make possible a refined life.

If the church cultivates an enlightened conscience concerning the actual and the desirable state of mankind, and concerning the human or moral quality of social projects, it will be, not only now but always, subject to the charge of unsettling the social order. Disturbing social complacency is a part of its business. Its natural affiliations are with parties, groups, and individuals that bring into the foreground of thought the needs of men, women, and children. The result, now and then, will be association with suspicious characters, dining with publicans and sinners, and getting a hearing for those against whom the good would like to stop their ears.

We can see this line-up of church people with others taking place daily. More than one bishop in good standing in his own communion has been associating with the socially discontented, sometimes with those whom the police and the courts are pursuing. Drafted men who are pacifists because they are Christians hob-nob in federal prisons with other pacifists whose philosophy of life and society is materialistic. Christian ministers and dogmatic freethinkers unite to oppose anti-evolution laws. Unchurched laborers, engaged in a struggle for elemental decency and fairness in employment relations, find understanding and public support in pastors of churches. In the struggle for the protection and restoration of our constitutional rights, Christian

ministers, Jewish rabbis, mystics, secularists, and
sceptics find unembarrassed fellowship.

These fellowships are not inventions, or products
of calculation, nor are they slips from consistency;
they are spontaneous creations of the respect for
persons that all of us profess. What, then, of church
fellowship as such? If it spills over thus, if it is continuous with fellowship based upon the simple humanity that is in men of all religions and none, why
the church at all? The reason for it is the need of
institutions, having continuous life, that "go the
limit" with the principle of the worth of persons. Our
faith in God is one aspect of this "going the limit."
Our worship, at its best, brings this divinely radical
faith into immediate relation to the undivine con-
servatisms of our conduct, our God becoming to us
at once a rebuker and a reinforcer of what we are.
Our work in the world, whether we call it missionary,
or evangelistic, or philanthropic, or mystical, or
educational, is to bring men, by any and every means
that works, to act as persons toward persons. Such
action, wherever it occurs, is the Kingdom of God
which the church, as well as each of us individually,
must seek first. The constant endeavor of the true
church, accordingly, is to empty itself into the
world; to pour its radicalism out into all social institutions and relations, making them increase while
it decreases; to make its own bounded self obsolete
as far as possible.

The need for churches, in this sense of church, lies
in the fact that the other institutions that organize
men either seek narrower ends than this, or else
compromise when they come up against the problems
and the difficulties of utter justice. I do not claim
that all institutions ought to seek wholeness for personality except within their own special set of relationships. Let a factory seek wholeness at one point,

a legislature at another, a clinic at a third, a public school at a fourth. Let them take over as far as possible the philanthropic, educational, and other functions that once belonged to the church. We still are in need of an association with one another that represents and reminds us of the "whole-idea"[1] of the personal. We need a fellowship of repentance, of radical self-commitment, of faith and hope that dare the utmost. But this means that the church is to be distinguished by the extremeness of its social radicalism. It is to be the mother of radicalisms, and the companion and support of all who, in any sphere of life, take persons as the true wealth of the world.[2]

52. It Might Reduce the Membership and the Wealth of the Church

Creative Christian education will lead the churches into the way of the Cross—the *way* of the Cross, whatever becomes of metaphysical theology concerning the crucifixion of Jesus. It seems to be a fact,

[1] A phrase borrowed from Hocking's *Meaning of God.*

[2] Wieman, in his *Methods of Private Religious Living* (New York, 1928), pp. 67-78, gives a helpful formulation of what he calls "two levels of community." Upon the first level, the standards and methods of co-operation are prescribed by custom and convention. Upon the second level, actual need, or some alluring possibility of mutual understanding, purpose, or support becomes the standard. The two levels, he goes on to say, conflict with each other, "so that it is impossible to be well adjusted to both." Now, the church always is a community on the first level. But what about the second level? Wieman appears to say that the whole meaning of the church has to be found upon the first level. "It cannot transcend its own mores. . . . It cannot lift society to something higher. . . . The work of the prophet and the innovator must be left to individuals and independent groups, not the church" (pp. 64 f.). I judge that Wieman has here in mind not any inability of the church to live upon the two levels at the same time, and in this sense to transcend itself, but its inability to supply social machinery or do social engineering. Certainly he holds that public worship "must inspire us to readjust our personal attitudes and progressively reorganize our lives individually and socially to the end of making that adaptation to God through which the best unattained but possible world shall be brought into existence" (p. 137).

and a significant one, that the decline that has occurred in the doctrine that men can be saved by a
substitutionary atonement has been followed by a
growing conviction that the highest values are
costly, perhaps tragically so, to both God and man.
Thus it is that the Cross, as a symbol of voluntarily
paying the cost of fidelity to the good, retains its
impressiveness.

The meaning of the Cross for the church has
dawned only slowly. We have assumed that the day
of persecution for our faith is long past, but we
have assumed it too hastily. In our own day individuals, in the aggregate no small number, have suf-
fered, some of them grievously, because their endeavor to be Christian contradicted some purpose of
society. Prophets have been stoned before our eyes,
some of the stones being cast by fellow churchmen.
There is no knowing how much more of this cross-
bearing awaits those who take their discipleship in a
radical sense and are practical about it. We should
not think that we can have a truly creative Christian education that will not expose its pupils to
this danger, nor should we fail to make this danger
explicit in our instruction. We stand for a cause that
is opposed to much that men value; if we stand for
this cause intelligently and practically, we shall
hinder accepted social processes, and we shall dis-
rupt accepted social relationships.

But this is only one aspect of the Christian's cross.
The principle applies to the church as an institution
as well as to individual members taken one by one.
"Woe to you when all men speak well of you." One
normal sign that the church as an institution is
really doing its work is an attitude toward it of apprehension or of antagonism on the part of those
whose interest in the *status quo* is too pronounced.
At this point an odd inversion in reasoning has oc-

curred. For approval of the church by conventional people, and even by those who are exploiting personality for profit, has been taken as a sign that the world is advancing toward the church's position, whereas the truth is fully as likely to be that the church is suffering arrest at the level of merely conventional goodness. It is the business of the church to keep ahead of the procession, to be unconventional.

It is to be expected that wealth will be hesitant, suspicious, and withholding. It may even organize against the church, as it endeavored to do against the Young Women's Christian Association in Pittsburgh. We need not be surprised if the economic-political order first endeavors to use the churches, and then, failing in the attempt, turns against them. In order to "carry on," the churches may have to become poor, and to decline in membership. If we are not ready to face this possibility; if we are not doing something that compels us to face it, there is lack of spiritual aggressiveness in the church. This can be said without in any degree assenting to the ascetic notion that there is virtue in suffering or in feebleness. Rather, the implication is that, like arctic explorers, we should make ourselves as comfortable as our enterprise permits, but go ahead with the enterprise, accepting hardships as a part of it.

If this kind of Christian education should prevail, what would then be the significance of joining the church or being confirmed in it? At present, the meaning of membership in the Protestant churches appears to be determined by one or the other of these two conceptions, or by a mixture of them: (a) The church is a body of saved persons who abstain from theft, fornication, profanity, and the like, and perform such religious duties as prayer, attendance at church services, participation in the eucharist, and the giving of money for the support of the church and its enterprises. In this case, becoming a member means becoming a saved person, whether by a conversion-experience, by assent to a plan of salvation, or by receiving a sacrament, and then taking up the obligations just mentioned. In practice the door is a wide one, and expectations not difficult of fulfilment. By the same sign, as far as the creation of a new world or a new church is concerned, membership has no pungent meaning. There is resistance to some worldly currents, and there are sturdy virtues, but the world is not turned upside down. (*b*) The second view of membership in the church is that the members are a society of mutual helpfulness in living a good life, and that practically anybody who is willing to help and be helped is eligible. Such a society, though it undoubtedly promotes decency, softens asperities, and strengthens men to bear their ills, is rather easy-going.

How to make membership connote, in addition to easier goodness, acceptance of the pains of creation, is by no means an easy question for the Christian educator. On the one hand, we desire children to grow up within the church, being happy in it, getting and giving a stimulus for customary goodness, and subjecting themselves to the influence of worship. On the other hand, we want them to be shaken out of customary goodness, to become on occasion opponents of it, and to be stirred by the unfinished tasks of the Kingdom so deeply that a hardy and adventurous life is taken as normal.

The solution of the problem here involved is not to be found at the door of admission to full membership; for nothing sudden, no abrupt demand for hardihood with which one is not already acquainted, can give a permanent set to the mind. The creative, trouble-making principle of Christianity must become a control of the whole educational experience of children and youth, and then, the door of full membership having been entered, this kind of education must go right on to the end. Such education might make for reduction in the number of church members. It would be likely to do so, not by condemning and rejecting many applicants, not by expelling members for unfruitfulness, but simply by failing to attract those who are not ready for spiritual adventure.

But what a power this diminished church would be!

53. It Might Usher In the Revival for Which Many Christian Hearts Are Longing

"The old-time religion is good enough for me," sing those who most vociferously believe that they believe in revivals. But the religion that they celebrate is not old, as they vainly imagine; measured by the Christian centuries, it is new-fashioned. It does not restore primitive Christianity, much less the religion of Jesus. Moreover, though it does not intend to deceive others or itself, it does nevertheless evade principles of Jesus that have the best historical attestation as his, and the best moral attestation as universally valid. Revivalism, as it is practised among us, takes the easy road. There are many objections to it—clap-trap auctioneering methods; slap-stick comedy; intolerance; shallow emotionalism; interruption of the solid ministrations of the church, educational and other; dubious financial gains—but the overwhelming failure of the revival, even when it succeeds, lies in the fact that it is insufficiently as well as inefficiently Christian. It does not enfranchise personality, but leaves it lacking in creative purpose; it even makes men dependent, crowd-minded, institutionalized. There is much talk of love, but the meaning is not the sternly as well as friendly ethical love that can create a just society. There is sincere desire to lead men into the good life, but both the method and the dynamic of radical goodness are lacking.

Yet the need for a revival of religion is manifest. In spite of the growth of the churches in numbers, wealth, culture, and all the power that these imply, every Christian who thinks twice is convinced that in a profound sense all is not well. Somehow, the world's work manages to run itself contentedly upon a secular basis, unconvicted by any call of the spirit. Even the part of the world's work that is done by churchmen is a thing separate from one's consciousness of God. It cannot be said that any issue between Christ and "the world" is being drawn with sufficient rigor to produce any general squirming either inside or outside the church.

With exception of minority-groups here and there, the outlook of our people upon our people is characterized by complacency, "practicality," caution, appreciation of "prosperity," "more of the same." The whole, with its defects, is defended upon the ground of the good that it contains. "What would you?" says Complacency, "Isn't education more wide-spread than ever before? Haven't we achieved manhood suffrage, and civil rights for the masses? Is not benevolence increasing in volume? Hasn't the workingman of to-day more physical comforts in his cottage than kings had in their palaces yesterday? Why not appreciate this increase of what all of us call good?"

By all means, let us appreciate it, being especially attentive to that in the good that makes it good. When Jesus looked upon the rich young ruler, he

loved him. But let us be wary, as Jesus was. The
capacity of the good for sitting down is immense; it
has an almost unbelievable readiness to make truces
with its enemies; it has a queer bent for becoming an
enemy of the best. If we want to know what we are
like, let us watch our conduct at crisis-points in the
struggle of righteousness. At the time that these
words are being written, the Cruiser Bill is upon the
President's desk, awaiting his signature. Could it
have been passed if half the church had been awake
and on guard? Militarism is creeping into colleges
and secondary schools—no, it is marching in, taking
over partial control of curriculum, appointments to
the teaching staff, and students. Before me lies "The
Letters of Sacco and Vanzetti," two Italian immi-
grant idealists, one a shoemaker, the other a fish-
peddler, who loved truth and their fellow men, and
hated violence, but were killed because they entertained a radical theory of social change. Who killed
them? The police? The court? The Governor of
Massachusetts and his advisers? The State of Massachusetts? Public sentiment? Yes, but not these
alone. The prisons of California have for twelve
years contained two men, Mooney and Billings, who
were convicted of murder upon what later proved to
be perjured evidence. The miscarriage of justice has
been clearly known for years, and the detective, the
prosecuting attorney, and the judge, all of whom
were misled by perjurers, have asked for the release
of the two prisoners. Who keeps them in prison?
The Governor of the State? Yes, for he hasn't found
time to examine the case! But who is back of the Governor? Who, likewise, is back of the official delay to
release the wrongly-imprisoned victims of the Cen-
tralia tragedy? Let us Christians not think that we
can end such questions by answering that "the interests" did it. For Jesus said, "I was in prison . . .

Inasmuch as ye did it not to the least of these, ye did it not to me." We Christians are not yet sufficiently keen for righteousness to prevent these terrible injustices when we could easily do it. We need a revival.

What may prove to be a foretaste of this revival is already here. For the church is not altogether without leaders and prophets who are spiritually realistic in the sense of Jesus' parable of the last judgment. There is a leaven at work, as we saw in a preceding section (36). In the newer type of preaching, in social creeds, in resolutions upon pending social questions, in multiplying documents that let in the light upon what it hurts us to look at,[1] and in social-emergency activities (sometimes of smaller groups, sometimes of large bodies), we see new life bursting out like the avalanche lilies that shoot up through the lingering snow upon the slopes of Mount Rainier.[2]

If any one should say, "Words, words! What we want is deeds," we should frankly acknowledge that there has been more thunder in the index than in the body of our work. Nevertheless, we should reply also that while some words are just talk, other words are themselves deeds. If any one doubts it, let him take note of two things—the fears of some "practical" men who think that our economic and political ways are about good enough, and persecutory actions directed toward those who criticize these ways from the Christian standpoint. Moreover, the educational

[1]Three periodicals of this kind, copies of which happen to be before me, are: *Social Service Bulletin* (150 Fifth Avenue, New York); *Information Service* (105 East 22nd Street, New York), and *Social Trends* (412 Chamber of Commerce Building, Indianapolis). Publications of this type give point to duty, and they put scientific method at the service of ethical insight.

[2]The fact that Ward's *Our Economic Morality and the Ethic of Jesus* (New York, 1929) is named as the "book of the month" by a committee of distinguished religious leaders suggests much as to the spread of the radicalism of Jesus.

aspect of these activities puts them far beyond the
category of mere talk. The force and the reach of
this new kind of churchmanship are not measured
by its effects in this or that immediate situation; the
truer measure is the extent to which the issues of a
truly Christian life and a truly Christian church are
drawn tighter within the fellowship itself. I do not
hesitate to say that here is creative education already
at work. It has begun to reach into the curriculum
for children and young people; it is bringing into
many lives a glorious new, though painful, realization of the meaning of God; into many other lives
it is bringing the unrest that presages a new idea
and a new sense of duty. There is resistance; there
is inertia; but, as the moisture of the atmosphere on
a rainy day gets into our homes even though doors
and windows be shut, so the troublesome truth enters
the soul of the church.

Creative Christian education, then, might usher
in the revival for which many Christian hearts are
longing, even though some might not recognize it
as the thing for which they have been praying.

CHAPTER XII

HOW CREATIVE CHRISTIAN EDUCATION MIGHT REVEAL GOD

54. Faith in God Is Declining Both Outside and Inside the Church. Why?

That faith in God is less common than it was, and that where it exists it is less lively, will scarcely be denied. There is, in fact, a rising tide of apprehension on the part of church leaders that something or somebody is misleading people on a large scale, and not a few efforts have been made to discover and to discredit the culprits.

The most significant phase of this situation is not what is happening outside of churches, but what is happening inside them. The realization of God as an actual presence and power is growing harder and harder for multitudes of persons who nevertheless have faith in him. Less than a week before this paragraph in its original form was begun, I received a letter from which I shall paraphrase a sentence or two that might be written by many devout souls. The writer of the letter is an active worker in the church, a person of spiritual sensitiveness and warmth, one who would run to welcome the Divine Spirit. Yet this believer could write: "I have been losing my sense of the reality and presence of God. The companionship with him, and the support, that Jesus felt I do not feel any longer. I do not understand why. Can you help me?"

A part of my reply was of the following tenor: "Your difficulty is a frequent one, and it is becoming more frequent. The people of our time, Christians

as well as others, are caught in a wave of questioning, doubt, or denial of the participation of God in
human affairs. I suppose this wave overwhelmed you
before you realized what was happening. The source
of your difficulty, in all probability, is not entirely,
or even mainly, within yourself. You are sharing a
common experience, for which a diffused and wide-
spread cause must be found."

What is this cause? Four explanations have been
offered, each of which contains a grain of truth, but
all of which, taken together, leave our problem unsolved. (a) Some say that a new mental attitude,
inimical to faith, has been created by the spirit and
the methods of the scientific movement. What is obviously true in this proposition is that some *kinds* of
faith walk out when the scientific attitude walks in.
To the extent that one's belief in God is dependent
upon a dogmatic, authoritarian, all-or-none, disbe-
lieve-upon-your-peril kind of teaching, the scientific
movement is and must be a withering wind. Some,
probably a large proportion, of the most radical dis-
believers either started life under such teaching, or
at least never in early life had intimate acquaintance
with religion of the free and ethical type.

But the doubting mood is wider spread than this.
There is less of positive revolt than there is of a
more or less hazy non-commitment in feeling as well
as in thought. To this mood the scientific movement
has made some contribution, particularly in the case
of professional men of science, whose business never
consists in believing, but often in doubting. Yet the
mainspring of this wide popular movement can
hardly be anything in the principles of science. For,
in the first place, there is a body of at least respectable thought that finds no inconsistency between scientific method and some sorts of theistic faith. Many
men of high repute in science have definitely affirmed

this, and they have even confessed their own faith. If, then, the strain from which we are suffering were primarily due to the scientific movement, more of our religiously disposed minds would turn to such types of theistic thought. That so few find anchorage here is evidence of an undercurrent that is more than intellectual.

We must remember, moreover, that the atmosphere of doubt is found far beyond the rather limited number of persons who concern themselves with the logic of the sciences or with the logic of theology. Something is going on that the people feel more than they think it, something that probably all of us feel first, and think afterward. The main cause must be sought, then, in the sphere of the spontaneous apprehensions in which we affirm, in advance of analysis, that in this or that direction lies reality.

(b) Some persons attribute great faith-destroying influence to particular ideas that have been offered by men of science as statements of fact or of natural law, such as the evolution of the human mind, or the evolution of the idea of God, or God as an idealization of human experience, or that universal cement mixer, the conditioned reflex. Probably each of these has given to a small number of persons a sense of insecurity in their faith, but if these ideas have had any large paralyzing influence upon faith, which is not likely, it is because they fell in with, or seemed to confirm, an antecedent mood. Some of these ideas, in fact, appear actually to have removed difficulties for the thoughtfully religious; others have been subjected to criticism; none that really negate theistic faith has had general acceptance among the critical. The deep anxiety about them on the part of some defenders of the faith is clearly misplaced—there are far stronger dragons to be fought!

(c) A popular explanation of the fogging of our sky is the influence of a machine age upon the whole mind. Here again there is some truth. For whatever habitually holds our attention gives a slant to our sense of what is real. Every man tends to make of his occupation a telescope through which to view his world. The increasingly general and increasingly tense absorption in mechanical processes certainly does tend to make the material world seem very real. But the industrial system has compelled men to consider one another as well as material things. The factory brings together men as well as machines, offering personal life as well as mechanism for contemplation. Why, then, has attention so generally fixed itself upon the machine?

Indeed, to say that faith grows dim because of our preoccupation with the mechanical phases of existence does not really explain, it merely states the fact that requires explanation. What we need to know is why our attention has been so nearly saturated with the mechanical. Why has our religion been so weak a competitor for attention? Has there been no spiritual object or event, wide open to the apprehension of our generation, that could compel attention? Has nothing happened that could create an impression that here forces other than mechanical are at work, forces that master, control, and use the mechanical? Let us put this question in a sharply individual form—it will help us appreciate the forces that are near us: As a matter of fact, what has happened within your memory, and yours, and yours, that could give you a sense that a mighty spiritual and ethical power is at work here and now?

(d) The easiest—and the least illuminating—explanation of the decline in theistic faith is that which attributes it to our practical materialism, in particular our love of money. Here again we have a description of the thing we want explained, not the explanation of it. The question is, How is it that in a world that contains Jesus and powerful churches highly organized that profess his principles, Mammon can come so near to strangling us?

All these attempted explanations of the present decline of faith in God look for causes outside the church, outside the religious tradition. Suppose we look inside. Considered statistically, our ecclesiastical organizations are most imposing. They have great numbers, great resources; further, they have potential moral energy sufficient to shake the world. In season and out of season they have affirmed the existence of God; they have prayed without ceasing; they have organized and systematized their efforts to maintain touch with him and to bring others into touch with him; they have built heaven-pointing churches in every community; they have poured out their earthly treasure in astounding amounts; finally, they have taught the young during their most impressionable years that God is. All this the churches have done and are doing. Why, then, does not God seem near? Why does even the church seem to be losing its hold upon him?

Either there is no such God as the Christian tradition claims there is, or else there is something so seriously defective in our religious technic that God cannot freely manifest himself through it. Let us pursue the second of these hypotheses a little way. The faith of the Christian attributes to him, as the supreme quality of his character, love, or radical regard for personality; consequently, as the writer of the First Letter of John so clearly and so eloquently sets forth, the sign and evidence of the divine presence is the presence of love in us. We cannot apprehend God, or reveal him to others, except in and through our own or others' ethical regard for persons. The crux of the

technic of religion, then, lies in this question: Are
we habitually alert to the influences that play upon
personality, and do we make the enfranchisement of
it in ourselves and others the goal and test of our
conduct? If we of the churches have no system for
keeping ourselves thus alert, and for bringing ourselves thus to the test, we might lose touch with God
even though we were filled with diffused good intentions.

A repetitious religion, a backward-facing religion,
a self-imitating religion must either keep its concept
of God below the level of ethical love or else put up
with a weakening self-contradiction within itself.
Here lies the clew to the present obscuration of God
within the churches. For personality cannot fulfil itself by repetition either of one's own self or of other
selves. What has happened among us, in fact, is partly that we have cherished an insufficiently ethical,
and hence insufficiently Christian, concept of God,
and partly that, having achieved such a concept, we
have not devised a method for making it work. But
an insufficiently ethical concept of God is a decadent
concept; it may flare into activity in situations that
seem to make it useful, but it becomes shame-faced in
the presence of clear thinking. Our total situation,
then, is this: We ourselves must make a new demonstration of ethical love in human relations, or else
lose our faith in God.

We need to remind ourselves that some kinds of
circumstance can easily make decadent ideas of the
divine speciously seductive. To the correspondent who
is mentioned in the first paragraph of this chapter I
remarked that we must not expect to be cuddled;
ethical love puts companionship with God upon a
basis different from this. If we make of him an imaginary compensation for the deficiencies of life, we reduce him to a mere residual that can be dispensed with

when things seem to go well. A surmise is justifiable that the present general decline in the feeling of intimacy with him is due in part to a new tendency toward objective-mindedness—the same tendency that appears in our discontent with the too facile idealisms of the mid-Victorian period. None but a robust God, it is safe to say, can permanently be taken as God at all.

The stark psychological fact is that we always are under the temptation to bend the idea of God so as to make it fit into our present habits and our uncriticised desires. A pious and highly intelligent Russian *emigré* told me what an unspeakably precious support the eastern orthodox religion had provided during the terrible days of persecution and flight. Verily, she said, God was "a present help in trouble." Later she went on to say that loyalty to the monarchist régime in Russia, and a purpose to restore it, are an integral part of this religion as it is practised by the *emigrés*. "You, with your traditions," she remarked, "cannot understand this." But surely we who watched the prayers of Christians of the United States and of the other belligerent nations during the Great War should have no difficulty in understanding how belief in God can mean belief in czarism.

But no concept of God can survive that does not involve a critique of czarism, and of Americanism, and of all our individual and party desires, from the standpoint of the effects that they have upon personality—upon all the personalities involved.

If the churches have such an idea of God, they lack a method for incarnating it in life and conduct. Two glaring evidences of this will suffice. The first is that church members as a class are within the industrial system as an unprotesting part of it; they share, upon equal terms with others, its denial of the supreme value of persons. Moreover, church organizations, in their capacity as employers, buyers, and sellers, have not achieved any moral distinction by their way of adjusting the economic relations of persons to one another. A second sign is that at the time of the Great War, the churches as a rule (though there are exceptions) made no clear demonstration of faith in one God who respects all men. Claiming to be mouthpieces of infinite love, our religious bodies made of themselves telephones of the modern, secular, nationalistic state.

Let us be candid with ourselves. To what extent, and how, does it appear to us that we really do believe in God? Do we really think that the church can engage in warfare and still believe, and make others believe, that there is a God whose character is like that of Jesus? Do we really think that we can acquiesce in an economic system that values profits more than it values persons, and yet convince the world, or ourselves, that we are in active communion with a God who values one person above the whole impersonal world? We are attempting a psychological impossibility.

55. This Decline Will Not Be Arrested by Existing Christian Education, Either Catholic or Protestant

It is true that existing Christian education, both Catholic and Protestant, *implies* that which, if it were brought into action, could arrest the present decline of faith in God. For truly God is the great theme of this education, and sincere endeavor is made to transmit the thought of Jesus about him. From the kindergarten age onward this is the interpretative principle that is applied to duty, the church, the Bible, at least in Protestantism. It is increasingly so, for Old Testament conceptions of the divine being are less and less influential, and New Testament conceptions are correspondingly more influential. If phrases were ideas, and if ideas were understood, and if understanding were purpose, and if purpose had experienced technic, then, indeed, were faith in the Christian God secure in the hands of existing Christian education.

There is no occasion to labor the "but" that here interposes itself. What we know of transfer of training, or spread of habit, gives no encouragement to the belief that our present teaching ever can be more than occasionally effective. Our experience in the church schools shows, likewise, that even the most appropriate symbols for radical goodness can interpret themselves into justification for conventional and obstructive goodness. Preaching, along with teaching in what is called the church school, shows the same sort of degenerate fruitage. In short, generalized instruction, separated from the concrete needs, difficulties, issues and alternatives, conflicts, victories, and defeats of personality in the world about us cannot save our faith. Nor can such instruction plus worship save it.

Anxiety has been expressed lest emphasis upon the "social Gospel" (as if there were any other!), or upon humanitarianism, or upon ethical conduct, should invert the true order of teaching, and leave the experience of God undeveloped. As a matter of fact, what leaves the experience of God undeveloped is, first of all, the endeavor of teachers and preachers to induce pupils and hearers to carry on dealings with God that are not at the same time dealings with men, as though God could be vitally apprehended otherwise than in the love that men have for one another. Then, in the second place, superficial handling of relations between men lends its own superficiality to faith in God. The deepening of personal life (which is social), and the deepening of our faith in God, must take place at the same point, and through the same process.

56. Why Theistic Philosophy Is Religiously Ineffective

May we expect the present decline of confidence in the existence and the availability of God to be successfully checked and turned back by philosophy? If we are to judge the future by the immediate past, the answer must be, No. For the philosophies that do the most to lay a rational foundation for faith appear to be religiously ineffective. This will be acknowledged, I think, by any one who reflects upon the situation. If—to do a little of this reflecting here and now—we compare the influence of metaphysics upon the theory and practice of education from, say, the beginning of the kindergarten to the present, with the influence upon the content of faith and the practice of religion in the same period, we come upon a startling difference. In one case we see the farthest-reaching thought of philosophers mingling with the homely wisdom of the masses in the conscious and planned reconstruction of old habits; in the other case we see habits changing, but we discover scarcely any guidance by metaphysics. In fact, there has been a disposition within Protestant churches to think that religion needs no guidance from philosophy, being somehow sufficient to itself. Why this gap? Even if we should assume (as I do not) that religion can learn nothing from non-theistic theories of the universe, how explain the fact that it learns so little from theories that definitely ascribe valid metaphysical meanings to religious faith? Of such theories we have had a long succession within this period, and within this succession a goodly sprinkling of penetrating thought.

Continuity between life and metaphysics is normal rather than exceptional, reality being that which we experience in our occupations and other interests, metaphysics being the analysis of this reality. The effect of such analysis is partly æsthetic—enjoyment of long perspectives, sense of the sublimely great, appreciation of architectonic thought-structures, the excitement of bloodless intellectual combat—but in addition, metaphysical outlooks become meanings for conduct, and a critique of conduct. Education has been one of the favorite fields for what might be called a practising metaphysics. Statecraft is another; ethical self-guidance a third; religion, of course. It is true that every philosopher tints his world-view by the colors that prevail at his time and among his people, yet the great tradition of philosophy is that of thought showing the way to reconstruction of habits.

There are three possible explanations for the present hiatus between metaphysics and Christian life in the churches. (a) It is conceivable that religion, in so far as it is worship, is more or less a flight from actuality into subjectivity. To the extent that this is true, religion and philosophy move in opposite directions. (b) It is conceivable that the kind of God that metaphysicians describe is insufficient for religious purposes. Any hint of this kind raises a double question: Whether on the one hand "religious purposes" are sufficiently profound, and on the other hand whether philosophers have ignored or passed over too lightly data that are important for any adequate theory. (c) It is conceivable that religion is employing an unproductive method of thought that blocks appreciation of what is done by other and more productive methods.

These possibilities, all of them sobering, deserve an amount of study that is here out of the question. Some suggestions that may be worth following up may, however, be possible. I shall take the risk of suggesting that each of these explanations contains an important truth, and that these three several truths point a single moral for Christian education.

First, then, is it not true that Christian worship, as it is now practised, does to some extent take refuge from the actualities of the world instead of facing them? And does not the enjoyableness of it make the rigors of critical thought seem unimportant?

In the second place, if the deities of metaphysics lack religious warmth, there must be a reason. It is easy to overgeneralize the aloofness of metaphysicians from the glow of religion. Think, for example, of Royce's "beloved society."[1] Yet it must be confessed, as Hocking has done,[2] that there generally is a gap between the object of religious adoration and the supreme being of all the metaphysical idealisms. The explanation of this is no doubt complex, but one factor, surely, is the fact that what we hold precious in our religion has been surrounded by touchy ideas. The "private property, keep off" sign that orthodoxy long maintained, set going a tradition, not yet dead, that visits of exploration are not invited. It should not be surprising that thinkers show a predilection for parts of the topic upon which they think they can get a hearing. Of course, no real philosopher can guarantee that his product will be warming rather than chilling, but certainly the prospect of metaphysical frost is enhanced if we exclude our warmest values from consideration. The philosopher does not get into the game with us, and consequently the ideas that he offers us are abstracted from the function of ideas—such functions, for example, as metaphysical ideas perform in education.

[1]In *The Problem of Christianity in Human Experience* (New York, 1913).
[2]In *The Meaning of God* (New Haven, 1912).

There is still another reason why the deities of metaphysics are religiously a-dynamic. It is the faltering of religion itself at the points where difficult creative acts are called for. That is, data proper to religion have not been present in sufficiently arresting form. It is a safe surmise that if Christianity had been quick to deal with the problems of personality that the industrial system has made so acute, the philosophy produced during the last hundred years would have been materially different. If the churches should now deal decisively with peace and the necessary causes of it, this mighty work of religion would be reflected in the metaphysical deities of the next generation.

As to the third point—the possibility that the church has practised an unproductive method of thought that makes the mind unreceptive toward a better method and its products—again it is necessary to confess judgment. This, in spite of the achieved adaptations mentioned in section 36. For the assimilation of biblical criticism and the theory of evolution (even now not nearly complete) was more a yielding to necessity than the adoption of a method that would make yielding to pressure unnecessary. If our thought-method were that of criticism and discovery instead of defense, we should welcome the ever-renewed reopening of the foundations. We should not only accept without resistance all the evidence offered us, but we should actively go after evidence that might at any time require uncomfortable tearing down and rebuilding.

Has our habit of defensive thinking prevented us from perceiving potential religious values that already are present in metaphysics? My own answer is a decided affirmative, but this answer should be taken simply as a stimulus to inquiry. The reasons for it cannot here be given. It would reward Christian thinkers, however, to make a survey of the unused resources of current philosophy.

All three of these part-explanations can be summed up in this, that what is called Christian thought assumes that its function is to assist in transmission rather than in creation. This assumption plays queer tricks. For example, at one moment it makes us anxious regarding tendencies in current philosophy; at another moment it leads us to declare that religion is independent of philosophy. Again, it stimulates to philosophical study that is intended to give due weight to religious realities, but even this philosophy, produced under the full glow of piety, appears to be religiously unfruitful. I have yet to learn of any quickening of religious life in the churches by the application of such systems of thought. Some thinkers of the type now under consideration have perhaps influenced religious attitudes by writings other than metaphysical, but only these now concern us. If, now, this impression of mine is correct, we have a further example of the deadening effect of the apologetic approach to the problems of the spiritual life.

We now have an answer to the question why even theistic philosophies are religiously ineffective. The reason is that the opportunity of thought to take part in re-creating religion is restricted by religion itself. The implications of this conclusion for the teaching of philosophy in institutions under the influence of the churches are reserved for a later section.

57. The Educational Sterility of Mysticism. How It Might Become Fertile

For the purposes of the present discussion I shall employ the term mysticism in a popular rather than critical sense (either philosophical or psychological),

not overlooking what Pratt[1] has emphasized, that
plain men, who are neither saints, nor seers, nor theologians, often declare that they individually touch
spiritual reality of a divine sort immediately and not
merely through instruction or logical reflection. They
claim to know directly and for themselves that there
is a true basis for worship, and that life can fulfil itself.

The descriptions of what is thus apprehended are
various and not always harmonious as between one
individual and another. Moreover, it is easy to prove
that derivation from instruction, tradition, or earlier
experiences plays a large rôle in what the subject believes to be wholly underived. It is possible, under the
influence of suggestion, to have an "experience" that
confirms any doctrine that one happens to have been
taught.

Nevertheless, after making allowance for all external influences, the mind that is in the mystical
mood remains certain that the derivative elements in
mystical experience are not the whole story. There is
something here and now, it claims, that exists or is
true on its own account, and not by the suffrage of
anything else. Now, this hanging on like grim Death
cannot be said to be derived; it is something more
than a case of transmission; there is here some sort
of original contribution by or through the individual.
Whatever else mysticism is or is not, it is one way of
asserting the finality of a person. It is also one way
of asserting that the finality of the individual is a social finality, for the mystic always feels that he is in
touch with something, however undefined, that is
akin to himself.

Let us endeavor to formulate this underived re-
mainder in mystical experiences: One goes to the
edge of all the good that is or ever has been actual;

[1] In his *The Religious Consciousness* (New York, 1920).

to the edge of all that oneself is and has been, and,
looking over, says that there is still more to the good,
and there is more to me, than ever has been actualized
or expressed; that the truth of me lies in the beyond
of me; that the goodness of the good lies in the beyond of the good; and that this "beyond" of the good
and of me is one "beyond." The vagueness of this
description is unavoidable. For the experience itself
denies the adequacy of all terms that get their definition from past events and learnings. That mystics
themselves, as a rule, affirm more than this must be
admitted, but these other things, which are taken to
be intuitions of specific truths, are demonstrably derived; and, moreover, the apparent confirmation of
them by a present emotional glow can be wholly ac-
counted for without reference to the truth of them.

But vagueness does not necessarily connote emptiness of meaning; it may connote meaning in process
of being generated. In this possibility of "meaning
in process of being generated" lies the crux of the
problem of what is called the validity of the mystical
experience. As a rule, the problem is handled clum-
sily by mystics themselves, both great and small. For
they endeavor to give articulateness to the "beyond"
that they experience by ascribing to it the things
that their religious environment has already defined,
as some notion of God, Christ, the Virgin, or some
non-Christian divinity. Hence the illusoriness that
pursues mysticism; it habitually takes a mental habit
as a fresh revelation. Sometimes, on the other hand,
refuge is taken in vagueness itself as the last word of
an experience that claims nevertheless to be revealing.
"Ineffability," which is non-communicability, was set
down by William James as one of the prime marks
of the mystic's experience. James was, in fact, much
nearer the truth than those who resort to mysticism
in defense of a particular set of beliefs already held.

But in fact no mystical experience contains anything that is more ineffable than the constantly used notion of "I, myself," or the notion, "experienced good." The incommunicableness is, in fact, simply that of the personal reference of human experience as such.

Because mysticism so generally interprets itself in the terms of conventional beliefs, or else declares itself incommunicable, it is educationally sterile. Incommunicable knowledge (even if we could grant that it exists) cannot be taught, while traditional lore can be taught so much more effectively by systematic drill and habituation that any help from mysticism becomes superfluous.

At two points, however, efforts to weave mysticism into education have appeared in Protestantism. The first is the endeavor of evangelicalism to prepare pupils for a mystical conversion-experience by teaching about it, then to bring about the experience by non-educational methods (chiefly suggestion), and then to use it as confirmation of the antecedent teaching. The scheme broke down for several reasons. For one thing, the standard experience could not be produced except in a part of the pupils; for another thing, the fruits ascribed to conversion were produced by education without conversion; in the third place, the doctrine that underlay the whole discovered its own lack of historical, psychological, and ethical foundation.

The other attempt to weave mysticism into education is in the sphere of worship. The theory is that by putting a learner, young or old, into an attitude of contemplation within a fitting environment (as, a Gothic chapel), divine truth will breathe itself into him. It happens that this method employs, more or less, some of the conditions that favor original thinking. But this is not, as a rule, desired, or expected, or accomplished. Rather, the learner is surrounded by

reminders of customary thoughts; he is under the influence of manifold and strong suggestion, the result
of which, if it succeeds, is to endow a tradition with
an emotion.

Yet mysticism might become educationally fruitful if it would only fix attention upon other phases
of itself. In the first place, the mystic engages in implicit criticism of the actual, of the past, but he seems
not to feel any responsibility for carrying this criticism explicitly through, nor for making it effective
at the points where it applies. Again, he is engaged
in a process of active self-adjustment at the points
where past experience does not yield him guidance,
yet he does not carry this adjustment through—he
either falls back into conventional ways or else seeks
relief from them by a repeated flight into an almost
objectless emotion. He affirms that there is more to
him than his present self, yet he does not take possession of this more in any specific or systematic way.
If, now, he would only take the next step, which would
evoke out of the "beyond" something definite and
critically approved to take the place of his present
self and his present world, he might become creative,
and he might show others the way of creation.

The history of mysticism justifies the judgment
that its function is not the intuitive apprehension of
truth. It commonly thirsts for absolute certainty, but
in fact it leads to the edge of the uncertainties involved in the creation of a new self and a new world.
It seeks rest in timeless being, but in fact it rests in
the temporal practices, views, and standards of its
environment.

What we have, then, as a net result, is the self-
affirmation of a being that, though he resides in time
and is subject to change, nevertheless participates in
determining the content of time. He is in the future
as truly as he is in the past and the present; that is,

he is creative. This self-affirmation offers itself as participation; that is, the creativity of the person is a shared creativity.

If the direct personal realization of God to which the mystic aspires were understood by him as self-realization in and through moral creativity, he would become a leader in Christian education. For his whole attitude would be stimulating to others, and not least to the young—stimulating to analysis and criticism of the actual, stimulating to fellowship with all aspiring personalities, and stimulating to mutual action toward a better world, the Kingdom of the creative God.[1]

58. The Relation of Experimentation to the Apprehension of God

Teachers of the Christian religion generally assume that a part of their function is to help pupils "have faith in God." What, then, is it to have faith? Is faith a kind of knowledge? Is it the same as belief or assent? Is it fidelity to a person or a cause? Is it the daring that acts even though knowledge fails? On the whole, it is treated as a kind of apprehension rather than as any more active state, and mostly as apprehension that is incomplete and therefore not fully at rest within itself. There has been a tendency, in Protestantism at least, to aspire to a sort of inner completeness in which faith shall be swallowed up and superseded by self-sufficing insight. One use of sacraments, for example, has been to enable the believer to realize that here and now, at particular

[1] This view of mysticism and Wieman's were worked out independently of each other. They have much in common, but there is, I judge, an important difference. For him the net validity in mystical practices lies in the waiting-attitude that precedes the dawning of a solution for a problem (*Methods of Private Religious Living*, New York, 1928, pp. 186–195); for me there is the validity of active affirmation of selfhood as a creative agent.

physical points, he is dealing with God himself, or rather, that God here directly communicates himself to the believer. Another point at which endeavor is made to transcend mere faith is common worship; a third is communion with God in private prayer, and a fourth is the conversion-experience and other mystical states and events.

It is an arresting fact that at each of these points where faith seems to achieve verification of itself suggestion is the instrument. In the sacrament, suggestion uses a material object to give force and apparent concreteness to an antecedent idea; in common worship a whole complex of sights, sounds, muscular acts, and memories gives vividness to what usually is lacking in vividness when one enters the sanctuary; in private prayer of the sort now under consideration one yieldingly contemplates the divine object, expecting certain subjective results; similarly the conversion-experience. If, now, we add that the usual method of evoking faith in the first place is likewise suggestion (by the reiteration of an idea), we shall perceive that we have upon our hands an educational problem of considerable magnitude. What about suggestion as an instrument for the apprehension of God?

Whatever is built by positive suggestion can be torn down by negative suggestion. For example, many a person who has watched his own experience in prayer in order to see just where and how God comes in, has found his devotions evaporating into a question-mark. Now and then this question-mark is taken as evidence that there isn't any God after all. What happens is that during the attempt to pray one carries in mind the thought, "Maybe God is not here, or here, or here," along with the thought "Maybe he is." The two suggestions simply neutralize each other. Suppose, now, that the environment of the learner constantly suggests maybe's. In this case, positive teaching by the method of suggestion could be counteracted and defeated on a large scale by nothing more content-ful than a maybe. The church as a whole might lose its confidence in God through the force of a question-mark. In fact, isn't this a factor in the present apprehensiveness of many Christians toward science and philosophy?

There is still another phase of faith-through-suggestion that, when once it is perceived, will test rather severely any conscientious teacher. Is yielding to suggestion a way in which a pupil can realize a wholesome selfhood? Let us assume that a teacher sincerely believes in God, and that he holds this belief to be of the utmost consequence. He then greatly desires that the learner shall entertain the same belief. Now, sincere beliefs, true beliefs as well as others, can be induced by the reiteration of verbal formulas, especially if it is accompanied by conditions, as in some services of worship, that awaken satisfying emotions. Is it, then, legitimate to work upon the pupil's mind by way of suggestion? Rather, since suggestion always is at work anyhow, the question is what besides suggestion is required, and what is the learner to be trained to do with suggestions, both pro and con. The basis for answering this question is to be found in our valuation of persons. If they are finalities for us, then the personal, discriminating, free-choosing mode of procedure on their part must be a constant goal of all our teaching. Therefore we defeat our central purpose if we lead the learner into an unquestioning faith. It is a function of the spiritual life, which is the personal life, to ask questions, to weigh alternatives, to resist suggestions until they are tested.

No intelligent teacher stops with faith in the form of mere idea or intellectual assent, of course, nor with this reinforced by emotion. It is recognized that a vital faith is a spur to action. Therefore, "What does God want us to do?" is asked with respect to one situation after another. Some excellent results in conduct follow; they should not be belittled; nevertheless, deducing rules for conduct from ideas received by suggestion has limitations and dangers. How—to consider a merely logical aspect of the matter—could all the details that we need for our guidance be first compacted into the concept from which subsequently we draw them out? What, moreover, is it, as a matter of fact, from which duty is deduced when the question is asked, "What does God want us to do?" Usually the deduction is made in a conventional manner from conventional standards; that is, by suggestion, with the resulting danger of making the learner into nothing more than a smug churchman.

Though many teachers would be shocked by a proposal that they start going in their pupils inquiry with respect to God rather than implicit belief in him, this is the really Christian way of dealing with the matter. In fact, the current method is condemned by its unconscious irreligiousness. For, if God exists, he must himself be the real teacher of his own existence, and the way to learn about him must be that of letting him express himself to us or in us. Wherefore, our problem becomes this: What sort of practices on our part give the best opportunity for the Great Valuer of Persons, if such there be, to disclose himself? There is only one direction in which we may reasonably hope for an answer to this question. The remarkable words attributed to Jesus, "If any man will do . . . he shall know," indicate this direction. We require a constant doing that carries within itself the question-mark of intellectual hospitality. This means experimentation within the areas of unsureness; it means engaging in problematic enterprises at the advancing age of the moral order. By the advancing age of the moral order I mean the line at which gains for personality already made in the historical process either are imperilled or else demand for their further development new and untried ventures. If there be a Great Valuer of Persons, he will be most manifest where we take risks on behalf of persons. He will be manifested in the grit with which lovers of men hold on through difficulties and defeats, in the richness of the fellowship that the adventurers have with one another, in the gains that are added to other personalities, and in our defeats when we compromise with the principle of personality.

Experimentation directed toward increased self-realization or enfranchisement of persons, then, is the method of apprehending the divine presence. Such experimentation can take place in any relationship between men, and upon any scale. Just now I received from an old friend a letter that illustrates the point. Each of us, it seems, has been a stimulus to the other. He has helped me worship, and he thinks I have helped him with some of his technical problems; through our intercourse each has gotten ahead as a person; moreover, we have labored together on behalf of the difficult cause of religious education. Why, now, does this description of a friendship seem cold-blooded, calculating, and certainly inadequate? Because this mutual furthering of personality is swelling with an interpretative afflatus. When two persons are most at home with each other, the walls of the home grow thin and diaphanous, permitting a glimpse of what seems like an all-enveloping Friendship. As the rose-glow of an evening sun can turn mountains, sky, and valleys into something more than just valleys, mountains, and sky, so when we most unreservedly take one another as persons, our world becomes suffused with new meaning. Does any experience whatever have more of a metaphysical tang than friendship?

But this interpretative afflatus requires, in turn, experimental testing. When we follow the friendship clew, what happens? Does good-will show capacity for propagating its kind? Does it grow through exercise, or, when exercised, does it peter out into something impersonal? Does it appear to have a vitality that hardship cannot quench? Is there any sense in which it is true, as one Christian put it, that "love never faileth"? and that, as another Christian expressed it, love is "the greatest thing in the world"? Every "Yes" that comes in response to such questions illustrates what still another Christian affirmed, "God is love."

Suppose we vault from the more restricted relations between persons to relations between nations and races. It takes some realism, some resistance to creatures of the imagination, to grasp the utterly simple fact that international affairs are affairs between specific persons—between men, women, and children on one side of a boundary-line, and men, women, and children on the other side—persons with whom we might shake hands, persons whose joys and sorrows we might feel as our own, persons who could feel our joys and sorrows as their own. Now and then, when a famine or a devastating flood or earthquake occurs, we realize this actuality of other peoples; they are persons like ourselves, and for the moment we experience friendship on an international scale. But anon this directness of appreciation sags back into symbol, ceremony, stand-offishness of one assumed national entity that is only quasi-personal toward another of the same sort. Then comes the opportunity for self-interest to use the national power without a feeling of responsibility for the effects upon men, women, and children, taken as persons.

Let us ask, then, how friendship or regard for persons works in these large relations, and how the absence of it works. Is there not plenty of evidence that good-will begets good-will and, when trusted, goes on toward effective and mutually happy control of the non-personal parts of environment? And, is there not sufficient evidence that when force rather than good-will is relied upon, it defeats itself and makes impossible the benefits that are sought by means of it? The most that can be claimed for the rule of force, as against regard for persons, is that, before the vessel strikes the rock that is ahead of her, some of the passengers may be able to get into the pantry and fill their paunches. Every national ship except the ship "Good-Will" is headed toward destruction. This is the lesson of experience, and it bears mightily upon the problem of the existence of God.

But the fact that many, many men, not a few of them in high station, are unconvinced that good-will has the last word, and the fact that the world's economic and political business is done, upon the whole, upon the contrary assumption, must also be taken into account as data. Such data do not suggest the presence of God; they create difficulty for belief in him, difficulty that may legitimately be set over against all experience of a contrary sort. What, then, about the outlook for faith? Simply this: We must go on with the experiment—we who, having made a beginning with the hypothesis of God, have found therein strength and stimulus to pursue the hypothesis to the end.

The experiment now before us has two phases: *First*, convincing people that the good-will policy is worth trying as a working hypothesis. This is to be done by assembling and rigorously analyzing facts that show just what happens when we pursue one policy or the other. Some apparently respectable policies would be shamed out of countenance if the effects of them upon men, women, and children were definitely shown. What strikes one in most discussions upon such subjects as peace and cruisers is the preponderance of theory and sentiment, and the paucity of facts that bear upon the main point at issue, which is, What and how much does good-will accomplish when it is intelligently put at work? *Second*, we must directly illustrate the power of good-will by exercising it in particular situations, being especially watchful of situations in which it is not customary. We shall find them all along the line that reaches from the family hearth or cook-stove through school, playground, church, neighbors, employment relations, and community relations, to the world-relations that are hanging in the balance between life and death.

It has long been said among Protestants that God, logically considered, is a hypothesis, the verification of which is found in religious experience. But the range of the religious experience in which verification is to be sought has not always been made clear, nor has the technic of testing been made clear. Recently Professor Wieman has helped us at this point by insisting that we must pursue definite and particular hypotheses as to what is good and what bad in each area of life, that these hypotheses must be such that they actually can be tested in practice, and that the outcome of each such specific testing of a specific way of living adds to our knowledge of what God is.[1]

The whole of Christian education might almost be

[1]Henry Nelson Wieman *The Wrestle of Religion with Truth* (New York, 1927), and *Methods of Private Religious Living* (New York, 1928). One can gratefully accept Wieman's help at this point without assenting to his definition of God, which makes no reference to personality or the moral order, and without taking anything as abstract as "integration" as the evidence of spiritual gain. According to my way of thinking, the problem of the ex-

described as experiments with the hypothesis of a Christ-like God. What constitutes an experiment depends, of course, upon a relation between an experience already had and one in prospect. In a child's life much is experiment that for an adult is no longer experimental at all. We have not half appreciated the extent to which, if the mind is to develop to its full capacity, childhood and youth must abound in experimental approaches. I have in my possession a photograph of a baby that is having his first experience of crawling upon a lawn. In the whole bodily attitude, and especially in the look upon the face, one beholds the young explorer. No arctic hero about to reach the Pole could express more of this spirit. Let this be a symbol of personality engaged in finding itself. We can no more solve our pupils' problems for them than we could carry this baby to his destination. The art in Christian education must consist in inducing pupils to make experiments that, being real at the stage of the learner's experience, will show where the truth lies, and at the same time leave the personality fresh for further experimentation. This qualification certainly implies that we prevent some kinds of experiment, but this preventive education will be easiest and most educative where the experimental attitude is most encouraged, not where it is least encouraged.

59. A Job for a Christian College

The anxiety of many parents and ministers concerning the influence of colleges upon students' faith is justified by the facts. If the churches are to

istence of God concerns the place and the possibilities of persons in our universe, and the test of the God-hypothesis (which requires the many sub-hypotheses mentioned above) concerns the ability of persons to maintain themselves as such, and to bring the conditions of personal living ever more and more under control.

remain what they now are, and if the colleges are to continue upon their present road, the two will go still farther apart than they are at present. This is true of the so-called Christian colleges as well as the others. The reason is not merely or chiefly that the content of academic teaching so often undermines what is taught in Sunday-schools and pulpits (though this is disturbing enough) ; the deeper fact is contrariety of a systemic sort. For the church and the college hold opposite notions of what it is to teach. In the church, education has the sense of bringing one into conformity with what has been transmitted from ancient times; but in the college one is constantly exposed to the process and the standard of critically examining what has been transmitted.

This is why the long-continued solicitude of the churches concerning what is taught in their own colleges has had such equivocal effect. If biology is taught at all, it has to be taught as a science. The teacher of it may endeavor to soften the resulting conflict with traditional religious thought, but in the end the whole opposition comes out. It must come out because of the nature of scientific method. If, in most denominational colleges, biology is now un-hampered, what about the teaching of the Bible? How are the teachers of it selected? What is expected of them? Do they feel entirely free to employ his-torical methods? At this point there has been much faltering, and it is not yet ended. But in the end these methods will be used without restriction be-cause the example and the pressure from other de-partments of instruction are such as to isolate and to brand as unacademic every compromise at this point. As to philosophy, how can it be taught at all unless it introduces students to strong thinkers who contradict many things that preachers and Sunday-school teachers aver? The method in the home church, as a rule, shields the pupil from contacts with unbelief, and even from the problems that agitate the minds of philosophers, whereas the college method of teaching exposes him to them.

If ever an account should be written of the various devices that have been employed to keep the colleges religiously in line, or to protect students from their colleges, and of how these devices have fared, the story would be an interesting one. It would tell of endeavors to have a safe curriculum, safe textbooks, safe professors; of rigid rules for conduct; required chapel services; revivals; college preachers; patronage of Christian associations; required courses in the Bible (sometimes suspiciously like camouflage for evangelism) ; the spurring of local churches to care for students, and (it may be added) at non-denominational institutions the establishment of denominational church homes or foundations for students.

As to the results, a palliative effect, or even something better than this, is here and there discernible. But alongside it must be placed the actual discrediting of church religion in the minds of many students. That these schemes or any combination of them ever will unify the religious work of the churches and the educational work of the colleges is simply incredible. In one church college after another, just as in other colleges, something runs away with the students, and in one church college after another the faculty and the administration approach more and more the types found in non-church colleges and universities. Recently the president of an old denominational institution openly declared that, while the college officially stands for the maintenance of religious life, it looks upon study and learning (in the curriculum sense) as the first concern of the student. Thus religion acquires the status of an "also," or an "as far

as it is convenient." Is there, in fact, even one college in which the dominant spirit of either faculty
or students brings religion and the academic approach to truth into a real, every-day, working
unity?

The difficulty is not all on one side, however—not
by any means. For, if we dig down into the dynamics
of the studies that college administrators and teachers regard as the main thing, we come upon two exceedingly important facts of motivation that have a
direct bearing upon religious and non-religious attitudes. The first of these facts is this: On the side of
students, their much-discussed indifference to studies; and on the side of faculties, an endeavor by means
of marking-systems, grades, and degrees, to force
students to study. This administrative mechanism
does not create love for truth or fondness for anything worth while, but rather desire to "get by,"
false pretense in all its degrees, and substitution of
the insignia of education for education itself. The
effect upon character is anti-ethical, anti-Christian,
and it is not successfully counteracted by any religiousness that the college may officially profess or
endeavor to promote. Now, Christian colleges have
no immunity from this charge of being on both sides
of the fence, for they, like others, make a marking
system the focal point of student motivation in relation to studies.

A second important fact in the motivation of studies is that many of them are being brought into
closer and closer working relations with the every-
day secular business of life. A close relation of this
kind would be desirable on either of two conditions.
If the occupations of which students are made conscious were inherently personality-building, or if the
studies of occupational data were such as to lead
students to judge the secular life from this stand-

point, then these studies themselves, though they
bore no religious label, would back up religion. But
there is plenty of reason for saying that neither of
these conditions is met. "Students are in college,"
one of them said to me, "for the purpose of making
an easier living afterward."

It is a fair question whether our colleges as a
whole, or even our Christian colleges, are doing more
to perpetuate, or more to overcome, the evils of our
economic and political life. Certain it is that academic learning is not generally brought into any
articulate relation to the great issues of life. In other
words, by abstracting knowledge from one of its
prime functions, the colleges forego their main opportunity to be religiously or ethically creative.

The job of a Christian college now begins to take
shape before our imagination. It is not to build a
buffer or effect a junction between the present conventional studies on the one side, and present conventional religion on the other, but to transcend both
by a fresh, vigorously intellectual attack upon the
problem of the real values in life and the ways in
which they are to be secured. The social studies, instead of being a new fringe upon an old curriculum,
would in such a college become central, and they
would be pursued as a critique of our conventional
ways of living, and as a step in reconstruction. In
this way the student might have an immediate part
in forming and testing the hypotheses whereby alone
we may hope to apprehend God. There could be religious vividness at the centre of the whole college
enterprise. This would require no shading of fidelity
to scientific method, no pressure upon anybody's
freedom. But it would have scant room for teachers
who do not sufficiently believe in freedom to defend
and promote the freeing of the human personality
in men, women, and children off the campus as well
as on it.

In recent years the notion has hovered about many minds of a possible system of religious education that should reach from the kindergarten of the church to the church college and university—one system, dominated throughout by a single, central motive. The vision is fascinating, and it is not inherently impracticable. But it is impracticable under present conditions, and it will remain so until there is a change in presuppositions at each end of the line, the church end and the college end. The church must transcend its present assumption that the function of education is to transmit a faith, and the college must transcend its assumption that its main job is to teach subjects abstracted from life's purposes. The development of purpose must be provided for in and through the pursuit of each subject of study—provided for, not by lugging in a homily, but by revealing the relation of the subject to life, and by making the subject a critique upon life.

Would it be wildly irrational to dream of a college that should live, move, and have its meaning in the hypothesis that there is a God? A hypothesis in process of being examined, revised, and tested; therefore a college that focuses all study upon the unsolved problems of human weal and woe, and specifically upon our unfinished tasks if we are to live together as persons supremely valuing one another? Such a college would neither imitate other academic institutions, nor be beholden to the church of yesterday, but only to the church that is engaged in transcending its yesterday by repentance and reconstruction. Because everywhere meanings in life and for life would be sought with critical pointedness, the present motivation of both teachers and students would constantly feel the touch of a spur. One can fancy a rebirth of philosophy in such an environment, and the intellectual excitement that would seize the collegiate mind, now blasé toward big things but straining itself over little ones. The sciences would thrive, being not only released from restraints but also inspired by interesting and developing tasks. Religion would not be an appendage of academic interests, or even a guest or companion, nor would religious thinking continue to be defensive, for the whole enterprise, suffused with a sense of the worthfulness of the personal, would be inherently and aggressively religious. Is not this the true job of the Christian college?

CHAPTER XIII

CODA

60. What, Then, Is Christian Education?

It is the systematic, critical examination and reconstruction of relations between persons, guided by Jesus' assumption that persons are of infinite worth, and by the hypothesis of the existence of God, the Great Valuer of Persons.

INDEX

Date Due

5/14/55			
MAY 2 5			
NOV 2 0			
MAR 1 6			
MR 26 '65			
AP 9 '65			
AP 22 '65			
MY 6 '65			
MY 20 '65			
DE 18 '73			
Jan 15			
MAR 11 '86			